His 98/8 £ 34.95

MANDE
POTTERS
&LEATHER-
WORKERS

MANDE POTTERS & LEATHER-WORKERS

ART AND HERITAGE IN WEST AFRICA

BARBARA E. FRANK

Smithsonian Institution Press
WASHINGTON AND LONDON

Copy editor: Virginia Wageman
Production editor: Duke Johns
Designer: Linda McKnight

Library of Congress Cataloging-in-Publication Data

Frank, Barbara E.
    Mande potters and leatherworkers : art and heritage in West Africa / Barbara E. Frank.
        p.   cm.
    Includes bibliographical references and index.
    ISBN 1-56098-794-4 (cloth : alk. paper)
    1. Pottery, Mandingo.   2. Leatherwork, Mandingo.   3. Mandingo (African people)—
Industries.   4. Art, African—Africa, West.   5. Sex role—Africa, West.   6. Sexual division of
labor—Africa, West.   7. Sex role in art.   I. Title.
    DT474.6.M36F73   1998
    738'.089'96345—dc21   97-27477

British Library Cataloguing-in-Publication Data available

Manufactured in the United States of America; color insert printed in Hong Kong, not at
government expense
05 04 03 02 01 00 99 98   5 4 3 2 1

∞   The paper used in this publication meets the minimum requirements of the American National
Standard for Information Sciences—Permanence of Paper for Printed Library Materials ANSI
Z39.48-1984.

For my family,
most especially my mother, Dorothy B. Frank,
and in loving memory of my father, Charles E. Frank

CONTENTS

PREFACE

I am often asked how I became engaged with Africa and the study of African art. What could possibly lead a middle-class kid on a journey of discovery from a small town amid the cornfields of Illinois to the dry and distant terrain of the West African savanna? What was it about the artistic heritage of another people that captured my heart and mind?

My parents were teachers of art and literature who instilled in their children a love of travel and an openness of mind and spirit. My father chose to take the family with him on a sabbatical leave to England when I was eight years old, my first remembered encounter with another culture. Several years later my family hosted a young woman from Madagascar for the academic year through the American Field Service exchange program. At the time Yari Robinson (Jeannoda) was a delightful, if somewhat exotic, older sister. She and her family have been part of our extended family ever since. It was our second AFS student who introduced me to the world of Islam and to the reality of poverty, hardship, and deep faith. Yusoph Latip came to us from Mindanao, the Muslim heartland of the southern Philippines. He taught my family and fellow students volumes about respect for other cultures and other religions.

In college I was drawn to the arts and humanities, taking courses across a broad spectrum, including film theory and criticism, English history, painting, printmaking, and sculpture. In the spring of 1977 I took a wonderful course on African art with Roslyn Walker. I accompanied her to a conference in East Lansing, where I was introduced to scholars whose work I had been reading—William Bascom, Frank Willett, Renée Boser-Sarivaxevanis, and Roy Sieber, among others. I was starstruck and I was hooked.

I went into the graduate program at Indiana University with a background stronger in studio art than in art history, a fascination for things cultural, and very little knowledge of Africa. An inclination toward historical issues and an interest in Islam led me to explore the impact of the faith and of the trans-Saharan trade on various artistic traditions, from textiles to architecture. An opportunity to work with Peg Gilfoy at the Indianapolis Museum of Art led me to doing a master's essay on the Berber textiles in the museum's Moroccan collection. The strength of the African language program at Indiana University, developed under the direction of Charles Bird, allowed me to acquire a rudimentary knowledge of Bamana prior to going into the field. These academic pursuits all steered my interest toward Mali, West Africa.

The greatest influence on the direction my work was to take came from Roy Sieber, my advisor and mentor. As those who have seen him move among either collections of the finest pieces of African sculpture or the disorganized array of stuff at a flea market can attest, his sensitivity to objects is unmatched. In addition, he insisted on an awareness of historical issues long before it became popular to do so. It was he who encouraged me to tackle the domain of Sudanic leatherwork, which the literature seemed to suggest was part of a homogenous Islamic tradition imported across the sands of the Sahara. The reality was more complex and more interesting than either of us had imagined.

Nevertheless, on the eve of my departure Africa remained an abstraction and my project an academic construct. Reality forced itself on my consciousness in unsuspecting ways. One of my last tasks before leaving for Europe was to complete my master's essay. The maps of Morocco were the final detail. I drew in the inverted V's indicating mountains randomly and with abandon, like the geographers of old filling great expanses of the unknown with fanciful animals and topographic features. Several months later, on the flight from Paris to Bamako, I looked out of the airplane window on what I took to be the Atlas Mountains. I shuddered to think of the distance between the reality of those peaks and the decorative pattern I had so recently submitted for my essay. As it turns out they were the Pyrenees of Spain, but the lesson was not lost. Reality is far more textured and complex than any hastily drawn map can convey. From the moment the plane touched down in Mali and the peculiarly sweet and smoky smell of Bamako entered my lungs, Africa was no longer an abstraction. My research had to respond to the bends, obstacles, and opportunities in my path, and my conclusions had to be drawn from that rich but disorganized reality.

My museum research and fieldwork on Mande leatherwork was supported by a Fulbright-Hays Dissertation Research Abroad Fellowship (1982–84). Having completed an extensive survey of leatherwork in selected American and European museums, I arrived in Mali with a sense of what nineteenth- and early twentieth-century Mande leatherwork looked like. I was confident that I could define a Mande style distinct from other leatherworking traditions across the Sudanic region, but I was daunted by its geographic extent. This widespread distribution came as no surprise to the leatherworkers I interviewed. Their own personal travel itineraries spanned similar geographic distances, as did the family histories they shared with me. In response, my research took on a similar itinerant pattern. I traveled widely, often with names of brothers or fathers or cousins to greet in distant towns. Although I cannot name them all, several hold a special place in my memory. It was Bakhodoré Sylla (Plate 25) who spoke with pride of his family heritage and honored me with my adoptive Soninke patronymic. The blacksmith Magnan Coulibaly (Figure 1) wanted to be sure I knew what locally made gunpowder sounded like and set some off at my feet while I was distracted with my camera bag. Bo Traoré (Figure 2), a leatherworker at the weekly market in Banamba, said nothing when I greeted him some five years after our first encounter, but smiled and reached into his pocket for a photograph I had taken of him. Perhaps my most remarkable encounter was with the blind Shekna Diakité (Plate 26) of the northern Sahel town of Nara. When he shuffled feebly across the compound on his wife's arm, I became concerned the interview be brief such that it

FIGURE 1. Bamana black-smith Magnan Coulibaly. Until his death in 1987, Coulibaly was widely respected for his cultural knowledge as well as for his ability at the forge. In tribute, a youth theater troupe included a skit satirizing his prowess in spiritual matters during a performance I attended in May 1988. Kolokani, Mali, 1983.

FIGURE 2. Bamana leather-worker Bo Traoré working on a sword sheath *(npanmuru-tan)*. This was the photograph Traoré pulled from his pocket when I greeted him nearly five years later. Banamba, Mali, 1984.

would not tire him. But he came alive with stories of the past, occasionally slapping the tape recorder with dramatic gestures of his hands, as kids from the neighboring compounds gathered around to listen.

Throughout my research, I almost always worked with an interpreter, even as my vocabulary of Bamana terms and phrases improved. Sometimes the interviews were formal, recorded on tape and later translated. Other times I simply observed, photographing the various processes and watching interactions with clients. Through James Brink I was put in touch with Kassim Koné, then completing his studies in English at ENSUP (Ecole Normal Superieure) in Bamako. I worked with Kassim whenever his studies allowed and relied on others when they did not. As those who have come to know him in recent years can attest, Kassim is a remarkable person. Without his friendship, scholarship, and deep respect for his own heritage, my engagement with the Mande world would have been a very different one.

En route home after sixteen months in Mali, I spent several weeks in Morocco finding that the contrasts far outweighed any comparisons. I was especially struck by the large scale of the tanning operations in Fez and Marrakesh, quite different from the one or two pots in a corner of a leather-worker's compound in Mali.

A Smithsonian Institution Pre-Doctoral Fellowship in Residence at the National Museum of African Art (1985-86) provided support for a year of writing and research on which my dissertation on Mande leatherworking was based. In 1988, with a Summer Fellowship and Travel Grant from the University of Tulsa, I was able to travel to Mali and Sierra Leone for an intense period of research on different craft traditions, including weaving, indigo dyeing, blacksmithing, and pottery, as well as follow-up research on leatherworking. In Sierra Leone, with Chernoh Njai as my cultural guide, I spent three weeks traveling to the Kono region, to Makenie, and as far north as Kabala. Although brief, the experience provided me with an important perspective from the edges of the Mande world.

In the process of completing the dissertation and working on an edited volume on Mande artists (Conrad and Frank 1995), I became increasingly aware of how little information was available on Mande women in general and female artists in particular. I wondered to what extent Mande women shared in the historical processes so critical to leatherwork—the grand themes of trade, Islam, state building, and slavery. I wondered how their perceptions might differ from those of the men with whom my first field experiences were shaped.

I returned to Mali for two seasons of research on Mande potters, with leave from the State University of New York at Stony Brook (SUNY) funded by a Fulbright-Hays Faculty Research Abroad Fellowship (1991) and by a grant from the Social Science Research Council (1992). In contrast to the itinerant nature of my previous research, I took a somewhat different approach, focusing primarily on two communities where there were active potters, one Bamana (Kolokani) and the other Maninka (Kangaba). In the Kolokani region I spent most of my time with the three wives of blacksmith-farmer Brehima Doumbia. Senior wife Assitan Ballo (Figure 3) is perhaps the most meticulous potter of the three; Seban Fané (Figure 4) is by far the most prolific; while the pottery skills of the youngest, Diarrasou Traoré (Figure 139), leave room for improvement. In Kangaba I spent most of my time the first season with Nansa Doumbia (Plate 1) and Nakani Kanté (Plate 2), the best potters of a large extended family. I had hoped to establish an apprenticeship with Nansa upon my return the following year. However, the sudden death of her husband on the eve of my arrival sent

FIGURE 3. Bamana potter Assitan Ballo forming the rim of a cooking pot *(daga)*. The pot rests on a bed of gravel in the broken bottom of an old water storage jar, which turns on a smooth dirt surface dusted with sand. Kunògò, Mali, 1991.

FIGURE 4. Seban Fané adding coils to the walls of a small water jar *(jidaga)*. Kunògò, Mali, 1991.

her into a prescribed four-month period of mourning, during which time she was prohibited from making pottery and discouraged from social interactions. As a result I was introduced to a potter from another Kangaba blacksmith family. Although her work lacked the finesse of that of Nansa and Nakani, Koloko Kanté (Plate 3) provided me with a different perspective. She is a woman with an especially powerful sense of her own identity and heritage and strong opinions of others.

Particularly important for comparative purposes was my participation on a ceramic collection and documentation mission with a team from the national museum in Bamako. Having been aware of the success of a textile collection and documentation project funded by UCLA's Fowler Museum of Cultural History, I proposed to Doran Ross (then Associate Director, now Director, of the museum) a similar pottery collection project. With seed money from the Fowler Museum, additional funds and supplies from the West African Museums Programme under Executive Director

Claude Ardouin, and the support of Samuel Sidibé, Director of the Musée National du Mali, the project took shape. It was Sidibé who recommended the Kadiolo region in southeastern Mali, where he had observed a high level of pottery production some years before. The team consisted of documentalist and *chef de mission* Mme. Dia Oumou Dia, draftsman Yusoph Kalapo, audio-visual technician Mamadou Samaké, chauffeur Oumar Traoré, and myself. We worked primarily in two communities. In Doguélédougou, Aramatou Kouyaté and Youssouf Kouyaté were especially generous with their time and patience. In Sissingué, Issa Diabaté, Seydou Diabaté, Kadidia Kouyaté, Kadari Kouyaté, and especially Fatoumata Kouyaté were among those who made our project a success in 1991 and were equally helpful when I returned to Sissingué in 1992 for additional research.

Throughout my fieldwork on potters, I relied primarily on female interpreters. Mariam Tangara, Madougou Kanté, and Korotoumou Traoré each brought their informative points of view to the process. I did fewer formal interviews with the potters but spent more time with them in informal conversation. In addition to taking still photographs, I recorded the various stages of the process with a video camera. The opportunity to devote full attention to bringing together these two quite different bodies of research into a single text was made possible by a NYS/UUP. Dr. Nuala McGann Drescher Affirmative Action Leave (1994), a National Endowment for the Humanities Fellowship for College Teachers (1995-96), and leave from the University at Stony Brook.

This research has been anything but an individual exercise. For their companionship and generous hospitality in the field, I especially thank Barbara and Gerald Cashion, Linda Caswell, Barbara Court, Nancy and Dan Devine, Ellie and Claude Girerd-Barclay, Robert Gutierrez, the late Gaoussou Koné, Joseph Opala, and the late B. Marie Perinbam. For their counsel, encouragement, and good humor over the years, I thank Martha Anderson, Lisa Aronson, Marla Berns, David Binkley, Claudia Chouinard, Kathy Curnow, Patricia Darish, Barbara and Bill Dewey, Henry Drewal, Margaret Ford, Kris Hardin, Eugenia Herbert, Chris Kreamer, Sue and Ray Lepore, Thomas Martin, Diane Pelrine, the late Philip Ravenhill, Elisha Renne, Christopher Roy, Ray Silverman, Robert Soppelsa, Carol Spindel, Janet Stanley, Craig Subler, and Vera Viditz-Ward. I have relied heavily on the advice, friendship, and scholarship of those whose own work has centered on and around the Mande world and whose interdisciplinary perspectives have contributed much to my understanding, most especially Claude Ardouin, Mary Jo Arnoldi, James Brink, David Conrad, Kate Ezra, Bernhard Gardi, Barbara Hoffman, Adria LaViolette, Peter Mark, Roderick and Susan McIntosh, Patrick McNaughton, Labelle Prussin, Richard Roberts, Julianne Short, and Peter Weil. At one time or another these people have all generously offered comments, criticisms, and encouragement on my work as presented in papers, chapters, and articles.

I owe special gratitude to Kathryn Green and Jack Ronald, who came through at a critical moment with substantive advice on the manuscript as a whole. I thank Pat and Chuck Sahertian for their assistance with production of some of the visual materials. To the members of my family who have been with me on this journey from the very beginning, and without whom I would not have had the courage to continue, my debt is immeasurable. I thank them from the bottom of my heart.

The path my research has taken has led to a rethinking of what an art history of the Mande peoples should be and of how scholars can contribute to reconstructing that history. I began this project trained to think about objects as they appear in museum cases or in slides, to recognize quality and to distinguish one style from another. Questions of how objects are produced were of interest to me as someone who has dabbled in studio art and enjoys the hands-on approach. Initially I did not view technology as anything more than background information, an avenue toward more serious discussions concerning artistic intent. Similarly, I was intrigued by artist biographies and genealogies, the complex web of interrelationships in a polygamous and endogamous setting, but did not fully recognize their importance. It was the artists who taught me that art history is more than plotting objects of leather or clay along a temporal continuum. It was they who taught me that technological styles and social identity are as critical as the objects so venerated in Western museums. It was they who taught me that artistic heritage matters. This book is about pots and leather, about pottery making and leatherworking, but most especially, about potters and leatherworkers. It is their art history.

A NOTE ON
MANDE ORTHOGRAPHY

In keeping with current practice, I have used the standard orthography for Mande terms established by DNAFLA (Direction Nationale de l'Alphabetisation Fonctionnelle et de la Linguistique Appliquée, 1979, 1980) of the Ministry of Education in Mali, which privileges Bamana over other Mande dialects. In general, the plural marker is indicated by a "w" at the end of the word; e.g., *numu* (singular), *numuw* (plural). There is a glossary of Mande terms following the notes (see also Bazin [1906] 1965; Bailleul 1981; and Koné 1995). Other foreign terms are defined in the text as they appear. Ethnic terms appear in Mande orthography, followed by variant spellings in parentheses at first mention. When a particular author or museum attribution is cited, the spelling as it appears in the original source is provided in parentheses following the standardized Mande term.

For most geographical locations, I have chosen to use the French orthography as it appears on most maps (Segou versus Segu; Djenné versus Jenne) but have included variant spellings at first mention. However, other place names appear in the now more familiar Mande orthography rather than in the outdated colonial French (Wagadu versus Ouagadou; Wasulu versus Ouasoulou). Proper names appear in French as they do on identity cards (Diawara versus Jawara; Diabaté versus Jabate; Kouyaté versus Kuyate), whether the reference is to a particular individual or to a general patronymic. This can lead to some confusion, especially when a name is understood in some contexts to be an ethnic label (Jawara) while in others a patronymic (Diawara).

An "e" or "é" at the end of terms and proper names should be pronounced as a separate syllable; it does not fall silent. The following is offered as a guide to the pronunciation of selected names and terms: Diawara (Jah-war-ah), Djenné (Jen-eh), Doumbia (Doom-bee-ah), Fula (Foo-lah), *fune* (foo-neh), *garanke* (gar-an-keh), Jakhanke (Jah-kan-keh), *jeli* (je-li), Kanté (Kon-tay), Koné (Ko-neh), Kouyaté (Coo-yah-tay), *numu* (noo-moo), *numumuso* (noo-moo-moo-soh), Soumanou (Soo-mah-noo), Sylla (See-lah).

1

MORE THAN OBJECTS

Artistry and heritage have a special relationship among the Mande peoples of West Africa, one that challenges Western notions of artistic freedom and artist identity and defies standard models of art historical scholarship. Mande society recognizes artists as exceptional in the fullest sense of the word. Blacksmiths, potters, leatherworkers, and bards are respected, feared, and disdained for the skills and capacities that distinguish them from others. The various and distinct roles these men and women play in both social and artistic arenas, and the exclusive assignment of these tasks to endogamous groups, are firmly embedded in Mande ideology. A man does not choose to become a leatherworker; a woman does not choose to become a potter. Their identity as artists is their birthright and their heritage. This is a system of considerable complexity and, I suggest, considerable historical depth. This ideology has survived precisely because potters and leatherworkers are active players in the continuation of these culturally defined roles.

BUILDING ART HISTORIES

In attempting to grasp the extraordinary diversity of African artistic expression, early art historical scholarship relied primarily on stylistic analyses to define and delimit different artistic traditions (e.g., Kjersmeier 1935-38). In keeping with Western notions of high art, the focus was almost exclusively on figurative sculpture and masks in wood, metal, and terra cotta, arranged according to geographical distribution in a vague ethnographic present. What emerged from this approach was a series of geographically defined style regions highlighting the sculptural traditions of particular ethnic groups.

The Western Sudan is one of a number of style regions that have become codified in museum displays and exhibition catalogues over the years (e.g., Sieber and Rubin 1968; Vogel 1981; Roy 1985).[1] Encompassing the major sculpture-producing areas of present-day Mali, Burkina Faso, and northern Côte d'Ivoire, this style label links together Bamana, Dogon, and Senufo traditions among others. Indeed, the sculptural traditions of these peoples tend to share certain stylistic conceptions of the human form. Their thin, elongated proportions and geometric, angular shapes are quite different from the more stout and rounded forms of the Baule, Dan, and others of the Guinea Coast style region to the south. Even as our knowledge of sculptural traditions has grown in complexity and sophistication over the years, and even as other media have entered our visual vocabulary, the Western Sudan remains a viable category in the art history of Africa.

Efforts to further refine stylistic labels, however, have concentrated on the identification of "tribal" or "ethnic" styles. Despite numerous caveats and criticisms of the fundamentally a-historical nature of such an obsession (Bravmann 1973; Kasfir 1984; Hardin and Arnoldi 1996; Ravenhill 1996), it has been virtually impossible to dislodge the privileged position of ethnic labels in discussions of artistic styles. In the 1968 exhibition catalogue of the Tishman collection, Roy Sieber and Arnold Rubin proposed that because both language and art are major factors for distinguishing among cultural traditions, language families might correspond to stylistic divisions within the larger regions. Accordingly, they divided objects from the Western Sudan into Mande and Gur sectors.[2] They suggest that such linguistic groupings might "reinforce hypotheses of historical relationships that cannot be documented by written history" (1968, 20). Few scholars have taken up the challenge to explore the historical implications of similarities and differences within or between language groups.[3] Even in the Tishman catalogue it is ethnic labels that identify most of the individual objects as Dogon, Senufo, or Bamana.

Indeed, Bamana sculptures are among the best known of African art traditions. The elegant antelope headdresses known as *ciwara* are almost ubiquitous in museum collections across Europe and the United States. They have long been a favorite of tourist markets, not only in the Malian capital of Bamako, but also in Dakar, Abidjan, Nairobi, Paris, and New York. Bamana figurative sculpture and masquerades are also well known, though not quite at the same level of cliché as the *ciwara*. The recent flood of Bamana mud-cloth *(bɔgɔlanfini)* designs on the fashion scene has brought Mande artistic traditions even more into Western aesthetic consciousness (Rovine 1995; see also Rovine 1997).

Yet despite this name and image recognition, surprisingly little is known of the history of these traditions. The literature is comparatively rich with information on ritual and social contexts of use, but our understanding of their development over time and space remains sketchy.[4] On the one hand, a preoccupation with Bamana art forms to the exclusion of those of other Mande groups has made it difficult to place them within broader regional patterns of interaction. Indeed, the name recognition of Bamana over Maninka, Maraka, Mandinka, Soninke, and other Mande groups may have led to the misidentification of objects, making the process of historical reconstruction even more challenging. Pressure to locate objects, as well as scholarly expertise in particular ethnic contexts, has provided little incentive to explore the complex relationships among the major traditions.

In the 1973 exhibition catalogue titled *Open Frontiers: The Mobility of Art in Black Africa,* René Bravmann offers one of the few serious challenges to the "one tribe: one style" paradigm. He examines artistic production and diffusion in two quite different settings: the Cameroon grasslands and the region around the administrative Cercle of Bondoukou of eastern Côte d'Ivoire and west central Ghana. Although Bravmann provides ethnic labels for some of the objects, his discussion focuses on the interchange of images and ideas in these pluralistic settings. He argues that the cultural imperialism of state building, the vitality of inter- and intraregional trade, and the mobility of art and peoples demand an approach that is responsive to the historical reality.

These are the themes that resonated throughout my research on Mande leatherworking. However, they were less important for understanding ceramic traditions. In fact, one of my goals was to develop a framework that would take into account the complexity of identities in a region and accommodate differences in the way history has shaped the lives and artistry of men and women. My analysis begins with objects, exploring distribution patterns of types and styles for clues to the histories of these traditions. For ceramics, a common ecological environment has tended to favor certain types of objects within different ethnic contexts, making clear delineations of a Mande style difficult. For leatherwork, though it is possible to distinguish a Mande style from those of others in West Africa, object types tend to reflect a shared Islamic heritage. Formal analysis of objects more often than not reveals a commonality of styles and types across ethnic boundaries. This provides a useful starting point but alone is not enough to understand the histories of these artistic traditions.

My approach then moves beyond the customary confines of art historical practice to give equal attention to the way these objects were produced. Because the processes of artistic production in West Africa are sophisticated, distinctive, and generally conservative, the technologies artists employ are, in fact, a better indicator of historical difference than are object styles. Although tools and materials may appear to be rudimentary, the technical knowledge required to successfully forge metal, form and fire pottery, and tan hides is anything but simple. Because these are culturally learned behaviors, significant variations in technological styles provide evidence of the different origins of these traditions.[5]

It is in the realm of social identity that a sense of distinctive heritage emerges most strongly. Here, ethnicity is one of a number of identities individuals assume, and not necessarily the most important one. Mande peoples have a term that captures some of the multivalent layers of identity. *Siya* is often translated as ethnicity or race, but it also means sort, kind, or category (Bailleul 1981). In response to the question, "What is your *siya*?" Mande individuals may choose to identify their ethnicity, artist group, clan, or lineage.[6] These layers of identity are part of a social ideology that sets artists apart from the rest of society. Identified collectively as *nyamakalaw,* certain Mande artists (blacksmiths, potters, leatherworkers, and bards) are historically distinguished from the class of farmer "nobility" *(hòrònw)* and from that of slaves *(jonw).* By tradition, *nyamakalaw* were prohibited from positions of political leadership and were protected from enslavement by their peculiar status, enabling them to act as intermediaries on behalf of their *hòròn* patrons. Their presence continues to this day to sanction baptisms, naming ceremonies, marriages, and funerals. Within the *nyamakalaw,* each of these endogamous groups continues to maintain a level of control over their particular areas of expertise.

The special capacity of Mande bards *(jeliw* and *funew)* is most clearly revealed in the domain of speech and music (Hoffman 1990, 1995; Conrad 1995). Their artistry has kept alive traditions of the heroic age of the empires of Ghana and Mali (Bird 1970; Bird and Kendall 1980). Their oral repertoires have been a gold mine for historians and linguists alike. Bards are also the principal musicians, providing their skills as singers and playing a wide variety of instruments from drums to balafons to guitars for social and ritual occasions (Charry 1992). In addition, leatherworking has long been practiced by certain *jeli* families.

As producers of figurative sculpture, blacksmiths *(numuw)* have been the focus of much of the art historical research in the region (Ardouin 1978; McNaughton 1988; Ezra 1986b; Brett-Smith 1994). Their ability to smelt and forge iron into hoes, axes, adzes, and swords made them essential

Table 1

Major Social and Occupational Divisions within Mande Societies, with Common Patronymics for *Nyamakalaw* Groups

Hòrònw / "Nobles"	*Nyamakalaw* / Artists		*Jonw* / Slaves and Their Descendants
farmers warriors clerics traders	*jeliw*	oral artists, praise singers, and musicians (male/female); some are leatherworkers (male) 　　Danté, Diabaté, Kouyaté, Soumanou	often weavers (male) and spinners (female)
	numuw	blacksmith-sculptors (male); potters (female) 　　Ballo, Camara, Coulibaly, Doumbia, Fané, Kanté, Sissoko, Soumaworo	
	garankew	leatherworkers (male); gum and lip tatooers (female); some are indigo dyers (female) 　　Diawara, Diaouné, Dembaga, Ganesi, Korkhoss, Mangassi, Samabali, Soumanou, Simaga, Sylla, Tambana, Tungara, Yafa	
	funew	oral artists, Islamic traditionalists (male) 　　Camara	

to the success of Mande farmers, warriors, and statesmen. In addition to the masks and figurative sculpture for which the Bamana are especially acclaimed, *numuw* also produce utilitarian items such as stools and tool handles. As McNaughton (1979, 1988) has shown, however, their capacities extend well beyond mundane affairs into the spiritual realm. They are the masters of Komo, the powerful men's society that once governed the spiritual and political life of Mande communities (see also McIntosh n.d.). They are often renowned as hunters, healers, and diviners.

While well deserved, the attention bards and blacksmiths have received has tended to overshadow the contributions of other artists to Mande social and cultural history. Like their blacksmith husbands, potters *(numumusow)* also have played a significant role in the economic, social, and spiritual lives of the community. Sacred ceramic vessels figure prominently in oral traditions concerning the occult resources of powerful characters in the Mande past (SCOA 1984, 213; Conrad n.d.; McIntosh n.d.). Komo shrines are also said to include ritual pots to contain the medicinal plants and herbs employed by Komo healers (according to Tereba Togola; cited in McIntosh n.d.). While we may never be able to prove it, it is not unlikely that these vessels were made by women, given widely held attitudes toward clay as a woman's medium. Today, despite the increasing availability of metal, plastic, and enamel wares, potters continue to produce an array of ceramic vessels for cooking, for cooling and storing water, and for burning incense. These women too are believed to have special powers and are treated with a mixture of respect and caution by other women in the community.

Less well known than any of their counterparts, leatherworkers *(garankew* and *jeliw)* have also played a vital part in Mande history. In the past they were called upon to produce saddles and trappings for cavalry forces, as well as shot pouches, sheaths, and quivers for Mande warriors. Equally important, if less visually dramatic, has been the role of leatherworkers in enclosing sacred scripts and other materials as amulets to protect the wearer from physical, spiritual, and psychological harm.

The lack of attention potters and leatherworkers have received by scholars is owing in part to a bias inherent in Western hierarchical notions of art (sculpture) over craft (textiles, leather, pottery). Only recently have nonsculptural African forms become the focus of art historical research and exhibition, not coincidentally, parallel to trends of the art market (Hardin and Arnoldi 1996, 9). The terms *craft, artistry,* and *art* are used somewhat interchangeably here for several reasons. First, Mande potters, blacksmiths, and leatherworkers view themselves essentially as craftspersons who produce in order to satisfy consumer demands, sell their wares, and generate income. When artistry is rewarded, the best of them rise to the occasion to create objects that achieve the status of what in the West would be called Art. They take pride in the quality of their work, but they do not have the luxury to create for the sake of creating. They live too close to the edge. As for their patrons, it is not that Mande peoples do not make aesthetic judgments about the objects they commission and acquire from these artists, but that there are other considerations entering into decisions of which artists to patronize. Patterns of interdependence between particular families often extend back at least several generations. These traditional bonds of reliance must be weighed against genuine friendships between individuals, as well as against critical judgments of the quality and utility of the finished product.

While a Western preoccupation with smiths and bards has certainly skewed our perspective (see Barley 1984), it is important to note that potters and leatherworkers are also to some extent marginalized within Mande tradition. Neither play a central role anywhere equivalent to that of blacksmiths in Mande cosmologies, nor are they especially prominent in the oral traditions told by Mande griots. Potters are thought of primarily as the mothers and wives of blacksmiths, at least according to Mande society at large. For all the exceptional strength they are believed to possess, there is no genderized paradigm of power equivalent to that of the smelting process their husbands once undertook (Herbert 1993). But this is not an issue of concern to the potters themselves. They are confident of their own exceptional powers and of their role in the cultural achievements of Mande society.

Similarly, the view Mande leatherworkers have of themselves may not be shared by the larger society. *Garanke* leatherworkers long settled in Bamana and Maninka towns continue to be referred to as foreigners or strangers, much like Fula and Moor families who have lived for generations on the outskirts of town. The public identity of *jeliw* as griots places greater emphasis on their oral artistry than on their craftsmanship with leather, but *jeliw* see no contradiction in these dual roles and will easily promote whichever identity is appropriate for the occasion. Thus Mande society today is more complex than our social models have allowed, and this complexity reflects a complicated social history. Focusing on the crafts of pottery and leatherwork allows for different voices to be heard in the process of constructing a more complete Mande art history, with broader definitions of both art and artist.

ECOLOGY AND ETHNICITY IN THE WESTERN SUDAN

The Western Sudan style region lies west of the bend of the Niger River and includes the rich flood plains of Inland Niger Delta and the dry, open savanna grasslands that stretch from the Niger

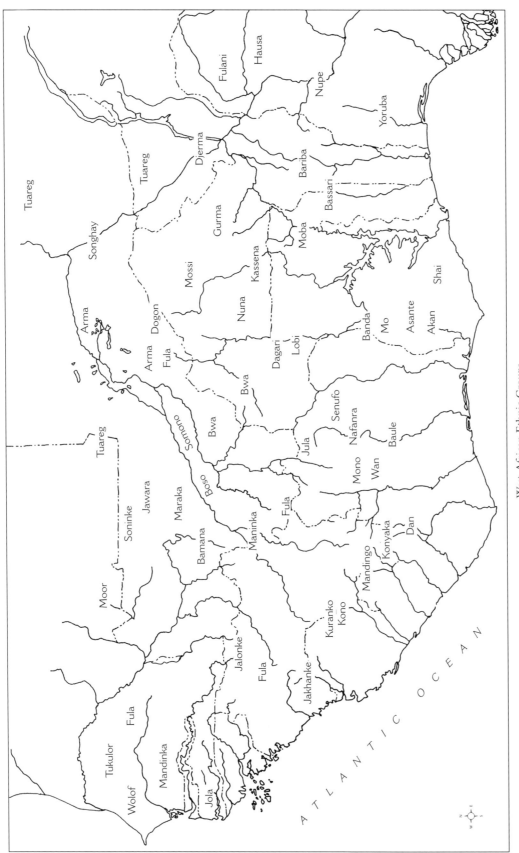

West African Ethnic Groups

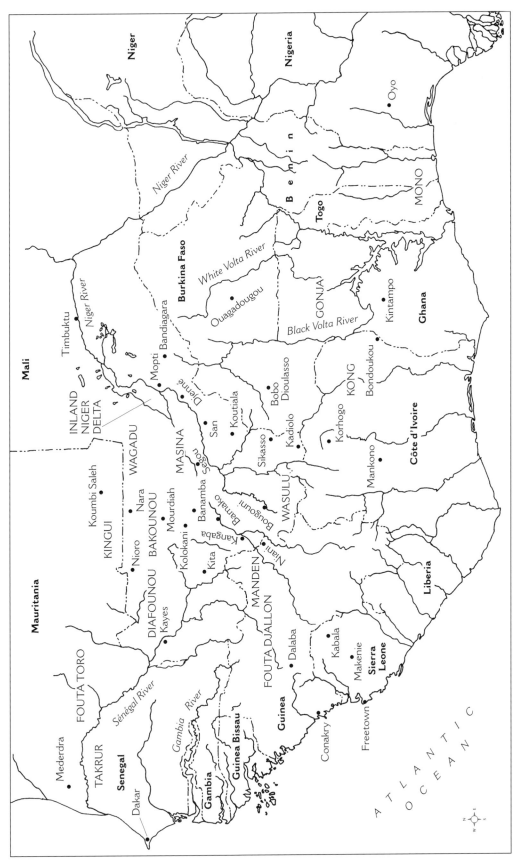

West African Towns and Place Names

Niger

Nigeria

B e n i n

Togo

MONO

Oyo

Mali

Burkina Faso

Ghana

GONJA

Niger River

White Volta River

Ouagadougou

Black Volta River

Kintampo

Timbuktu

Niger River

Bandiagara

Mopti

Djenné

INLAND
NIGER
DELTA

Bobo
Dioulasso

KONG

Bondoukou

Koutiala

San

Kadiolo

Korhogo

Côte d'Ivoire

WAGADU

MASINA

Sikasso

Mankono

Koumbi Saleh

Nara

BAKOUNOU

Mourdiah

Banamba

Ségou

Bamako

Bougouni

WASULU

KINGUI

Nioro

Kolokani

Kita

Kangaba

Niani

Mauritania

DIAFOUNOU

Kayes

MANDEN

Liberia

FOUTA TORO

FOUTA DJALLON

Dalaba

Kabala

Mederdra

TAKRUR

Senegal

Makenie

Sierra
Leone

Sénégal River

Gambia River

Guinea

Conakry

Gambia

Guinea Bissau

Freetown

Dakar

A T L A N T I C

O C E A N

N
W   E
S

to the upper reaches of the Senegal and Gambia rivers in the east.[7] Bordering the northern edge is the Sahel, where desert merges with the savanna grasslands. To the south, savanna gives way to woodlands, and the vegetation becomes relatively lush and green.

One of the most important factors relevant to the study of craft traditions is the availability of appropriate raw materials. For leatherwork, the savanna grasslands are ideally suited to the raising of livestock, including sheep and goats, source of the most common types of skins employed. In addition, hardy acacia trees growing throughout the region provide seed pods that are the principal source of tannin. Other vegetal materials used in tanning and dyeing skins also are available locally, whether cultivated especially for leatherwork, such as the red millet used in dyeing, or gathered wild.

The region is rich in clay deposits, the best and most accessible being those of the flood plains of the Inland Niger Delta. All other materials used in pottery production are also locally available, although a great deal of physical effort may be required for their collection. Historically, the availability of fuel resources would have fluctuated along with broad ecological trends (Brooks 1985). Today, Bamana and Maninka potters rely on an ever diminishing supply of fuel. They now must walk farther and often settle for less effective types of wood. In the Inland Niger Delta region, where supplies of wood have always been less accessible, straw and grasses continue to provide the primary fuel for pottery firing.

A second factor important to the study of craft traditions, especially leatherworking, is the relative ease of travel. There are few natural barriers. Throughout the Western Sudan the land is open and relatively flat, allowing caravans of camels, horses, donkeys, and oxen loaded with trade goods to pass. The Niger River has long been a major waterway for the shipment of supplies and for movements of peoples across ecological zones. Although perhaps not as conducive to travel, the savanna woodlands and forests to the south and west did not prevent mobility of Mande peoples into these regions. Indeed, it may well have been the availability of wood and other resources that drew blacksmiths and perhaps other artists south.

The Western Sudan historically has been a crossroads where peoples of diverse origins and ethnicities have interacted with each other for centuries. The main players in this story are the various Mande groups, including Bamana, Maninka, Jula, Soninke, and Somono, and their non-Mande neighbors, including Fula, Dogon, Bwa, Senufo, Moor, Songhay, and Tuareg (see Map 1).

Mande languages are spoken in various forms over much of the western part of West Africa (see Greenberg 1966). According to Charles Bird (1970), the northern subgroup (known as Mandekan) is exceptional not only for its extensive geographic spread as a first language, but also for its relative cohesiveness despite widespread distribution. This region stretches north and west toward the border of present-day Mauritania, east to the southern portions of the Inland Niger Delta and western Burkina Faso, south into northern Côte d'Ivoire, and across Guinea into eastern Senegal. Within this area, three major dialects correspond to the major ethnic divisions—Bamana (Bambara) to the north and east, Jula (Dyula) to the south, and Maninka (Malinke, Mandinka) to the south and west. In addition, Mande languages have been extended beyond the core region as a first language by minority populations who have migrated and as a second or trade language by others.

Soninke is also included in the northern group of Mande languages, but its relationship to the other Mande languages is somewhat ambiguous. Dalby (1971, 7–8, 13, n. 25) suggests that Soninke may be an early Mande language that diverges from the others due to influence from another non-Mande source. In fact, Bird (1970, 151–52) identifies Soninke as containing features of both northern Mande and Fulfulde, a reflection of the long interaction between Soninke and Fula peoples.[8] The Soninke heartland is located along the northern edge of the Sudan in the Sahel region between the upper Senegal and Niger rivers (Kendall, Soumare, and Soumare 1980). This region was the seat of the empire of Ghana (known in oral traditions as Wagadu), which flourished from the third or fourth century A.D. until its decline in the eleventh to twelfth centuries. This is the arena from which Soninke traders and clerics (and, very likely, leatherworkers) dispersed south and west in search of commercial opportunities.

With the fall of Ghana and the rise of the empire of Mali in the fourteenth century, a process referred to as the Mandingization of these Islamic trading clans resulted in the emergence of new identities, including the Maraka (Marka) of the Inland Niger Delta region, the Jula (Dyula) to the south, and the Jakhanke (Diakhanke) in the west (Sanneh 1976, 1979; Curtin 1972; Brooks 1985; Green 1984; Perinbam 1980; Person 1963, 1972). Although these clans kept Soninke patronymics and maintained a sense of distinctive heritage, they gave up their original languages and adopted Maninka dialects in deference to the hegemony of the Mali empire.[9]

Other Mande-speaking groups include the Somono, whose emergence as a distinct social group dates back at least to the seventeenth century when they were conscripted or recruited as boatmen under the leadership of the Bamana state centered at Segou (Roberts 1981; LaViolette 1987). Today they (along with the Boso) continue to navigate the Niger River and its tributaries, earning most of their income from fishing and river transport. However, in the region of Djenné (Jenne) there are significant numbers of Somono blacksmiths and potters as well.

Mande peoples have long maintained generally peaceful and productive relationships with other ethnic groups throughout the Western Sudan.[10] Most important among these groups are the Fula (Fulani, Peul), who speak the West Atlantic language known as Fulfulde (Greenberg 1966, 8, 24–30; Fagerberg-Diallo 1984). As a result of centuries of migrations in search of pasture for their herds, Fula peoples are widely dispersed across the West African savanna, from Senegal to Cameroon. There are major concentrations of Fulfulde speakers in the Fouta Toro (Futa Toro) region of Senegal along the Senegal River near the border of present-day Mauritania; in the Fouta Djallon (Futa Jallon) of the Guinea highlands; and in the region known as Masina (Macina), between Segou and Timbuktu, encompassing the rich flood plain of the Inland Niger Delta. Given their mobility and their association with herding, it is not surprising to find Fula leatherworkers competing with others at markets throughout the region, in towns small and large. In addition, Fula women are among the most prominent of potters in the Inland Niger Delta region, and their wares are renowned well beyond their homeland.

The Voltaic neighbors of the Mande include various Dogon and Bwa peoples who speak different dialects of Gur-related languages.[11] The Dogon live in small farming villages along the Bandiagara escarpment and the adjacent plains, while the largest concentrations of Bwa speakers are in the region of San. Dogon and Bwa leatherworkers venture out to the major markets of the Delta region and occasionally try their luck in the larger cities of Segou, Bamako, and Sikasso. By contrast, Dogon and Bwa pottery has a much smaller circulation, primarily serving local needs.

Senufo peoples also speak a Gur language. They live south of Sikasso in southern Mali, into southwestern Burkina Faso, and throughout the northeastern part of Côte d'Ivoire. They are farmers, hosts to Jula clerics and traders as well as a number of artisan groups, some of whom claim Mande origins.

Along the northern fringe of the Mande region are various Berber-related nomadic peoples, including Moor to the northwest and Tuareg to the northeast. Moor and Tuareg peoples, along with the Hausa of northern Nigeria, are especially well known for their leatherworking traditions.

Sonrhaï is the first language of the majority of the population in the urban settings of Djenné and Timbuctou, the heart of the great Songhay empire that dominated the region after the fall of the Mali empire. Sonrhaï is also the language of the Arma, descendants of mixed marriages between local Songhay women and the soldiers of the Moroccan invasion force that brought the Songhay empire to an end in the sixteenth century. The Arma are especially important because they are associated with the Islamic crafts of slipper making and embroidery. Whatever their biological ancestry, Arma leatherworkers today trace the origins of their craft to Morocco, and their tool kits and associated terminology are Arabic in origin.

This complex matrix of identities is what has long given the Western Sudan its dynamism. If shifts in language, ethnicity, religion, and craft specialization occurred in response to changing spiritual, economic, or political demands, such accommodations were not done lightly. The region is not a melting pot. Indigenous ideologies continue to promote notions of distinctive identity. In short, social and cultural differences matter.

TRADE, ISLAM, STATE BUILDING, AND SLAVERY

Preservation of social and cultural heritage in this pluralistic setting did not inhibit the exchange of objects and ideas. The development of long-distance trade networks facilitated the diffusion of material goods, some locally produced, some imported across the Sahara, and others introduced by Europeans along the Atlantic coast. With the trans-Saharan trade as a powerful impetus for securing gold and other commodities, Islamized Mande traders dispersed from the economic and cultural centers of the Western Sudan into the savanna woodland areas to the south and west, expanding preexisting commercial networks and establishing new trade routes. These traders and the clerics who accompanied them introduced non-Muslim populations to the Islamic faith. Islam brought new attitudes concerning the power of the Arabic script, new styles of dress, new types of objects, new symbols of power and authority, and a distinctive architectural style. However, while Islam drew on indigenous imagery and expertise, it also ultimately precipitated the decline and disappearance of at least some artistic traditions associated with animist practices. The state-building activities of Mande warrior groups also led to the movements of craftsmen. Newly emerging states needed blacksmiths and leatherworkers for production of trade items, for supplying farmers with agricultural tools necessary for a strong economy, as well as for the production of weapons of war, horse trappings, and regalia. Slavery was an important part of the economy of these states. The extent to which the services of craftspeople may have been conscripted bears consideration. These factors—trade, the introduction of Islam, the expansion of Mande military and political power, and slavery—affected Mande social and cultural institutions in different ways, sometimes providing opportunities for expansion, other times limiting their success and even preventing their survival.

The trans-Saharan trade brought the peoples of West Africa into direct contact with those of North Africa, Egypt, and the Near East. As early as the beginning of the ninth century A.D., a reference to Ghana as the land of gold appeared in the account of an Arab geographer (al-Mas'ūdī, cited in Levtzion and Hopkins 1981, 30, 32, 379-80, n. 8), a tribute to the commodity that was to sustain interest in establishing and maintaining relations with the Western Sudan for generations of Arab traders and later European explorers.

In addition to gold, exports from the Western Sudan included slaves and ivory as well as malagueta pepper, kola, and leather. The twelfth-century account of the Arab traveler Abū Ḥāmid al-Gharnāṭī identifies tanned and dyed skins as an export from the Sudan:

> Various kinds of goatskins dyed in a marvellous manner are exported from the land of the Sūdān, each skin being tough, thick and pliant, and in a pleasing colour from violet to black. . . . They are used to make boots for kings. They do not let the water through, nor do they damage easily or perish, despite their pliability and softness and their pleasant smell. One such skin is sold for ten dinars. The thread with which the shoe is sown perishes, but the leather does not, nor does it crack. It may be washed in a bath of hot water, and again becomes as new. The owner may have inherited it from his grandfather through his father. It is one of the marvels of the world (Levtzion and Hopkins 1981, 133).[12]

Indeed, it has been suggested that a major portion of the leather acquired by Europeans as "Moroccan" was actually produced in West Africa (Hopkins 1973, 49). By the nineteenth century, tanned and dyed skins were certainly among the leather manufactures produced by the Hausa for export to North Africa. However, although they never developed the kind of large-scale tanning and dyeing industry for which the Hausa are so well known, it is plausible that Mande leather-workers also contributed to this trade.

Europeans seem to have been more interested in acquiring raw materials for their own manu-facturing base. During the seventeenth century, the English, Dutch, and French competed for what had become a lucrative export trade in hides and skins, according to some reports second only to gold (De Moraes 1972).[13] It is difficult to determine the impact of this trade, if any, on leatherwork in the region. In the first place, Europeans sought the larger hides of cows and oxen, rather than goat- or sheepskins, and they acquired these skins untanned. Fula herders are identified in contemporary accounts as the source of the hides, and although leatherworkers may have been employed in the preparation of skins for shipment, there is no mention of their participation (De Moraes 1972, 113).[14]

Goods imported from North Africa and Egypt included dates, spices, perfumes, copper and brass metalwares, books, paper, rich fabrics, cotton calicoes, and horses.[15] Ceramic wares are not mentioned in the Arabic accounts as items of trade or gifts. Nor is there any evidence that objects of leather such as sandals, shoes, or boots were among the items of personal adornment and dress introduced into the Sudan via the trans-Saharan trade. By the fourteenth century, however, Arab horses along with Arab-type saddles and trappings were in great demand for the cavalry forces of the Malian Empire. When the Portuguese began to establish trade relations with peoples along the Senegambian and Guinean coasts, they soon recognized that the items most in demand were goods already familiar from the trans-Saharan trade—textiles and metalwares, as well as horses and Arab- or Moorish-style trappings (Crone 1937, 17; see also Elbl 1991).

The development of trade and the movements of peoples within West Africa were far more important for the diffusion of some Mande artistic traditions than these external trade relationships. The earliest phases of the Mande diaspora began with the migrations of Muslim Soninke trading clans as part of the expansion of trade networks during the heyday of Ghana. As noted above, this southern dispersal was accelerated by the decline of the empire in the eleventh and twelfth cen-

FIGURE 5. Sudanese-style mosque with ceramic caps *(coorow)* remaining on several pinnacles. They are commissioned from local Jula potters. Dioumaténé, Mali, 1991.

FIGURE 6. Ceramic pinnacle cap *(cooro)* collected in 1991 from an abandoned mosque in Gouéné, Mali. Musée National du Mali, Bamako.

turies, and continued as these commercial networks came under the control of the empire of Mali during the thirteenth and fourteenth centuries.

The traders' expanding network of markets would have been an attractive incentive for the migration of Mande leatherworkers. Unlike most other artisans, who produced items in their compounds or workshops and brought the finished product to market to sell, leatherworkers very likely arrived with their tools and some supplies, setting up a workshop on the spot. In addition, they probably worked directly on commission from clients and would have been more likely to travel than to stay put and supply others with goods in quantity. The development of new trade routes and associated markets would have provided these craftsmen with a setting for soliciting the patronage of new clients.

The spread of Islam along these trade routes also presented leatherworkers with opportunities to practice their artistry. Mande clerics, traders, and presumably craftsmen settled as strangers among non-Muslim, non-Mande populations. The religious character of the communities they established gave them a sense of identity and community with the larger Islamic world. They were, however, primarily interested in trade, not in proselytizing among their pagan neighbors. According to Bravmann:

> In a very real sense, this economic class could be described as a group of "merchant-clerics," for many of its members clearly served in a dual capacity. In general, their aims were twofold: the control of regional and interregional trade routes, especially to monopolize the distribution of luxury goods and necessary products that could not be obtained locally; and the introduction of superficial and material elements of Islamic culture to individuals or groups (1974, 7).

These Mande ambassadors introduced the concept of the magical power of the Arabic script (Goody 1971; Prussin 1986, 1995; Quimby 1972), creating a demand for Islamic amulets well beyond the needs of the local Muslim minority. Leatherworkers would have been called upon to enclose these amulets in leather casings for both Muslim and non-Muslim clients. Leatherworkers would also very likely have been commissioned by the clerics themselves to make covers or slipcases for the Koran and other precious manuscripts.

The impact of trade and Islam on ceramic traditions is more difficult to assess. There is little evidence that ceramic wares served as items of long-distance trade.[16] Nor did Islam introduce or create a demand for new models. Most of the types of objects produced by potters associated with Muslim practices have non-Muslim parallels. Small bowls used for ritual ablutions prior to prayers are identical in form to those produced for serving sauces.[17] The ceramic pinnacle caps and other architectural pottery forms that are a distinctive feature of some Sudanese-style mosques (Figures 5 and 6) are more elaborate than those documented on animist shrines but similar in concept. In other words, none of the objects Mande potters make are exclusively Islamic, such that their origin may be attributed to Islam.

Furthermore, Islam may well have contributed to the demise of some ceramic traditions. The figurative terra cottas identified with the archaeological cultures of Djenné (Figure 7) and Bankoni presumably were part of a pre-Islamic animist belief system (McIntosh and McIntosh 1979; McIntosh 1989).[18] They are thought to have served as altars, or as images of ancestral figures to whom prayers might have been offered. This tradition, along with that of the burial of human remains in large ceramic urns, appears to have faded with the coming of Islam.

The essentially peaceful activities of traders, clerics, and craftspeople were followed by the more aggressive expansion of Mande warrior groups. Craftsmen, especially blacksmiths and leather-workers, played an important role in the growth of Mande military and political power. During their heyday, the empires of Ghana and Mali (and later Songhay) were major patrons of the arts. A reference from the Arab writer al-'Umarī's fourteenth-century account suggests that the cavalry were provided horses and equipment: "Among their chiefs are some whose wealth derived from the king reaches 50,000 mithqāls of gold every year, besides which he keeps them in horses and clothes" (Levtzion and Hopkins 1981, 266). The success of the Malian cavalry was repeated by off-shoots of the empire, as Mande warriors established states dependent on horses, including Kong and Gonja to the southeast and the Mandinka (Mandingo) kingdoms of the Senegambia (Goody 1967, 179-205; Green 1984; Innes 1976; Levtzion 1968; Quinn 1972).

There is little information in the written record concerning the production of equipment for warfare and state support for, or control over, craftsmen. However, the nineteenth-century Fula state of Masina apparently maintained its cavalry, supplying both horses and equipment. According to Marion Johnson:

> In addition to this standing cavalry force, a seasonal army of cavalry and infantry was conscripted annually; . . . These men were given an allowance to equip themselves with lances, swords etc, and with saddlery and harness; artisans are said to have been provided with slaves to help with this work. . . . On longer campaigns, the army was accompanied by smiths, saddlers etc. paid by the state (1976, 485).

FIGURE 7. Terra-cotta figure excavated in 1981 by the McIntoshes at Djenné-djeno, with amulets around the neck and a knife and sheath worn on the upper arm. Musée National du Mali, Bamako. (Photo: Roderick J. and Susan Keech McIntosh)

Presumably, leatherworkers would have been essential to Mande state-building activities in the production and repair of equipment for warfare, including sword and knife sheaths, saddles and other horse trappings, boots, quivers, shot pouches, and powder horns. They also would have taken part in the production of regalia for established chiefs, including crowns, staffs, and fly whisks.[19]

While the movements of traders, clerics, and warriors have received a great deal of attention, those of artisans remain poorly understood. George Brooks (1985) has suggested that Mande smiths accompanied, and perhaps preceded, traders and clerics into the forest regions as entrepreneurs developing new markets for their products and in search of fresh supplies of timber for charcoal. The smiths would have been well received by local farmers in need of tools for agricultural production, and they would have been especially important as a source of weapons for the territorial ambitions of Mande warriors. It seems likely that there was a similar dispersal of Mande leatherworkers. The various factors described above provided the setting for such a diaspora and a heightened demand for the services of leatherworkers. This does not appear to have been the case for potters.

The movements of some artisans certainly reflect the entrepreneurial drive of individuals, but not all such movements were voluntary. The institution of slavery, widespread in West Africa for at least several centuries of the pre-colonial era, seems to have escalated during the course of the nineteenth century. Throughout this period, the regions of southern Mali, southwestern Burkina Faso, and northern Côte d'Ivoire suffered tremendous disruptions due to the slave-raiding activities of the warriors of the Maninka ruler Samory and of the Bamana states of Segou and Sikasso (Kenedougou). Without the protection of centralized power, farming populations across the savanna region offered little resistance (Rondeau 1980, 104; Klein 1992; Roberts 1987, 113).

Today *nyamakalaw* repeatedly stress that their ancestors were protected from enslavement by their peculiar status. There are hints in the historical record, however, that their services were sometimes conscripted. As noted above, male leatherworkers and blacksmiths certainly would have been in demand for maintaining the effectiveness and power of the various slave and free armies, producing and repairing weapons and horse trappings. In his extended study of Samory and his military organization, Yves Person (1968-75, 2:919-23) mentions the establishment at major garrisons of teams of artisans, primarily blacksmiths, who were provided grain and thus expected to work full time on the production of weaponry. Person also mentions tailors and leatherworkers among the artists garrisoned by Samory, but suggests that their numbers were much less important than the blacksmiths. Roberts (1981, 187; 1987, 126) reports that the grandfather of one of his Maraka informants from Sansanding (Sinsani), along the Niger River northeast of Segou, maintained a plantation exclusively of slave ironworkers. According to Green (1984), blacksmiths and bards were conscripted by the Watara rulers of the state of Kong in northern Côte d'Ivoire. Meillassoux (1975, 202) mentions that blacksmiths and weavers might have been exempted from agricultural labor in return for the products of their particular expertise, and that the same might have been true for basketmakers, potters, and cloth dyers.

But what about women in general and women potters in particular? Throughout the Western Sudan more women and children were taken captive than men, and a much higher percentage of those remaining in West Africa were also women and children (Robertson and Klein 1983; Klein 1983). The men were more likely either to be killed during the raiding, drafted into the army, or transported to the coast for the Atlantic trade. Female slaves were preferred and in fact demanded higher prices because of their productive capacity. It was not the ability of female slaves to produce offspring that made them valuable, since it was more expensive to raise a child from birth to a productive level than to purchase a slave outright. Rather, it was their labor in the fields, combined with the enhanced performance of male slaves when provided wives, that made female slaves a desired commodity. Females slaves also supplied a wide range of domestic services (drawing water, preparing food, cleaning, etc.) to both slave and free populations.[20]

While agricultural and domestic labor would have been reason enough to keep the demand for women high, female slaves had other skills that augmented their value. During the dry season, when there was little work to be done in the fields, they were encouraged to engage in craft activities, especially those related to textile production. Even old women whose usefulness in the fields had all but disappeared could command high prices if they were adept at spinning (Meillassoux 1975, 202, 249-50; Roberts 1984, 1987, 108, 125-26). The value of skills such as spinning and dyeing (done by women) as well as weaving (which remained a man's task) can be tied directly to the commercial importance of the trade in textiles. However, the value of other craft activities such as pottery production is more difficult to assess.

Person (1968-75, 2:920) notes that the wives of the blacksmiths stationed in military camps by Samory spent time carefully pounding gun powder in their mortars, but makes only brief reference to their "past" roles as potters. Meillassoux (1975, 202) includes potters among those who might be exempted from agricultural labor as slaves, presumably to provide pottery in exchange. Indeed, potters must have been needed to supply the cooking vessels used to prepare food for the armies of the various warlords and the workers in the fields. Potters also would have made the jars for cooling water and brewing beer. For the time being, the question remains open as to whether these services were provided by slaves or by free women, but if the skills of other craftspeople were tapped, it seems likely that those of the potters would have been as well.

Trade, Islam, state building, and slavery—these are the major themes of West African history. Artists were certainly affected by the economic and political fortunes of the great states that rose and fell in the Western Sudan, just as they were by religious and social changes wrought by the spread of Islam. But the impact was not universal. Different crafts were affected in different ways, and the gender of the artists surely contributed to the particular roles they played in this history.

GENDER AND CRAFT SPECIALIZATION

The notion that certain artistic activities are gender-specific is deeply embedded in contemporary Mande ideology. While men do blacksmithing, leatherworking, weaving, and wood carving, women do pottery, indigo (and other) dyeing, spinning, and basketry. Men and women may on occasion assist each other in some phases of production. For example, women are often the ones to draw and transport the water needed for blacksmithing and tanning, an extension of their domestic responsibility to fetch water for other personal and household needs. Similarly, blacksmith men sometimes help their wives digging the clay pit, transporting clay, and marketing the finished products. Potters may assist their fathers or husbands at the forge, especially when there are no male siblings or male children of an appropriate age. Many of the potters I interviewed spoke of working the bellows as children or as young wives, a physically demanding chore often required of young apprentices. Two of the women (exceptional in other ways as well) said that they had themselves forged iron, even though this is supposed to be an exclusively male activity. In general, however, such collaborations and crossovers are seen by both men and women as exceptions to the rule.

The historical implications of these social patterns have not been fully explored. For example, because Mande tradition assigns men the exclusive responsibility for sculptural traditions in wood and metal, it is generally assumed that they too were the makers of terra-cotta statuary (Frank forthcoming; cf. Berns 1993). However, this presumption fails to take into account that, with few exceptions, women hold a virtual monopoly on ceramic production throughout the Mande heartland and the Inland Niger Delta regions. It seems likely that women produced both domestic and ritual pottery, and at least plausible that they were also the makers of the terra-cotta sculptures.

Evidence for the participation of women in a diaspora of Mande cultural institutions is uneven, at best. On the one hand, the presence of Mande women as indigo dyers throughout Guinea and into Sierra Leone suggests that they may have traveled with their husbands, offering their skills to a new clientele. However, in other settings, indigo dyeing is dominated by men. Among the Maraka of the Middle Niger valley, the craft is acknowledged to have once been a woman's domain. Men took control of the process in the nineteenth century when it became a commercial venture (Roberts 1984). Labelle Prussin (1986) contends that Islam is partially responsible for causing a major shift in gender roles by excluding women from certain artistic processes. As the mobility of craftsmen increased and opportunities for trade expanded, Islamic restrictions limited the participation of women in certain craft specializations. The shift among some populations from nomadic to sedentary life styles — from tent to mud brick architecture — also meant less control for women over the domestic domain of building. Prussin argues that leatherworking, textile production, and dyeing originally were women's art forms, taken over by men as a result of the introduction of Islam. She contrasts the women tanners and leatherworkers of the nomadic Tuareg and Moor with the appearance of Arma craftsmen whose history is quite clearly tied to an Islamic and North African heritage. Among Mande peoples, leatherworking as a male domain was already well established by the time of the arrival of the Arma in the late sixteenth century, but as argued above, Islam and trade provided greater opportunities for male craftworkers than for women.

Evidence that female potters traveled with their blacksmith husbands is also mixed. On the one hand, the association of pottery and blacksmithing among the Senufo, Dogon, Wolof, and other non-Mande neighbors supports the notion of a historical link to Mande practices. However, exceptions to this pattern in both Mande and non-Mande settings suggest that at least in some instances itinerant blacksmiths either married local women, or the women abandoned their trades once they had departed from the homeland. In southeastern Mali, for example, the wives of Mande blacksmiths specialize in basketry but do not make pottery. Ceramics are the domain of Jula women, whose origins are probably not Mande (Frank 1993 and chapter 6 herein). Among the Kono, a Mande-speaking people of Sierra Leone, pottery production is restricted by age and gender to elder women but is not associated with blacksmithing (Hardin 1996, 40-41, 48, n. 10). Similarly, Mande (Konyaka) immigrants among the Wan and Mono of northwestern Côte d'Ivoire included blacksmiths but not potters (Biot 1989, 44).[21]

Clearly, the widespread distribution of a distinctive style of Mande leatherworking is only in part due to the fact that leather goods travel more easily than ceramic wares. It is also due to the greater freedom of movement enjoyed by men, historically and to the present day. The movements of women in the past as well as today tend to be dependent on marriage ties between particular families and communities, not on distant trade or market opportunities. As a result, external influences on their artistry have been more limited.

It may never be possible to fully reconstruct a datable chronology of either Mande leatherwork or pottery. However, relying exclusively on monolithic ethnic styles to define artistic traditions prevents scholars from recognizing the complexity of their histories. Exploring objects, technologies, and artist identities within a broader regional framework reveals the richness of Mande artistic heritage and allows us to restore these men and women to their deserved but different places in Mande art history.[22]

2 THE PLACE OF POTS

Pots from the Mande heartland have strong, simple shapes. Proportions tend to be robust, and the pots are shorter and broader than most in the spectrum of West African ceramic traditions. Painted patterns are bold and textures are rough (Plates 4-6, 8). Only rarely does one find in the field pots with figurative imagery in relief, such as those identified as Bamana in museum and private collections (Plate 7; Figures 25, 26). Today, decorative touches are confined to rims with impressed lines, molded ridges around the belly of the vessel, and surface patterning generally reserved for the lower surfaces (Figure 8). Upper surfaces often are burnished smooth. Water jars intended for public display are painted with geometric designs in red slip, while cooking and other kitchen storage vessels are treated hot from the fire with a vegetal solution that gives them a richly varied, shiny black surface.

While I argue that these features constitute a Mande style, it is one that is more regional than ethnic. What examining the distribution of ceramic styles and object types reveals are long patterns of interaction among different ethnic groups, along with a shared social and ecological environment.

POTS IN PREHISTORY

Ceramic artifacts have long served archaeologists as markers of cultural identity. Their durability and ubiquity in archaeological contexts provide tangible evidence of the presence and evolution of distinct cultural traditions as well as cross-cultural contacts over time and space. While art historians have generally concentrated on the study of figurative sculpture, archaeologists have found valuable historical clues in their analyses of ritual and domestic pottery and pot sherds.

At a series of sites in the Inland Niger Delta, pottery has proved to be especially sensitive time and culture markers (Bedaux et al. 1978; McIntosh and McIntosh 1980, 112-29, 436-37, 452-56; McIntosh 1995, 130-213). Thin-walled, rimmed spherical or hemispherical pots with fine sand-tempered paste-and-twine impressed decorations from the earliest phases of occupation (c. 250 B.C.-A.D. 350) at the site of Djenné-djeno (Jenne-jeno) display clear affinities with pottery docu-

FIGURE 8. Bamana potter Assa Coulibaly adding textured decoration to the belly of a water jar *(jidaga)* with a twisted-string roulette. Banamba, Mali, 1988.

mented at earlier Saharan sites, suggesting a northern origin for the tradition. Oral traditions concerning the peopling of the region support such an hypothesis.[1] This fine ware disappears from later phases (A.D. 350-850 and A.D. 850-1400) at Djenné-djeno and elsewhere in the Inland Niger Delta. The later assemblages reveal the evolution of a more diverse array of decorative techniques, rim variations, and vessel types within what remains a relatively conservative tradition (McIntosh and McIntosh 1980, 451; McIntosh 1995, 163-64; Gallay 1986; Bedaux et al. 1978).[2] Twine decoration, slip-painted designs, and carinated rims (ones that angle sharply inward) are hallmarks of this northern style.

These characteristics are quite distinct from those of archaeological pots from the southern savanna and forest regions, which have flared, everted rims; coarse grog-tempered paste; and deeply grooved or modeled relief decorations. The antiquity of stylistic differences between northern Sahel/Sudan and southern savanna/forest regions appears deeply rooted in West African prehistory.

This interpretation has been supported by recent excavations at Korounkorokalé, a site some thirty kilometers southwest of the capital city of Bamako. Archaeological finds from this site establish a very early date, 4240 to 3800 B.C., for ceramic production in the savanna/forest region. According to Kevin MacDonald (1995, forthcoming), stylistic evidence suggests that this pottery is not an offshoot of the northern ceramic tradition. Although some of the decorative elements are similar to those of the Saharan assemblages, the open, unrestricted vessel shapes and thin walls are sufficiently different from their northern counterparts to constitute a distinct tradition (see McIntosh and McIntosh 1980, 436-37).

The later ceramic assemblage at Korounkorokalé (tentatively dated to A.D. 880-1200) is important for the stylistic characteristics it appears to share with at least two other ceramic assemblages. Distinctive "Y rims," thickened rims, and decoration with accordion-pleat, knotted-strip, and multistick, cord-wrapped roulettes have also been found in ceramic materials excavated in the region of Segou and Markala and believed to date to A.D. 1100 to 1400 (MacDonald 1995). MacDonald also notes some parallels with the ceramic materials published by Filipowiak (1979) for the site of Niani, Guinea, dating to c. A.D. 1000. What is significant about all of these finds taken together is that they appear to constitute a distinct Mande/Maninka ceramic tradition contemporary with the rise of the empire of Mali.

What makes the contrast between Inland Niger Delta and Mande heartland pottery from archaeological sites all the more important is that such differences exist despite indications of trade and contact between these two regions and elsewhere. Evidence of this interaction appears in the presence of a particularly distinctive footed bowl form found at various Sahel, Sudan, and savanna forest sites (Bedaux 1980; Bedaux and Raimbault 1993, 284). The earliest of these appears to be from Niani, while other examples have been found at Korounkorokalé, Djenné-djeno, among the Tellem materials excavated along the Bandiagara cliffs, and as far north as Koumbi Saleh.[3] Rogier Bedaux has suggested that the form originated in Niani and may have reached the other areas by trade. However, he notes that subtle changes in the process of manufacture in the later bowls from the Tellem finds reflect local production of an otherwise imported form. This suggests that each of these sites supported a distinct local ceramic tradition, interested in and capable of incorporating a new and foreign form into the repertoires.

Similarly, the occasional appearance of slip-painted and carinated pottery forms in the ceramic sequences at various southern forest sites (Gonja and Kintampo) has caused speculation on possible connections with the Inland Niger Delta region (Davies 1964, 1969; Mathewson 1968; see also Shinnie and Kense 1989, 130). The McIntoshes urge caution in attributing this style specifically to the Inland Niger Delta:

> With particular reference to carinated form and painted decoration, we do not know how widespread these attributes are, either along the Niger or to the west of the Middle Niger in the Sahel belt, during the first millennium A.D. It is possible that all these characteristics are part of a generalized first millennium Soninké potting tradition throughout the Sahel. If so, attributing their presence in savanna contexts to contact with the IND [Inland Niger Delta] or Niger Bend is unwarranted (McIntosh and McIntosh 1980, 455).

The possibility of identifying a Sahelian Soninke ceramic tradition as distinct from an indigenous Maninka forest one is intriguing, but conclusions must await more sustained and comprehensive archaeological work in the Mande heartland, the Inland Niger Delta region, and elsewhere. Nevertheless, the notion of distinctive regional styles corresponding to a broad northern/southern division provides a general framework from prehistory to explore in the contemporary setting.

LIMITATIONS OF THE HISTORICAL RECORD

Turning from the archaeological record to search for information concerning more recent pottery production into the historic period, one finds little in the accounts of early European travelers to assist in establishing style boundaries.[4] In 1623 Richard Jobson, traveling up the Gambia River into what he referred to as "Mandingo" territory,[5] noted the work of blacksmiths, leatherworkers, and potters. His account attests to the existence of potters, but he associates them with masons, not blacksmiths:

> Another profession we finde, and those are they who temper the earth, and makes the walles of their houses, and likewise earthen pots they set to the fire, to boyle and dresse their food in for all other occasions, they use no other mettle, but serve themselves with the gourd, which performs it very neatly (Jobson [1623] 1904, 155).

Unfortunately, he provides no information as to the gender of the potters, their technology, or the range of products they created.

The Scottish explorer-adventurer Mungo Park (1799, 22, 281), who traveled into the interior through much of the region of what is today western Mali, mentions the use of earthen vessels for containing water and cooking, as well as for indigo dyeing. However, pottery is not one of the local trades he describes. Similarly, Anne Raffenel's catalogue (1856) of the Bamana industries he observed lists blacksmithing and smelting, leatherwork, weaving, and indigo and other cloth dyeing, but does not mention pottery production.

Not until the colonial period, as ethnographer-administrators and missionaries made their forays into the realm of local cultural practices, did descriptions of ceramic process and product begin to appear. One of the earliest is by Frantz de Zeltner (1915) based on interviews with and observations of an elderly Soninke woman in the region of Nioro. He noted the absence of discussion of pottery in the literature, yet remarked that regional and indeed ethnic styles were suggested by stylistic differences, despite a superficial uniformity. He described Bamana pottery as rough, less than spherical, and without decoration, handles, or feet. He contrasted this with the incised decoration of vessels from Mopti and the painted geometric designs of those of the Inland Niger Delta. His description of the decorative phases of the pottery-making process included impressions made with netted fiber over a pot sherd, twisted-string roulette, and dentelated-calabash roulette. He also provided what appears to be a fairly complete list of vessel types and indigenous nomenclature (de Zeltner 1915, 229, 233).

Efforts to define style regions are hampered by the lack of well-documented materials preserved in museum collections in the West, in contrast to the relatively greater quantity of leatherwork.[6] United States museums generally have tended to favor Anglophone countries (Nigeria, Ghana, Liberia, Sierra Leone) over their French-speaking Sudanic counterparts in terms of collections, but even these are not extensive when it comes to ceramic wares. African ceramics have recently been the focus of several exhibitions drawn from private collectors and dealers, but often with little in the way of field documentation.[7]

More important is a growing body of literature from ethno-archaeological studies of contemporary pottery and potters (see titles by Bedaux, Gallay, Huysecom and Mayor, LaViolette, Raimbault, among others). Because of their site-specific nature and attention to detail, these studies are an invaluable resource for comparison with my own research and field observations. Approaching distribution patterns of ceramic styles and types from a regional perspective allows for de Zeltner's hypothesis to be tested. Was de Zeltner on the right track when he suggested that ethnic

FIGURE 9. Repertoire of some of the pottery types made by Bamana and Maninka potters. Cooking pot *(daga)*, cooking pot *(barama* or *nègèdaga)* with feet and handles based on a metal prototype, couscous steamer *(nyintin)*, saucepot *(nadaga)*, tripod brazier *(singon)*, water pitcher *(garigulèti)*, chicken watering pot *(sheminfaga)*, washbasin *(faga)*, water jar *(jidaga)*, two styles of incense burner *(wusulanbèlè)*, and large water jar *(jifinye)*.

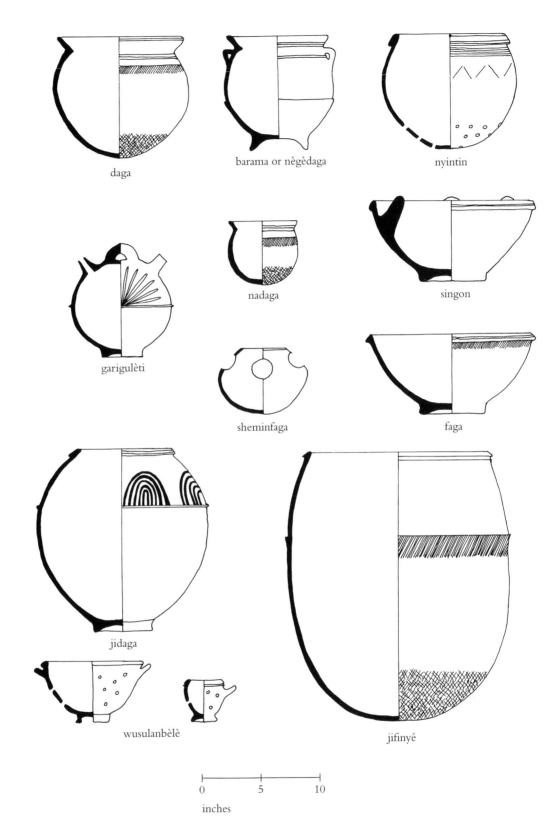

daga

barama or nègèdaga

nyintin

garigulèti

nadaga

singon

sheminfaga

faga

jidaga

wusulanbèlè

jifinyé

0   5   10

inches

FIGURE 10. Four green pots ready to be fired. From left to right: two small cooking pots *(nadagaw)*, a washbasin *(faga)*, and a small water storage jar *(jidaga)*. An already fired large water storage jar *(jifinye)* is upturned in the background. On the far right is an old vessel used as a mold. Kunòyò, Mali, 1988.

FIGURE 11. Unfired pottery cooking pot (left; *barama* or *nègèdaga*) made in emulation of a metal prototype (right), complete with lug handles and tripod legs. Kunòyò, Mali, 1991.

styles existed? Are any of the vessel forms or decorative techniques employed by potters distinctive enough to identify with particular ethnic groups? Does the distribution of stylistic features allow for speculation of independent origins, the development of styles over time, or the movement of certain designs and forms over space, in short, the stuff of traditional art history?

DEFINING A MANDE STYLE

The vessels Mande potters have produced for at least a century fall into a dozen or so standard types (Figure 9).[8] The most common type of vessel in various sizes is the cooking pot called *daga,* also a generic term for all pottery. Small ones are called *nadaga* (saucepot) and larger ones are sometimes referred to as *tobidaga* (cooking pot). These are generally round-bottomed vessels with small, restricted rims and little decoration beyond perhaps a textured lower surface and a line or two impressed into the rim (Figure 10). Curiously, given their ubiquitous presence in village markets, it is relatively rare to see women actually using them to cook, since aluminum kettles have largely taken their place. Ironically, these now common metal pots probably were based on ceramic proto-types. The path has come full circle with the making by some potters of ceramic skeuomorphs (copies from one material to another) of the metal pots called *nègèdaga* (literally, iron pot) or *barama* (one of the terms used for metal cooking pots) (Figure 11).

A second type of cooking vessel is the *nyintin,* or *basidaga* (Figures 12–14), used primarily for steaming couscous but also for smoking the pungent locust bean paste known as *sumbala.* It is similar in shape to the regular *daga,* but the rounded bottom is pierced with holes. The pot may be lined with cloth to contain the grain and then placed above a pot of boiling water.

Another type of pot that comes in different sizes is the *faga,* a low, wide, usually footed bowl with an unrestricted rim (Plate 8; Figure 10). Larger ones are generally used for washing clothing and dishes. Smaller ones may be used for serving food, although this function has been largely usurped by the more colorful and now ubiquitous enamelware and plastic bowls. Small ones also may be used for washing faces and hands, including ritual ablutions before prayer, in which case they are called *sèlidaga* (literally, prayer pot).

The *singon* is a brazier with a low bowl-like shape similar to the *faga,* but with three prongs extending into the interior (Figure 15). These prongs serve as tripod supports for a cooking vessel. The *singon* also can be used as a portable heater inside sleeping rooms and vestibules. Some potters also make an object they refer to as a *furuno* or *furunè* (from the French *fourneau*) that serves a similar function. These come in a variety of sizes and configurations and are often skeuomorphs of imported or locally made metal braziers (Figure 16).

The largest vessel currently produced is the *jifinye* or *finye,* destined for the kitchen as a storage container for water (Figure 17). Ovoid in shape with slightly restricted rims and round bottoms, they stand as much as three feet high. Like *dagau,* they usually have no decoration other than lines impressed into the rim and lower surfaces textured with twisted-string and corncob roulettes. These pots are identified as the type of vessel once used extensively for brewing millet beer, an activity now rather rare in predominantly Muslim Mande areas of Mali. Tanners and indigo dyers once made extensive use of pots of this form in their respective trades.[9]

The vessel forms described above are all given a special treatment as part of the firing process (see chapter 4), which renders their surfaces a rich, shiny black. While they may be admired for

FIGURE 12. Maninka potter Nansa Doumbia punching the holes in a large couscous steamer *(nyintin)* she had been commisioned to make. This was one of two she made at the same time in the event a problem arose with one of them during firing. Both of them turned out fine, and she was easily able to sell the second pot. Kangaba, Mali, 1991.

FIGURE 13. Pots ready for firing, including two small incense burners *(wusulan-bèlèw)*, two large couscous steamers *(nyintinw)*, two tripod braziers *(singonw)*, and several cooking pots *(dagaw)*. Kangaba, Mali, 1991.

FIGURE 14. Woman cooking couscous with a ceramic *nyintin* over a metal pot. They are wrapped with cloth where they meet in order to make the seal between the two pots as tight as possible. Kangaba, Mali, 1991.

FIGURE 15. Maninka potter Nansa Doumbia making a tripod brazier *(singon)*. Kangaba, Mali, 1991.

FIGURE 16. Unfired pottery brazier *(furuno),* left, a skeuomorph of the metal prototype, right. Kunògò, Mali, 1991.

FIGURE 17. Group of vessels ready for firing, including nine large water storage jars (*jifinyew*), five smaller water jars (*jidagaw*), four cooking pots (*dagaw*), four couscous steamers (*nyintinw*), four washbasins (*fagaw*), two saucepots (*nadagaw*), two footed cooking pots (*nègèdagaw*), two braziers (*singon* and *furuno*), one water pitcher (*garigulèti*), and four incense burners (*wusulanbèlèw*), primarily the work of Seban Fané. Kunògò, Mali, 1991.

their pleasing shape, neatly done patterns around the belly, or smooth, burnished upper surfaces, they are viewed as serving primarily utilitarian and not aesthetic purposes.

However, there are several other types of pottery that are intended for public display (Figure 18). These have more decorative details and are more varied in form and design motifs. Most important are the medium-sized water jars (*jidagaw*). They often are placed prominently under a tree in the family compound, or just within the veranda, easily accessible to serve visitors the obligatory cup of cool water. These vessels usually have one or more molded ridges encircling the body of the pot, dividing the surface into at least two domains. The upper shoulders are polished smooth and painted with bold red slip designs. The lower surfaces are sometimes textured with corncob and twisted-string roulettes, but they are more often smooth and painted all over with red slip. Older examples sometimes have simple molded designs (Figures 19, 20) or animal shapes—snakes, turtles, crocodiles, lizards—modeled on their upper surfaces (Plate 7; Figures 25-28).

More skilled potters also make large water jars with wide, flared rims in emulation of those from the Inland Niger Delta region (Plate 6; cf. Plate 10, Figure 21). These usually are given smooth, burnished surfaces and painted red slip designs. A small, restricted water vessel with a short, slightly flared neck is identified as a *dunden*, a term also used for calabash water bottles of a smaller size but similar profile. Another relatively rare vessel produced by Mande potters is one that seems oddly shaped until its purpose is realized. *Sheminfagaw* (literally, chicken drinking pots) are roughly spherical in form with a very restricted rim and a series of small openings around the shoulder

FIGURE 18. Slip-painted water jars *(jidagaw)* and water pitchers *(garigulètiw)* for sale alongside the road to Kangaba. Medina, Mali, 1991.

FIGURE 19. Bamana water jar *(jidaga)* with an unusual molded brickwork design. Collection of Douglas Dawson. (Photo: courtesy Douglas Dawson)

FIGURE 20. Water jar *(jidaga)* with a simple molded serpentine design, in the compound of a home. Kolokani, Mali, 1991.

FIGURE 21. Pots for sale at the Dibida market in Bamako. In the background are three Mopti-style water jars painted with red slip designs on white clay and with a smooth transition from neck to rim. The others in the background are locally made variants with carinated or angled rims. In front of them are cooking pots *(dagaw)* and braziers *(singonw)* imported from Segou. In the foreground are locally made flowerpots with fluted rims. Bamako, Mali 1991.

FIGURE 22. Maninka potter Assetu Doumbia finishing the firing of a group of watering vessels for chickens and guinea hens *(sheminfagaw)*. Bamako, Mali, 1991.

FIGURE 23. Water pitcher
(garigulèti) with incised and
impressed patterns, in a family
compound. Kita, Mali, 1983.

FIGURE 24. Flowerpot and
two *garigulètiw* made by
Maninka potter Mafin Kanté.
Bamako, Mali, 1991.

(Figure 22). These pots are for watering chickens and guinea fowl; the narrow openings prevent other animals from depleting the water supply.

At least two other types of pots are routinely left the red color of the clay. The *garigulèti* (from the French *gargoulette*) is an enclosed water pitcher with a stirrup handle and one or two spouts (Figures 23, 24). Like the water jar, they are sometimes painted with red slip designs, but most rely on the beauty of the unusual shape for aesthetic effect. They are considered difficult to make and, in my experience, are rather rare.

By contrast, it would be unthinkable for a young woman to leave home to join her husband's household without a *wusulanbèlè,* used to burn incense to sweeten the air of the bridal chamber and elsewhere as need be. These small burners come in a variety of shapes, from small pierced cups with handles to bottle-shaped forms with a single opening on the side (Figure 13). The *wusulanbèlè,* the *jidaga,* and the *jifinye* are essential to a young woman's trousseau.

To put the stylistic features of Mande pottery into historical perspective reveals a basic conservatism; the majority of cooking vessels produced today are probably little changed in form from those of at least a century or more ago. Indeed, there seem to be many parallels between contemporary pottery and archaeological materials excavated at different sites in the region (cf. Filipowiak 1979). The only hint of change over time is an apparent shift in recent times away from modeled figurative imagery to slip-painted designs, especially on decorative water jars. There are examples in museum and private collections attributed to the Bamana (or to the Boso) that have modeled imagery on their surfaces (Plate 7; Figures 25, 26).[10] These are rarely seen in the field today. On one occasion I by chance came across a discarded water jar with relief modeled designs (Figures 27, 28). I was told that it had been made "many years ago" by Sitan Coulibaly, a well-known potter who had recently passed away.[11] The potter with whom I was traveling said that while she is capable of producing such forms, it is not worth the extra time and care involved since her clients do not request nor would they appropriately compensate for such elaboration. She recalled that such designs were more common when she was a young woman. Virtually all those I saw produced during my fieldwork were slip painted. This may reflect the influence of the so-called Mopti water jars from the Inland Niger Delta region, which are now widely available in the larger cities and highly prized as wedding gifts.

POTTERY STYLES AND ETHNIC IDENTITY

Given the notion of Mande pottery as a broad regional style, it is when one tries to further limit elements of style to particular ethnic identities that problems arise. On the one hand, the distribution of styles does not necessarily correspond to the distribution of object types. Furthermore, of the range of objects Mande potters make, none can be said to be exclusively Bamana or Maninka in either type or style.

The most complex and unusual object made by some of the more skilled Mande potters is the small stirrup-spouted water pitcher called *garigulèti*. As noted above, they are rather rare compared to the production of the larger water jars, incense burners, and cooking pots. I saw no more than a dozen or so in production or in use. However, I documented them in widely separated areas—in the repertoires of Maninka potters of Bamako, Medina, and Kangaba, of Bamana potters near Kolokani, of Jula potters in the south near Kadiolo, and in a Bamana household in Kita. *Garigulètiw* turn up in lists and diagrams of objects types produced by potters throughout the northern stretch

FIGURE 25. Bamana pot with molded figurative imagery in low relief. Collection of Keith Achepohl. (Photo: courtesy Keith Achepohl)

FIGURE 26. Bamana pot with high-relief molded male and female figures alternating with lizards, snakes, and other water animals. Collection of Charles D. Miller III.

FIGURE 27. Discarded water jar with molded figurative imagery including snakes, tortoises, iguanas, and lizards. This pot was made some forty years ago by Maninka potter Sitan Coulibaly. Hamdalaye, Mali, 1992.

FIGURE 28. Detail of Figure 27.

among the Tukulor (Toucouleur) of Senegal (Wane 1969, 58) and the Jola (Diola) of the Casamance (Linares de Sapir 1969; Thomas 1957, 552-53) to the west; among the Soninke and Jawara (Diawara) to the north (Boyer 1953; Gallay 1970; Saint-Père 1925; Völger 1979); among the Somono and Fula of the Inland Niger Delta (LaViolette 1987; Gallay 1986); among the Dogon (Gallay 1981); among the Lobi in Burkina Faso (Schneider 1990); and as far east as the Hausa of northern Nigeria (Dupuis and Echard 1971), the Djerma of Niger (Völger 1979), and the Fulani of northern Cameroon (David and Hennig 1972, 1-29). In form, the *garigulèti* seems to emulate a Mediterranean prototype, and it is in fact often used by Muslims for ritual washing before prayers. However, there is at present no evidence to conclude that it was introduced by means of trade or other direct contact with the Islamic world north of the Sahara.[12] The fact that it is known primarily by variants of the French term suggests that its distribution may ultimately reveal more about the shared impact of French colonialism than about interactions among peoples in the distant past.[13] Along with the *furuno,* this may be a form of relatively recent introduction, easily incorporated into the repertoire of the better potters, whether they be Mande or not.

When the repertoires of the different potter groups throughout the region are compared, one finds that while they have much in common, there are some variations. Perhaps the most limited in number of forms is the repertoire of contemporary Dogon potters, with subtle variations in size and proportions that are sufficient for the surprisingly broad range of functions the vessels serve (Bedaux and van der Waals 1987; Gallay 1981; Huysecom and Mayor 1993).

The repertoire of Soninke potters (Figure 29) is similar to that of Bamana and Maninka potters (Boyer 1953; Gallay 1970). It includes water jars with impressed, incised, and molded designs; braziers; water pitchers; couscous steamers; and cooking pots. In addition, Soninke potters build large unfired clay granaries (*bono, mara* in Soninke; see Gallay 1970), which are made in sections. Some Bamana potters told me that they too used to make such storage containers, but that there was no longer much call for them.

The Somono seem to have the largest and most diverse repertoire of object types (Figures 30, 31; cf. Plate 9), which include not only the expected cooking pots, serving vessels, and storage containers, but also a wide variety of architectural ceramics such as rainspouts, window grills, roof vents, and toilet shafts (LaViolette 1987; Huysecom and Mayor 1993). They also make pot lids, tripod braziers, braziers based on metal prototypes, and pancake griddles. Somono potters occasionally produce a number of domestic items that are known from archaeological contexts but are not in great demand today. These include supports for beds, stool forms, and a special washbasin that incorporates a small stool as part of its design.

The range of objects produced by the Jula potters of the Kadiolo region is also quite extensive (Figure 32). They make most of the types of vessels found in the Bamana/Maninka repertoire— *daga, jidaga, jifinye, faga*—but with more variety in styles and sizes (Figures 33, 34). In the not too distant past they were producing huge vessels (as much as four to five feet high), called *dolodagaba,* which once were used to brew and store locally made millet beer and now serve as vessels for water and grain storage.[14] In addition to making a couscous steamer similar to those available in the north, Jula potters make one with holes punched all the way to the rim (also called *nyintin*). The best among them make *garigulètiw* as well as griddles for pancakes (*ngomifagaw*), pots for watering chickens (*sheminfagaw*), special vessels for preparing and storing sacred medicines (*furadagaw* and *bamadagaw*), rainspouts (*coolow*), and unusual stirrup-handled caps (*coorow*) for the pinnacles of the old

FIGURE 29. Examples of Soninke (Diawara) pottery and tool kit among the Jawara (Diawara). Five water jars, a brazier, a double-spouted water pitcher, a cous-cous steamer, a cooking pot, a salt cellar, and three granaries (after Boyer 1953, 105). The circle depicts the potter's tool kit: corncob, gazelle horn, wooden sticks, calabash roulette, polishing cloth, and calabash scrapers.

FIGURE 30. Somono potter Niamoye Nientao completing a water jar *(jidaga)*. Djenné, Mali, 1983. (Photo: Adria LaViolette)

FIGURE 31. Somono potters with their wares on market day. These include, from left to right, pot lids, cooking pots *(dagaw),* washbasins *(fagaw),* braziers *(singonw),* more cooking pots, and water jars *(jidagaw).* In the background (center) are a rain-spout *(coolo)* and a pancake griddle *(ngomifaga).* Djenné, Mali, 1983.

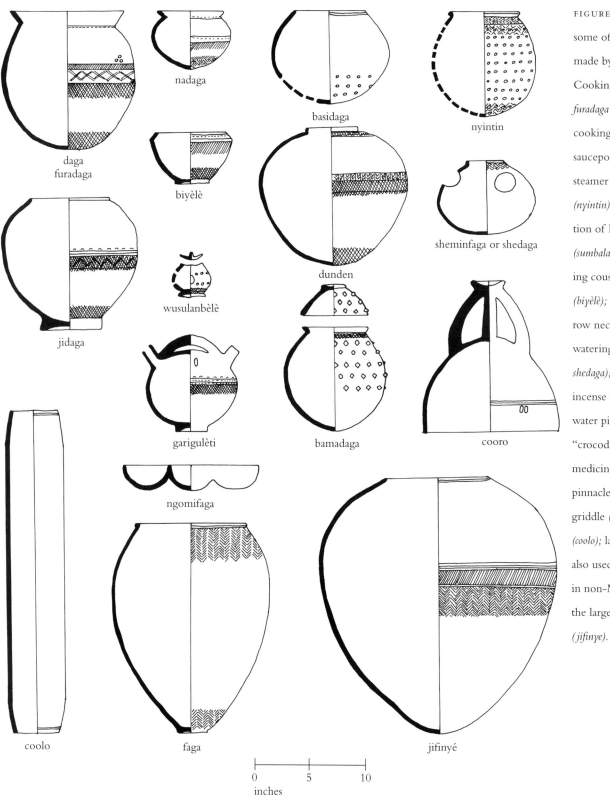

daga
furadaga

nadaga

basidaga

nyintin

biyèlè

dunden

sheminfaga or shedaga

jidaga

wusulanbèlè

garigulèti

bamadaga

cooro

coolo

ngomifaga

faga

jifinyé

0   5   10
inches

FIGURE 32. Repertoire of some of the pottery types made by Jula potters. Cooking pot *(daga),* called *furadaga* when it is used for cooking herbal medicines; saucepot *(nadaga);* couscous steamer *(basidaga);* strainer *(nyintin)* used in the preparation of locust bean paste *(sumbala)* as well as for steaming couscous; sauce bowl *(biyèlè);* water jar with a narrow neck *(dunden);* chicken watering pot *(sheminfaga* or *shedaga);* water jar *(jidaga);* incense burner *(wusulanbèlè);* water pitcher *(garigulèti);* "crocodile" pot for storing medicines *(bamadaga);* mosque pinnacle cap *(cooro);* pancake griddle *(ngomifaga);* rainspout *(coolo);* large washbasin *(faga)* also used to close the tombs in non-Muslim burials; and the large water storage jar *(jifinye).*

FIGURE 33. Water jars *(jida-gaw)* typical of the work of Jula potters. Sissingué, Mali, 1991.

FIGURE 34. Pots made by Jula potter Awa Kouyaté, including (from left) a water jar *(jidaga),* a chicken watering pot *(sheminfaga),* a medicine pot *(bamadaga),* and a small saucepot *(nadaga).* The "crocodile" pot *(bamadaga)* is used for storing herbal medicines. The raised nodules are said to warn people not to touch the vessel. Sissingué, Mali, 1992.

FIGURE 35. Jula potter Kadidia Kouyaté scraping excess clay from a ceramic rainspout *(coolo)* after it has become leather-hard. Sissingué, Mali, 1992.

FIGURE 36. Kadidia Kouyaté forming a pancake griddle *(ngomifaga)*. Sissingué, Mali, 1992.

Sudanese-style mosques of the region (Figures 32, 34–36; see also Figures 5, 6). While the terms used for these forms are Mande ones, in style and type the Jula repertoire has much more in common with that of Senufo potters to the south (cf. Spindel 1988, 1989).

An examination of the distribution patterns reveals that some ceramic types appear to correspond to a northern Sahel/Sudan versus southern savanna/forest division, as reflected in the early archaeological assemblages. The three-prong brazier form *(singon)*, for example, appears among Soninke, Bamana, Maninka, Somono, and Fula repertoires across the northern stretch; it is only rarely made by Jula potters and not at all by Senufo or other potters to the south and east. Similarly, the lidded medicine pot known as *bamadaga* (literally in Jula, crocodile pot), with its distinctive nodules raised in warning to those who might dare to tamper with it, is distributed widely in the south from Guinea to Benin.[15] It is not among the repertoire of Mande or other potters in the north.

However, other objects appear to fall into east/west rather than north/south distribution patterns. Long, tubular rainspouts are produced by Somono, Jula, Sonrhaï, Fula, and Senufo potters following a distribution that extends all the way from Timbuktu to northern Côte d'Ivoire. Ceramic pancake griddles have a similar eastern distribution from desert to forest. These unusual forms are not unknown to Bamana and Maninka potters, but they associated them with other objects imported from the east.[16]

Turning from object type to decorative techniques, the picture becomes even more complex. Of the different finishing processes employed by Mande potters in the heartland, none are uniquely Mande. The rich black surfaces of the pots made by the Bamana and Maninka potters with whom I worked were not essential for the Bamana potters of Kalabougou, nor for the Somono potters of the Inland Niger Delta.[17] Knowledge of how to blacken pots in the way that Bamana and Maninka potters do is more widespread than the practice itself (see chapter 4 herein). The decision of whether or not to treat the pots in this way may depend in part on the scale of operation. The Jula potters of the village of Doguélédougou (near Kadiolo), for example, fire as many as six to eight hundred pots in huge communal firings without blackening a single one. However, they will at the same time stack and fire a small pile of thirty to forty saucepots to be blackened. An intense black achieved in similar ways is a common characteristic of Dan pottery of Liberia, Baule and Akan pottery in Côte d'Ivoire, and Mo pottery in Ghana. The technique is also known in Burkina Faso, Togo, Benin, Nigeria, and Cameroon.

The shift by Bamana and Maninka potters away from low-relief designs to painted red slip patterns on water jars and incense burners may be owing to the recent influence of Inland Niger Delta styles, such that painted designs are now the norm. Similarly, Somono potters themselves have shifted from an earlier, more time-consuming stamp-and-comb patterning toward painted slip designs (LaViolette 1987).

Perhaps the most distinctive device used by Mande potters to impress a woven design into the base of a pot is a piece of netted fiber *(jò)* that is placed over a broken pottery sherd, clay tamper, or large stone (Figure 37).[18] This is done while the base of the vessel is being formed over the mold and once the desired thickness has been achieved. The practice imparts a crosshatched pattern that may or may not be retained through the remaining building process, depending on the type of vessel and the choice of the potter.

Otherwise, most of the techniques Mande potters use to impart a textured surface to their pots are also used by other potters in varying degrees and combinations. Mande potters often enhance

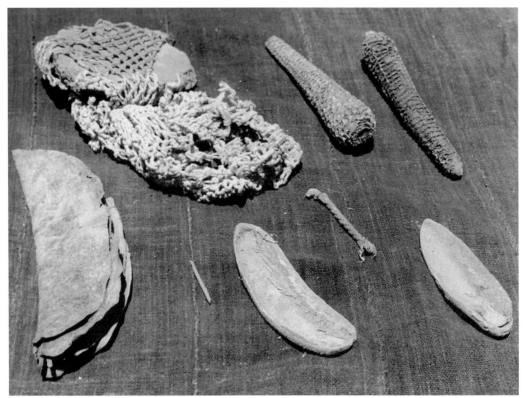

FIGURE 37. Partial tool kit of Bamana potter Seban Fané. Top: broken pottery sherd with netted-fiber covering used as a tamper, two corncobs; bottom: sheaf of baobab leaves, which is dipped into water and used to smooth the surface and especially the rim of a pot; toothpick-sized stalk used to impress lines into the surface; two stiff seed pods used for scraping; and a twisted-string roulette. Kunògò, Mali, 1988.

the rough textured surface after the vessel is formed by means of corncob and twisted-string roulettes. While corncobs are found in tool kits throughout the region, they generally serve as scrapers. Their use for decorative purposes by other potters seems to be limited.

Twisted-string or twisted-fiber roulettes are perhaps the most common decorative tool potters have available to them (Soper 1985). Rolled once across the wet surface of the clay, these roulettes leave a series of diagonal linear impressions. Evidence of their use dates back to the earliest archaeological finds at Djenné-djeno and Niani (McIntosh and McIntosh 1980; Filipowiak 1979). Distinctions among different pottery traditions lie in the extent to which the tool is used and how it is combined with other decorative techniques. Bamana and Maninka potters use it sparingly, right at the transition from shoulder to belly of the vessel, and occasionally just below the rim, places where it has the most visual and tactile impact.

Simple twisted-string and twisted-fiber roulettes also exist in the tool kits of Soninke, Bobo, Somono, and some Fula potters (Gallay 1970, 1991-92, 35) where they are used in combination with other decorative techniques that tend to obscure their presence. Jula potters of Kadiolo choose among as many as seven or eight different plaited-fiber and carved wooden roulettes in addition to twisted-string roulettes like those used in the north (Figure 38).[19] One renders a herringbone pattern, another a diagonal pattern, another a plantlike motif, still another diamonds. These potters do not hesitate to combine patterns, even layering one over another, before using yet another tool or found object to elaborate their complex array of patterns and textures.

Another tool that appears to be fairly widespread is the dentelated calabash wheel, which figures prominently in Soninke tool kits and in fact was one of the tools mentioned by de Zeltner

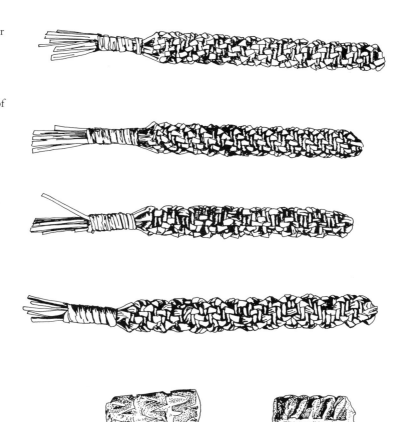

FIGURE 38. Four plaited-fiber roulettes and two carved wooden roulettes, decorative devices used by Jula potters of the Kadiolo region to give pattern and texture to the surfaces of almost all of the types of vessels they produce. They also use dentelated calabash wheels similar to those found in other Mande potter tool kits (see Figure 29), as well as a variety of bottle caps, toothpaste tube caps, and old flashlight parts.

(1915) at the turn of the century (see also Boyer 1953; Gallay 1970). While they are not unknown in the Mande heartland, even those potters who have them in their tool kits rarely use them. Thus while these tools for impressing designs into the surface were used to a greater or lesser degree by Mande potters, none were exclusively "theirs," nor were any clearly borrowed from other potters.

Stylistic variations are more regional than they are ethnic based. In places where several ethnic groups compete with one another, a homogeneity of style is encouraged. The objects made by Mande Somono potters in the region of Djenné and Mopti are stylistically more similar to those of their immediate Fula competitors than to those of their distant Bamana or Maninka relatives to the west. The "Mopti" water jars produced by both Somono or Fula potters that make their way into the markets of Bamako, Koutiala, and Sikasso are easily distinguished from locally produced wares by their tall proportions; large, graceful flared rims; fine white clay body; and bold red slip designs (cf. Plate 10; Figure 21). Similarly, Jula and Senufo repertoires are more like each other in style and range of types than either is like Mande pottery to the north.

Thus while pottery from the Mande heartland shares certain qualities distinct from pottery traditions elsewhere in the region, it would be misleading to suggest that pottery styles and types alone are sufficient to identify the ethnicity of the producer. Bamana and Maninka potters themselves recognize different styles and associate them with places rather than peoples. The more skilled among them are generally more than willing to try to satisfy patron demands by emulating new and different styles. Even within the relatively conservative domain of pottery, the limitations of the "one tribe-one style" paradigm are clear.

3

BEYOND THE FRINGE

More than twenty-five years ago, William Fagg described fine leatherwork from West Africa as

> one of the attributes of the great and fairly homogeneous Moslem culture which stretches from
> Senegal to Northern Cameroon, taking in the Manding-speaking tribes as well as the Hausa . . . ,
> two tribal groups whose artifacts are often so similar as to call for a special category, Hausa-
> Manding, for undocumented objects conjecturally identified in the study collections of the British
> Museum (Fagg 1971, n.p.).

In my research on Mande leatherworking, I set out to examine whether West African leather traditions—and by implication cultural traditions generally—are homogeneous and dependent on
Islamic tradition, or whether it would be possible to identify one or more Mande styles of leatherwork, distinct from both immediate and distant neighbors. In fact, while some object types appear
across the entire stretch of the Sudan and many have parallels in the Islamic world, styles are more
distinctive. Objects produced by Mande leatherworkers share certain features that set them apart
from objects associated with other major leatherworking traditions in the region. However, as with
pottery from the Mande heartland, it is not possible to distinguish Bamana, Maninka, and Soninke
styles from one another.

Mande-style leatherwork has a very broad distribution not only throughout the Western
Sudan, but into the savanna and forest regions west and south of the Mande heartland. Given the
fact that much of this leatherwork is associated either with Islam or with warriors and cavalry, its
geographic extent is not surprising. This is a tradition in which both patrons and artists were on the
move, traveling great distances and disseminating, among other things, a Mande aesthetic.

LEATHER AND ARCHAEOLOGY

Scholars interested in early ceramic traditions have a great deal of material to work with in the
quantities of pottery and sherds that have survived in archaeological contexts, and there is promise

of more as archaeological work continues in the region. The same is not true for leatherwork. In the Western Sudan, as in much of sub-Saharan Africa, few objects of leather have survived beyond the last two centuries. However, excavations carried out in the region of Bandiagara in Mali have yielded an assortment of leather objects associated with phases dated from the eleventh to the sixteenth centuries (Bedaux 1972; Bedaux and Rompen n.d.). Among the some two hundred and fifty objects found were items of dress including aprons, bracelets of plaited leather, sandals, and boots, as well as a variety of leather bags, knife sheaths, and leather-covered wooden quivers. The decorative techniques evident on these objects are similar to those employed by Mande, Dogon, and other leatherworkers today, including painted red and black designs and incised geometric patterns. The significance of these finds is that they establish an early date for knowledge of leatherworking in the region and suggest a continuity in form and style of leather objects up to the present day. In style, type, and technique, only the plaited leather bracelets are without parallel in contemporary leatherwork from the region.

Archaeological excavations also have provided clues in the form of terra-cotta figures wearing what appear to be amulet necklaces, knife sheaths, and quivers. Perhaps best known is a spectacular headless reclining figure (Figure 7), which was discovered at the site of Djenné-djeno (McIntosh and McIntosh 1982; *African Arts* 1995; see also Devisse et al. 1993, 233). Suspended from the neck of the figure is a pendant in the form of a large rectangle flanked by two smaller ones, not unlike the amulet necklaces commissioned from leatherworkers today. The figure also wears a dagger in a sheath strapped to the upper arm. Similar arm daggers appear on some Soninke Kagoro (or Dogon?) figures and on Bamana sculpture used by the Jo and Gwan societies of southern Mali (Ezra 1986b, 1988, 30-31; de Grunne 1991). While upper arm daggers are not among the corpus of Mande objects in museum collections from the last century,[1] the form of the sheath itself resembles contemporary examples.

Similarly, the quivers on the backs of terra-cotta and wood sculptures have stylistic parallels in surviving examples of leatherwork. Equestrian sculptures, however, rarely provide much in the way of clues to the particular styles of horse trappings. If there is any indication of a saddle, it is usually identifiable as an Arab type with pronounced pommel and cantle, but there is rarely a suggestion of particular form, much less decoration. Limited though they may be, such images do provide a visual counterpart to the written references in the historical literature.

LEATHER IN HISTORY

Despite the association of leather with Islam, knowledge of working with skins and leather in the Western Sudan clearly predates contact with the Islamic world. Early Arabic accounts and later European descriptions corroborate the widespread use of skins as clothing and supply evidence of the existence of at least some types of leather objects. Some of these accounts refer to the skins of wild animals, worn with the hair or fur still attached. One of the earliest was Ibn al-Faqīh, who in A.D. 903 said of the people of Ghana, "Their clothes are [made of] panther skins, panthers being abundant there" (Levtzion and Hopkins 1981, 28).[2] Others refer to the wearing of skins without being precise as to the type of skin, or whether they were tanned, tailored, or given special decorative treatment.[3]

The impact of the trans-Saharan trade and contact with the Islamic world are reflected in the adoption of new styles of dress, replacing skins with cloth. According to Ibn Saʿīd of the thirteenth century: "The apparel of the Sūdān of Takrūr and elsewhere is chiefly skins; wherever one of them attains status [having a retinue *(iḥtasham)*] he wears his skins dyed. Those who mix with white men and become particular adopt clothes of wool and cotton, which are imported for them" (Levtzion and Hopkins 1981, 185).[4]

Early European accounts seem to echo information provided by the Arab travelers. The fifteenth-century Venetian explorer Cadamosto, writing about the peoples of the Senegambian coast, observed: "These people dress thus: almost all constantly go naked, except for a goatskin fashioned in the form of drawers, with which they hide their shame. But the chiefs and those of standing wear a cotton garment—for cotton grows in these lands" (Crone 1937, 31).[5] His observation would seem to suggest that, at least in the areas he visited, the wearing of cloth garments was the exception, not the rule.

By the early seventeenth century, cotton cloth had become the primary means of dress. Richard Jobson, traveling in the Senegambian interior in the early seventeenth century, noted that there was little difference between the dress of the ruler and that of his subjects, because cotton was the only locally available material. The wearing of skins by "savages" of the interior was thus an exception worth noting:

> The men likewise shewed a more savage kinde of people then we had seene; many having breeches made of rawe hydes, either of Deare, or other cattle, the grace whereof was the taile of the beast which remaineth on the skinne, did sticke right forth upon the hinder part of the mans buttocks, resembling the manner as the beast wore it (Jobson [1623] 1904, 119-20).

Development of the trans-Saharan trade in imported textiles was one of a number of factors that contributed to the replacement of skins with cloth as the principal mode of dress. The introduction of cotton and the horizontal loom made locally produced cloth available to a larger segment of the population. And the spread of Islam resulted in the adoption of new styles of dress marking change in status and acceptance of the faith.

Islam also brought to West Africa a new spiritual resource accessible by means of protective amulets (see Quimby 1972; Prussin 1986, 1995).[6] Verses from the Koran, cabalistic signs, and magic squares drawn on small pieces of paper provided an effective alternative that could be used in addition to non-Islamic means—a literal and symbolic layering of power bases. Amulets are not mentioned in Arabic accounts, but early European travelers were certainly impressed by the strength of belief in their efficacy. Jobson observed:

> Now for the manner of their apparell, it is soone related, they being for the most part bare-head, only bedecked or hang'd over with gregories [gris-gris, or amulets], as they are likewise over their bodies, legges and armes, . . . The Gregories bee things of great esteeme amongst them, for the most part they are made of leather of severall fashions, woundrous neatly, they are hollow and within them is placed, and sowed up close, certaine writings, or spels which they receive from their Mary-buckes [marabouts, or Muslim clerics], whereof they conceive such a religious respect, that they do confidently beleeve no hurt can betide them, whilst these Gregories are about them, and it seems to encrease their superstition; the Mary-buckes do devide these blessings for every severall and particular part, for upon their heads they weare them, in manner of a crosse, aswell from the fore-head to the necke, as from one eare to another, likewise about their neckes, and cross both

shoulders about their bodies, round their middles, great store, as also uppon their armes, both above and below the elbow, so that in a manner, they seeme as it were laden, and carriyng an outward burthen of religious blessings, whereof there is none so throughly laden as the Kings, although of all sorts they are furnished with some, both men and weomen, and this more I have taken notice of, that is any of them be possest of any malady, or have any swelling or sore upon them, the remedy they have, is onely by placing one of these blessed Gregories, where the grief lies, which they conceite will helpe them: and for ought I can perceive, this is all the Physicke they have amongst them, and they do not onely observe this for themselves, but their horses doe usually weare of these about their neckes, and most of their bowes are hanged and furnished with them ([1623] 1904, 62-64).

Jobson and others also were impressed by people's willingness to pay high prices for the protection amulets provide.[7] His colorful description supplies evidence that amulets were worn by both men and women, that they were essential accouterments of warriors, and that leather was the principal material used in covering them.

Benjamin Anderson, who traveled into southeastern Guinea from Liberia in the late nineteenth century, identified the providers of amulets as Mande:

It is sufficient for the "Kaffirs," (unbelievers,) as they are denominated by the Mandingoes, to buy the amulets, necklaces, and belts containing transcripts from the Koran sewed up in them, to be worn around the neck, arms, or waist as preservatives from the casualties of war, sickness, or ill luck in trade or love ([1870/1912] 1971, 40).

Amulets with verses from the Koran were thus certainly not limited to use by wearers who professed the Islamic faith. Non-Muslims and Muslims alike sought the expertise of clerics and leatherworkers.

As for other items of personal adornment and dress, small pouches, wallets, and bags probably were as ubiquitous as amulets, yet they do not appear in Arabic documents and receive only passing notice in European accounts.[8] There are, however, references to leather sandals and boots among the accouterments of the Sudanese elite. In the twelfth century, al-Idrīsī described the king of Ghana in this way: "His garments consists [sic] of a silk cloth *(izār ḥarīr)* which he wraps round himself or a mantle *(burda)* in which he envelops himself; loose trousers cover the middle of his body, and he wears sandals made of *sharkī* on his feet" (Levtzion and Hopkins 1981, 110).[9]

Leather sandals were well established as an item of trade between Hausaland and Timbuktu, and probably elsewhere, by the sixteenth century. According to Leo Africanus, this trade supported a thriving craft industry in Gobir (the northernmost Hausa state). He writes: "Heere are also great store of artificers and linnen weauers: and heere are such shooes made as the ancient Romans were woont to weare, the greatest part whereof be carried to Tombuto [Timbuktu] and Gago [Gao]" ([1600] 1896, 3:828).

By the time of Heinrich Barth's visit to Kano in the mid-nineteenth century, the manufacture and export trade of sandals from Hausaland was second only to indigo-dyed cotton cloth in volume of exports. According to Barth: "The chief articles of native industry, besides cloth, which have a wide market, are principally sandals. The sandals are made with great neatness, and, like the cloth, are exported to an immense distance" (1857, 1:513).[10] In fact, it is the Hausa-style sandal that is most widespread in West Africa.

It is uncertain when the practice of wearing sandals became common among the Mande and their neighbors. Cadamosto, who provides rather detailed descriptions of the dress of the inhabitants of the Senegambia in the fifteenth century, reported that men and women always went barefoot (Crone 1937, 32, passim), and neither of his contemporaries, Duarte Pacheco Pereira ([d. 1533] 1937) or Valentim Fernandes ([fl. 1494-1515] 1938), mentions sandals or shoes. In the early seventeenth century, Jobson related that most of the "Mandingos" with whom he came into contact were barefoot, but added, "except it be some few of them, who have a peece of leather under their foot, cut like a shooe-sole, butned about the great toe, and againe about the instoppe ([1623] 1904, 63). This description matches Mande-style sandals collected some two centuries later that are quite distinct from the more familiar Hausa style sandals. In any case, by the nineteenth century sandals appear to have become a common feature of dress for men and women throughout much of West Africa and the Sahara.

Because of their association with horses and cavalry, boots have long been considered prestige dress in West Africa. The twelfth-century account of Abū Ḥāmid al-Gharnāṭī refers to leather exported from the Sudan used to make the boots of kings.[11] It is tempting to suggest that this is a reference to boots made by local craftsmen for Sudanic kings. However, he could just as easily have been referring to one of the ways skins exported from the Sudan were used in North Africa and elsewhere. One of the clearest references to high status signaled by the wearing of boots in West Africa is that of Ibn Baṭṭūṭa, a guest at the court of the king of Mali in the fourteenth century. He remarked on the special position of Dugha as the king's spokesman, intermediary, and counselor, and said:

> Dūghā the interpreter stands at the gate of the councilplace wearing fine garments of silk brocade (zardakhāna) and other materials, and on his head a turban with fringes which they have a novel way of winding. Round his waist he has a sword with a golden sheath and on his feet boots and spurs. No-one but him wears boots on that day (Levtzion and Hopkins 1981, 290).

Curiously, there are no references in the Arabic accounts to the wearing of slippers, items of dress that to this day have strong Islamic associations.

One of the most important roles of the leatherworker was as a provider of equipment for war, producing not only shields, sword sheaths, shot pouches, powder horns, and quivers, but also all the trappings for cavalry forces. Foremost as accouterments of military power, many of these items also functioned as emblems of chiefly regalia. Tough leather shields are mentioned frequently by Arab authors. These accounts often repeat information provided by previous writers concerning the effectiveness of a particular kind of shield, impervious to blows from swords.[12] Jobson described mounted Mande warriors bearing round shields, or bucklers. He reported, "we have seene of them likewise on horse backe, the horses being of a small stature, bridled and sadled after the Spanish fashion, each man having his Assegie [spear or javelin], and upon the right side of his horse a broad Buckler hanging" ([1623] 1904, 57). Unfortunately, if this type of shield was at one time common in the Mande region, examples have not made their way into museum collections.

Swords as well as lances and other iron weapons are also mentioned periodically in Arabic accounts. According to al-Bakrī, in the eleventh century pages carrying swords and shields decorated with gold were part of the sumptuous display of the court of the king of Ghana (Levtzion and Hopkins 1981, 80). Sword blades may have been among the items imported from North Africa via Saharan trade routes, and they were certainly among the goods brought by Europeans to trade along the coast. Describing warrior dress of the Senegambia in the fifteenth century, Cadamosto noted:

They also carry some Moorish weapons, in the style of a short scimetar, that is, curved: they are made of iron, not of steel, for they obtain iron from the kingdom of Gambra of the Blacks beyond, but they cannot make steel. If there is iron in their land, they do not know of it, or are not skilled in working it (Crone 1937, 33).

Presumably leatherworkers were called upon to provide sheaths for these swords, whether the blades were produced in the interior or imported. Moroccan leatherwork may well have provided a model. Such weapons were hardly rare by the late nineteenth century, as Anderson remarked:

So far as the matter of carrying arms is concerned, it is always better to observe the usage of the natives. Arms always form a part of the dress of barbarians. The more formidable you can make yourself appear, the better for your peace and safety on these highways of African travel. To seem harmless does not always invoke forbearance; it sometimes suggests plots and attempts on life and property. . . . Every person I met on the road was girded with a heavy iron sword, a quiver thrown over the shoulders full of poisoned arrows, and a powerful bow ([1870/1912] 1971, 114-15).

In addition to the sword, an important element in the dress of warriors and hunters was the bow and quiver full of arrows. Among the many references in Arabic documents to these accouterments is Ibn Baṭṭūṭa's fourteenth-century description of the mounted warriors of the king of Mali: "Each *farārī* has his followers before him with lances and bows, drums and trumpets. . . . Each *farārī* has a quiver suspended between his shoulder blades and a bow in his hand and rides a horse. His companions are some on foot and some mounted" (Levtzion and Hopkins 1981, 290-91). Once again, this description finds a parallel in later accounts. In the seventeenth century, Jobson wrote of Mande warriors: ". . . the better sort of them, doe carry their bowe in their hands, and at their backe a case, very artificially made, which may hold within it some twenty foure of their arrowes" ([1623] 1904, 57).

As these brief references suggest, horses and cavalry were important in the political, economic, and cultural life of West Africa. Horses and their trappings provided the elite with a means of displaying their wealth, power, and prestige.[13] Since it was saddles with stirrups that made cavalry such an effective force in warfare, it seems logical to speculate that such trappings were equally in demand.[14] The earliest evidence for the use of imported equestrian equipment is the fourteenth-century account of al-'Umarī, who reported that the army of the king of Mali included substantial well-equipped cavalry forces. He wrote:

The king of this country imports Arab horses and pays high prices for them. His army numbers about 100,000, of whom about 10,000 are cavalry mounted on horses and the remainder infantry without horses or other mounts. . . . The people of this kingdom ride with Arab saddles and in respect of most features of their horsemanship resemble the Arabs, but they mount their horses with the right foot, contrary to everybody else (Levtzion and Hopkins 1981, 266).

In addition to trade, horses and trappings are also mentioned as gifts between rulers as part of diplomatic protocol. According to al-'Umarī, the Malian ruler Mansa Musa, while on pilgrimage to Mecca, received from the sultan in Egypt lavish robes of honor as well as "saddled and bridled horses for himself and his chief courtiers . . . and two horses saddled and bridled and equipped with decorated mule[-type] saddles" (Levtzion and Hopkins 1981, 270).

Horses, saddles, and trappings were among the items brought by the Portuguese to trade for gold, ivory, and hides along the Senegambian coast. Cadamosto reported that horses were sold fully equipped with their trappings (Crone 1937, 36, 49). The Portuguese also presented horses and trappings as gifts to various local leaders with whom they wished to establish good relations (Crone 1937, 30, 130). The king of Portugal is said to have sent diplomatic missions to various rulers, including one identified as Mandi Musa, King of Timbuktu. João de Barros (1496-1570) wrote: "They took him as a present horses, beasts of burden, and mules with their harnesses and several other gifts much appreciated in that land, for they had been sent before" (Crone 1937, 143). Although some of these horses and possibly the trappings were acquired in Portugal or Spain, they may also have been obtained at ports along the Moroccan coast where the Portuguese had established trading houses.[15] Thus the same types of equipment that formed the trans-Saharan trade may have found their way to the coast via the Portuguese and other European powers that followed them.

There are numerous references in the literature to the establishment of centers for the local breeding of horses, reducing the demand for imported horses; however, there is much less information on the production of equipment.[16] It seems likely that not long after the introduction of these new objects, local craftsmen were called upon to repair imported saddles and trappings. As the demands of patronage grew, artisans responded by expanding their repertoire of forms using locally available materials and technology, copying the imported prototypes, but giving them their own style.

DEFINING A MANDE STYLE

Without the actual objects, discussions of the styles of early leatherwork must remain speculative. However, nineteenth- and twentieth-century objects preserved in museums provide a means of examining continuity and change in styles for well over a century. While a large proportion of the leather objects came into these collections with rather sketchy data, others are quite well documented, allowing the provenance of particular styles and types to be identified. The broad distribution of some types of objects suggests extensive interaction throughout West and North Africa. However, there are some techniques especially distinctive of Mande leatherwork, making it possible to define a broad regional style and to distinguish Mande leatherwork from that of the Moors, Tuareg, and Hausa.

Perhaps the most ubiquitous objects produced by leatherworkers are amulets *(sèbènw),* worn to protect the wearer and to produce positive outcome in all endeavors (Figures 39, 40). These leather-covered charms are sought to provide protection against illness and death, as well as to assure success in matters of love and money. They are critical at certain moments of a person's life, when the individual enters a particularly vulnerable stage or undertakes some challenge that is potentially dangerous. Women receive special amulets during pregnancy and especially before childbirth, as do newborn infants. Leatherworkers are called upon to cover amulets for young boys and girls during the transitional and vulnerable time of circumcision and excision. While the contents of an amulet are considered secret, once covered and contained they become a visible part of dress. This is most apparent on young children who wear little in the way of clothing (Figure 41). The ones worn by adults are often concealed by clothing, although there is no special effort to do so. Some are worn openly and may be strung with beads or other items for additional aesthetic and prophylactic effect.

If amulets serve a wide range of functions, they also are varied in form and material. In his description of the various trades or occupations, Jobson referred to the leatherworker as

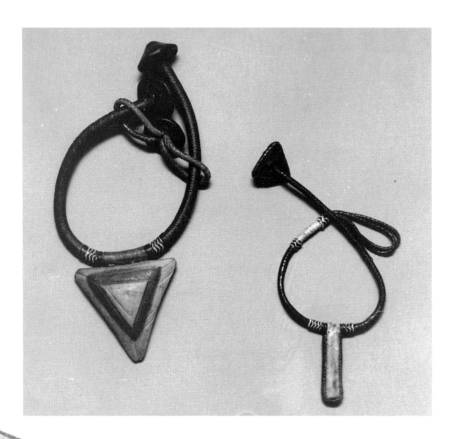

FIGURE 39. Two nineteenth-century Mande (Mandingo) amulet necklaces *(sèbènw)*. The triangular one was acquired from the Colonization Society of Washington in 1894 and the other from Professor O. F. Cook in 1893. Department of Anthropology, National Museum of Natural History, Smithsonian Institution, Washington, D.C. (E168868 and E167994).

FIGURE 40. Amulet necklace *(sèbèn)* made for a client by Soninke leatherworker Oussoubi Mangasi. Kolokani, Mali, 1983.

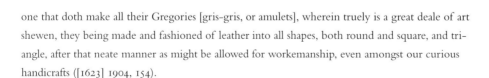

one that doth make all their Gregories [gris-gris, or amulets], wherein truely is a great deale of art shewen, they being made and fashioned of leather into all shapes, both round and square, and triangle, after that neate manner as might be allowed for workemanship, even amongst our curious handicrafts ([1623] 1904, 154).

The form of the amulet depends to some extent on the contents. Non-Islamic amulets tend to be irregular, taking the shape of the horns, teeth, or other substances enclosed. In contrast, Islamic amulets take the geometric form of the packet of paper they enclose. They are usually rectangular or square, sometimes triangular. The particular shape is determined at the time the amulet is written, when the paper is neatly folded and wrapped with thread by the cleric, who whispers in prayers

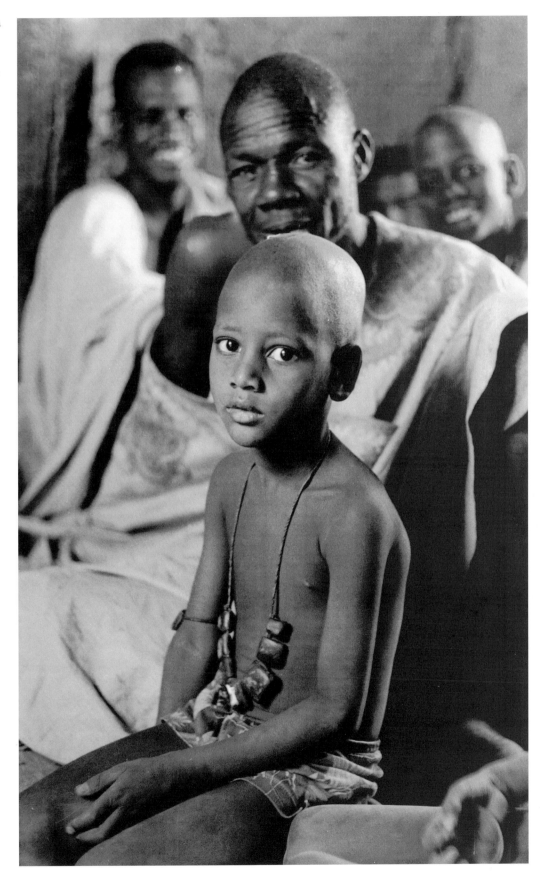

FIGURE 41. Young boy with a string of amulets around his neck and another tied around his arm. Fatoma, Mali, 1984.

Tuareg

Hausa

Asante

Morocco

Timbuktu

Guinea

Timbuktu

Liberia

FIGURE 42. A sampling of wallet styles. Top: Tuareg, Hausa, Asante, and Morocco; bottom: Timbuktu, Guinea, Liberia, and Timbuktu. Tuareg: Department of Anthropology, National Museum of Natural History, Smithsonian Institution, Washington, D.C. (E423863); Hausa: after Heathcote 1974, 100; Asante: Department of Anthropology, National Museum of Natural History, Smithsonian Institution, Washington, D.C. (E350047); Morocco: after Meakin 1902, 198; Timbuktu: after Barth 1857, 1:350; Guinea: Ethnography Department, Berne Historical Museum, Berne, Switzerland (Sen 114); Liberia: after Büttikofer 1890, 2, pl. xxviii; Timbuktu: after Dupuis-Yacouba 1921, 71.

as part of the process. The amulets are taken by the client to the leatherworker in this form to be covered with strips of cloth and leather. The leather is secured with a homemade paste and sewn with the tendons of a cow or a thin leather strip. While some amulets have simple painted designs, the vast majority are of a single color, usually black, with impressed, molded, or stamped designs.

These are visually rather simple objects. Because variations in the styles and shapes of amulets do not correspond to particular ethnic styles, a Mande style cannot be distinguished from that of other ethnic groups in the Western Sudan. However, there are some styles that are rarely, if ever, produced by Mande craftsmen, such as the more elaborate cotton and wool embroidered amulets of the Tuareg of southern Algeria and other northern Saharan groups.

The various pouches and bags in museum collections are more easily identified with a particular tradition than are amulets. One of the most common forms is that of a wallet *(jèmè, jèmèni)* suspended on a cord around the neck, consisting of one or more pockets with often highly decorated flaps and an outer case that slides down over the wallet (Figure 42). This type of object is complex

FIGURE 43. Three wallets *(jèmè* or *jèmèni)* in the collection of the National Museum of Natural History. The one on the left is identified as a "messenger" case from Liberia, collected by Commodore Rohrer before 1917 when it entered the museum's collection. The wallet in the center is labeled "Gola, Liberia" and was acquired from Professor O. Cook in 1893. Museum records state that the skin is probably that of a striped-back or banded duiker. The third wallet was discovered in the collection without accession data but is typical of such wallets from Liberia. Department of Anthropology, National Museum of Natural History, Smithsonian Institution, Washington, D.C. (E301522, E168023, and E406414).

enough in configuration to suggest a common origin, even though it appears across West and North Africa. Yet size, proportions, materials, decorative techniques, and design motifs vary enormously. One style is consistently identified as Mande, or more precisely, Mandingo, and is most often from Liberia (Figure 43). This style tends to be relatively large. The top edge has an oval- or diamond-shaped projection flanked by extensions of the casing on either side where the cord passes through and is attached to the inner pocket. The outer case is of brown leather with impressed lines marking off geometrical patterns created by painting with black dye. These chevron and rectangular patterns are laid out on a grid system on either side of a line dividing the bag into two equal but not bilaterally symmetrical halves. The back usually remains undecorated. However, occasionally the back is covered with short, wavy lines suggestive of Arabic script, lending support to the notion that these wallets serve a protective function as well. The inner bag usually has just one pocket, often of white rawhide, sometimes with a single embroidered tassel in the center of the bottom edge, where it projects beyond the casing.

There is a second type of pouch consistently identified as Mande that is even more distinctive in both style and type (Plate 29; Figures 44, 45). Museum records report that this type of bag *(bòrò* or *bòrè,* the generic term for bag) was used variously for amulets, medicine, gold, tobacco, and other small items, and sometimes as a shot pouch *(kisèbòrò* or *nègèdenbòrò)* carried by warriors. The bag is roughly horseshoe in shape and small, with either one or two central pockets. Outer flaps fall on either side and, being of the same size and shape, conceal the bag beneath. These flaps are decorated with designs that are stamped, impressed, molded, or painted. On some bags the leather is

molded around a small inverted triangle in the center of the flap, possibly enclosing an amulet. Both sides of the flap are decorated with the same technique and often the same design. The surfaces of the inner pouch are usually plain; only occasionally are they given simple painted or impressed designs. From either side hang one or two long, wide bands decorated with painted, incised, and peeled designs and bundled together with thin strips of fringe. The bottom of the bag is usually secured by means of a pair of large semispherical buttons, with cords on which there may be elliptical and cylindrical leather beads, with a bundle of fringe hanging from the bottom. The carrying strap is long, as if the bag is to be worn across the chest, and attached by means of large buttons. These buttons and beads are a distinctive feature of Mande leatherwork (cf. Figures 57, 64, 73); they may be plain black or brown, or sometimes covered with red cloth, but are often leather intricately woven with palm fibers. According

FIGURE 44. Small Mande-style pouch with incised and peeled designs on the flap and wide bands. The cylindrical bead suspended from the flap is embroidered with palm fiber. Deutches Ledermuseum/Deutsches Schuhmuseum, Offenbach am Main, Germany (1754). (Photo: Deutches Ledermuseum/Deutsches Schuhmuseum)

FIGURE 45. Leather pouch acquired as an exchange with the Glen Island Museum of Natural History. It is identified in museum records as "Morocco?" based on the finely woven red wool cord. However, while the cord may well have come from Morocco, the leatherwork is typical of Mande-style pouches. Department of Anthropology, National Museum of Natural History, Smithsonian Institution, Washington, D.C. (E169023).

FIGURE 46. Drawing of two bags identified as powder flasks from Liberia (Stockholm Ethnographical Collection). (After Ratzel 1896–98, 3:100.)

FIGURE 47. Leather pouch with one hundred tightly woven cords, incised and peeled designs on the lower section, and impressed cross-hatching on the amulet forms attached to the bottom. Collected by Reverend Gurley in Liberia probably in the mid-nineteenth century. Department of Anthropology, National Museum of Natural History, Smithsonian Institution, Washington, D.C. (E5155)

to Prussin (1995, 45), in the Fouta Djallon region of Guinea, these buttons are themselves identified as amulets (*hatumere* in Fulfulde). It may well be that the geometric patterning so typical of Mande leatherwork simultaneously serves a protective and a decorative function.

There is a third kind of leather bag that is consistently identified in museum records as Mande (Mandingo, Maninka, Mandingue), but with an even more limited provenance—the southwestern Mande area where Guinea, Liberia, and Côte d'Ivoire meet (Figures 46, 47). Like the previous examples, museum records suggest that these pouches served as containers for medicine and amulets, or possibly as powder flasks. This type of bag is cylindrical in form, with an opening at the top, closed by means of a cylindrical tube that slides down over the bag. The lower section of the bag is of a different material than the top, usually stiffer and more durable

FIGURE 48. Mande-style sandals (sabaraw). Left: after Ratzel (1896–98, 3:280); right: after drawing from the catalogue card, Museum für Völkerkunde, Hamburg (C1875).

FIGURE 49. Pair of sandals collected by Captain C. Armitage in Gambia, given to the British Museum in 1924. Department of Ethnography, Museum of Mankind, London (1924.6–7.23). (Photo: Labelle Prussin, courtesy Trustees of the British Museum)

FIGURE 50. Bamana man, wood engraving by Edouard Riou for a nineteenth-century travel account. The man is shown wearing amulet necklaces (sèbènw), with a powder horn (marifamugu binyèn), small dagger (muru) and sheath (murutan), and a small pouch (bòrò, kisèbòrò, or nègèdenbòrò) probably used for money, tobacco, or shot hanging from his belt. (From Gallieni 1885, 385.)

and often decorated with incised and peeled designs. The carrying strap is made of tightly woven cords attached at the top of the bag and fastened by means of a large button through a loop attached to the bottom of the bag. These buttons, and, on some examples, the cylindrical closure and sections where the cords or the loops are attached, are often decorated with palm-fiber embroidery typical of Mande leatherwork.

Large round or conical buttons are also a feature of a particular style of sandal (sabara) common throughout the Mande region (Figures 48, 49, 73). Mande-style sandals are small and peanut-shaped, coming to a slight point at the tip of the toe and the heel. The sole is often as much as an inch thick, usually made of several layers of cow or oxen hide. Only the top layer is of sheep or goat skin, decorated with fine painted and impressed lines and occasionally with stamped designs. A row of stitching around the edge attaches the top layer to the rest of the sole and secures the straps on either side. The straps may be plain, drawn with delicate black designs, or impressed with fine lines.

Short knives or daggers (muruw) probably have been a common feature of the dress of Mande men, especially hunters and warriors, for centuries (Figures 50, 51). It is still common today to see men in the countryside wearing knives attached to their belts, and knife sheaths (murutanw) are one of the items most frequently commissioned from contemporary leatherworkers.

There are several styles of knife sheaths usually identified in museum collections as Mande (Figure 52). In one of these styles, the sheath ends in a cylindrical knob, approximately the same diameter as the rim where the handle meets the sheath. The sheath is decorated with molded, impressed, and stamped designs and may employ different colors of leather or skin with the hairs still attached. The handle of the knife is also covered with leather. In addition, the sheath often has small buttons and loops to which are attached a carrying cord or bundle of cords similar to those on the long, cylindrical pouches described above. Another style has a tapered sheath decorated with molded, impressed,

FIGURE 51. Bamana man wearing the traditional cotton pants and tunic with a knife and sheath *(muru* and *murutan)* hanging at his side. Banamba, Mali, 1988.

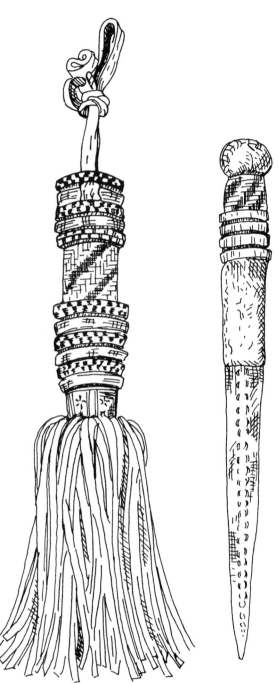

FIGURE 52 (opposite left).
Knives and sheaths acquired
in 1910 from George W. Ellis,
Jr., and identified as being
from Western Sudan.
Department of Anthropology,
National Museum of Natural
History, Smithsonian
Institution, Washington, D.C.
(E261685 and E261682).

FIGURE 53 (opposite right).
Mandingo dagger and sheath
(muru and murutan), after
drawing from the catalogue
card, Museum für
Völkerkunde, Hamburg
(49.50.2)

FIGURE 54. Soninke leatherworker Sekou Tambana with
a recently completed knife
sheath (murutan) embroidered
with white plastic strips in the
manner of palm-fiber
embroidery seen on museum
examples. Kita, Mali, 1983.

FIGURE 55. Knife and sheath
(muru and murutan) with
impressed designs and
embroidered with plastic, just
completed by Maninka
leatherworker Souleymane
Kouyaté. Kangaba, Mali, 1988.

FIGURE 56. Group of objects collected in the Fouta Djallon region before 1902 when they were published in an article on local arts and crafts. They are identified as Fula (Foulah); however, most of the leather-workers in this region are of Mande (Jakhanke or Soninke) origin. They include Mande-style knives or daggers, two with sheaths (top left and right); a sword and sheath (center); an amulet necklace possibly for a horse, given the length of the cord (center right); and a shot pouch and powder horn (lower left). (From Normand 1902–3, opp. 66.) (Photo: courtesy Labelle Prussin)

FIGURE 57. Mande-style sword and sheath *(npanmurutan)* with molded ridges encircling the sheath, impressed designs, and palm-fiber embroidery around the sheath near the grip and on the oval and circular buttons. The wide panels that hang from the sheath have incised and peeled designs. Deutsches Ledermuseum/Deutsches Schuhmuseum, Offenbach am Main, Germany (2652). (Photo: Deutches Ledermuseum/Deutsches Schuhmuseum)

FIGURE 58. Leatherworker having just completed a Mande-style sword sheath *(npanmurutan)* in Ditinn, region of Dalaba, Guinea, 1953. (Photo: P. Potentier, Photothèque, Institut Fondamental d'Afrique Noire, Dakar, Senegal [C54-41])

and stamped designs, and ends in either a small, rounded knob or a bundle of fringe. This style is often embroidered with palm fibers (Figures 53–55).

A distinctive Mande style of sword sheath *(npanmurutan)* also is well represented in museum collections (Plate 30; Figures 56–58).[17] This style follows a straight or often slightly curved blade, accentuated toward the pointed tip by a widening of the sheath into a leaf shape. This flat area provides a surface for painting as well as impressed and stamped designs and occasionally embroidery. The central portion of the sheath is divided into sections by a series of raised molded ridges encircling the sheath and marking off separate sections. These ridges act visually as frames for decorative patterns, sometimes painted designs, sometimes embroidery with palm fibers. Four large buttons (two on either side) are attached to the cords that provide loops for the shoulder strap. These buttons are sometimes plain, but are more often embroidered with palm fiber. From these buttons hang one or two wide panels decorated with incised and peeled designs and a bundle of fringe. On some examples, a tassel of fringe is suspended in the center.

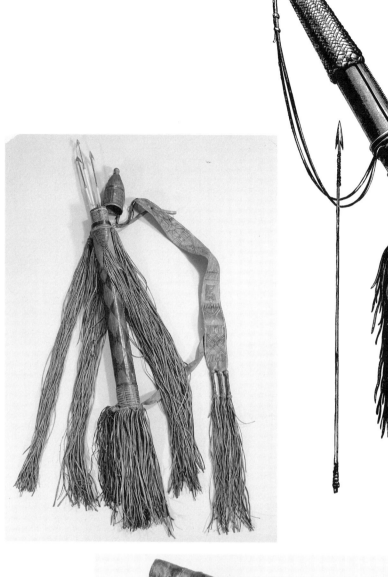

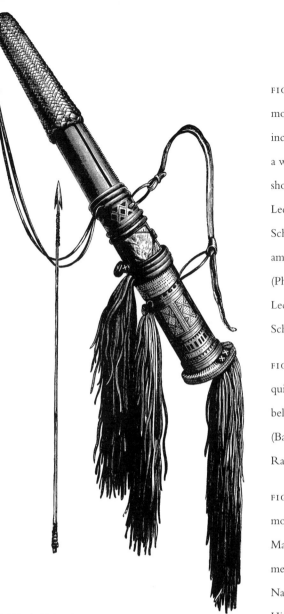

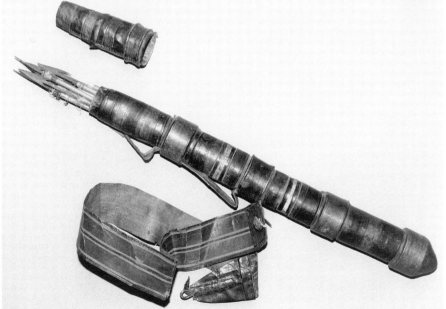

FIGURE 59. Quiver with molded ridges, fringe, and incised and peeled designs on a wide band that serves as a shoulder strap. Deutsches Ledermuseum/Deutsches Schuhmuseum, Offenbach am Main, Germany (10247). (Photo: Deutches Ledermuseum/Deutsches Schuhmuseum)

FIGURE 60. Drawing of a quiver and arrow identified as belonging to a Bamana (Bambarra) chief. (From Ratzel 1896-98, 3:308.)

FIGURE 61. Quiver with molded ridges typical of Mande leatherwork. Department of Anthropology, National Museum of Natural History, Smithsonian Institution, Washington, D.C. (E168875).

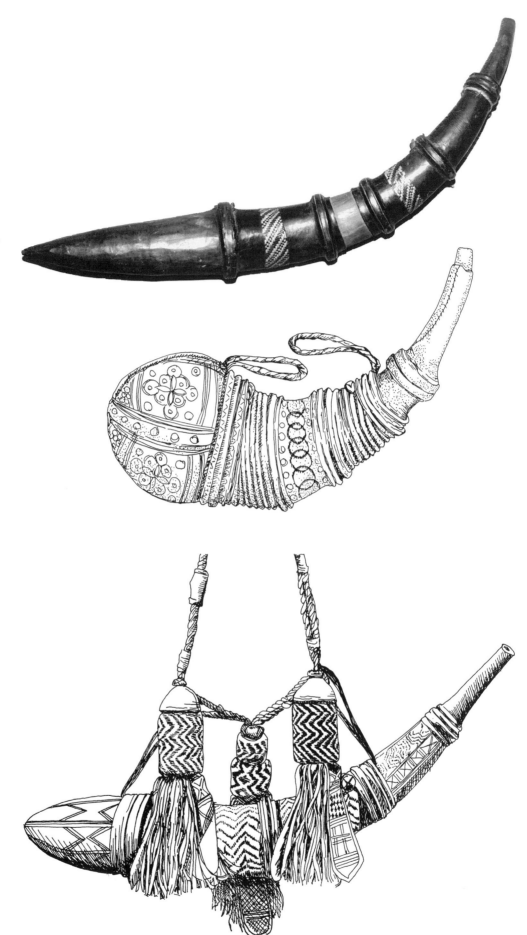

FIGURE 62. Mande-style powder horn *(marifamugn binyèn)*, with molded ridges and palm-fiber embroidery. Acquired in 1931 from the estate of Victor J. Evans. Department of Anthropology, National Museum of Natural History, Smithsonian Institution, Washington, D.C. (E360077).

FIGURE 63. Powder horn *(marifamugn binyèn)* identified as Mandingo, with molded ridges and impressed and painted designs, after drawing from the catalogue card, Museum für Völkerkunde, Hamburg (49.75.1).

FIGURE 64. Drawing of a Mande-style powder horn *(marifamugn binyèn)*, with incised and peeled designs, molded ridges, and tassels with palm-fiber embroidery. Deutsches Ledermuseum/ Deutsches Schuhmuseum, Offenbach am Main, Germany.

Although they figure prominently in Arab and European descriptions, quivers (Figures 59-61) are not nearly as well represented in museum collections as are swords. The most consistent feature of Mande quivers is a series of molded ridges that encircle the shaft. More elaborate examples have designs between the ridges and long fringe attached to the bottom and along the side or at the point where the cap is secured. A nineteenth-century illustration of one identified as having belonged to a Bamana (Bambarra) chief has what appear to be round buttons with designs that may be palm-fiber embroidery, a typical feature of Mande leatherwork (Ratzel 1896-98, 3:308).

The wide range of powder flasks and horns *(marifamugu binyènw)* found in Morocco is not par-alleled in West Africa (Figures 62-64). The most common in the Mande area are of cow horn and wood partially covered with leather. The small end provides the opening, while the larger end is usually closed with a pointed tip or sometimes a bulbous form carved from wood. The surface of the horn is visible between sections of leather, encircled with ridges, like the sword sheaths described above, that provide a means of attaching a carrying strap. The decoration is usually palm-fiber embroidery or incised and peeled patterns, or both. Those with a bulbous end are usually painted with designs. The most elaborate examples also have bundles of fringe and (amulet?) tassels.

Of all of the items produced by Mande leatherworkers for their clients, saddles and horse trap-pings are the most diverse, the most clearly derived from imported forms, and the least amenable to sorting out a Mande style from other West African traditions. With few exceptions, saddles *(kerikew)* across West Africa are of the Arab type (Plates 31-34; Figures 65-68). The high pommel in front and broad cantle behind provide protection for the rider and, along with the stirrups, secu-rity in the saddle. One variation is small with a vertical pommel ending in a round, flat disk (Plate 31). The cantle is small, rounded, and more or less perpendicular to the sideboards of the saddletree. This style appears over a wide area in the possession of horsemen of different ethnic origins, including Bamana, Soninke, and Fula.

A second variation is larger with a similar pommel and a low, flared cantle with slightly squared edges that slants back from the seat (Plates 33, 34; Figures 65, 66). It is identified by Pierre (1906, 56) as the Masina (Macina) type and is perhaps the most common one in the Middle Niger region. Although it is associated primarily with the Fula, saddles of this type are also used by Bamana, Dogon, and Soninke horsemen. This is also the most decorative style; the large surfaces lend them-selves to sometimes intricate and elaborate painted designs.

A third style has a forward curving pommel with a flared, forked cantle (Plate 32; Figures 67, 68). It is identified as Bamana (Bambara) by Pierre (1906, 56) and as Jawara (Diawara) by Boyer (1953, 96). In Banamba this style is said to be older than the other saddle forms in the region. It is associated especially with warriors; the forked back is used for hanging their accouterments.[18]

For each of these types, the saddletree is attached to a quilted saddle pad that serves to protect the back of the horse. The form ranges from small and circular to large and rectangular. However, the size and shape of the saddle pad does not necessarily correspond to the saddle style. In fact, although they are usually stitched together, they may be acquired separately, and an old saddle may be given a new pad, or vice versa.

Among the other accouterments provided by the leatherworker for horses there are several that are especially distinctive of the Western Sudan, though not exclusively Mande. These include a band of fringe *(bunsan,* the generic term for fringe) worn across the horse's forehead, said to help keep flies away from the horse's eyes (Plate 35). Although rare elsewhere in West Africa, similar

FIGURE 65. Horse and trappings belonging to a Soninke leatherworker. The cantle is flared and slants toward the back. Touba, Mali, 1984.

FIGURE 66. Saddle and trappings belonging to a horse owner near Djenné. The saddle has a large, flared cantle that slants back from the seat. Senoussa, Mali, 1983.

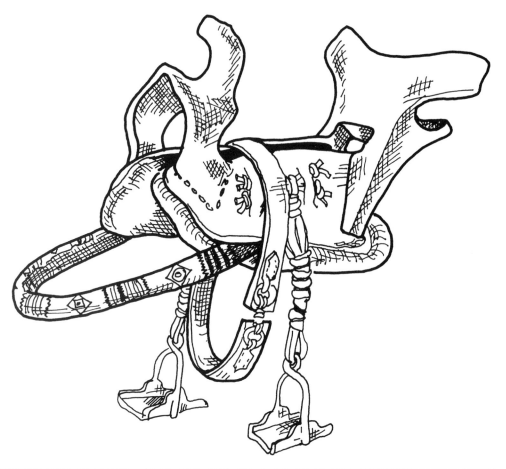

FIGURE 67. Drawing (after Boyer 1953, 96) of a saddle-tree with a forward curving pommel and a flared, forked cantle, from the Soninke (Diawara) region.

FIGURE 68. Saddletree photographed in the region of Bakounou, Mali. (Photo: courtesy Musée National du Mali, Bamako [1.BC.2a Bakounou 82 K.S. 3-#14])

FIGURE 69. Belt (?) with palm-fiber embroidered buttons, fringe, and wide panels with cut and peeled designs. It probably was part of an elaborate set of horse trappings. Identified as Mandingo, it was acquired in 1893 from a Dr. Traün of Hamburg. Staatliche Museen, Preussischer Kulturbesitz, Museum für Völkerkunde, Berlin (IIIC5668). For a detail, see Plate 38. (Photo: Museum für Völkerkunde)

bands of fringe are part of the elaborate accouterments of horses in Morocco, once again suggestive of a particular North African connection. Large fringed belts also may have been worn across the chest of the horse (Figure 69).

In the Western Sudan, the tassels hung around a horse's neck are said to serve a protective as well as decorative function and are often identified as *sèbènw* (Figure 70). In the fifteenth century, Cadamosto found that horses purchased without such protection would be provided straightaway with the appropriate amulets. He reported:

> When a chief buys a horse, he sends for his horsecharmers, who have a great fire of certain herbs lighted after their fashion, which makes a great smoke. Into this they lead the horse by the bridle, muttering their spells. Then they have it rubbed all over with an ointment, and keep it for fifteen to twenty days without anyone seeing it. Then they fasten to its neck charms compressed into a small space and covered with red leather. They believe that with these they are safer in battle (Crone 1937, 49–50).[19]

The stylistic features that link neck amulets found in museum collections and still seen in the field with other Mande style objects are the tightly woven cords and the use of embroidery with palm fibers on the tassel and buttons used to secure the necklace.

Other accouterments employed in the Western Sudan, such as the bridle, reins, and assorted halters *(karafejuruw* or *falamuw),* are not especially different from those used elsewhere in West Africa and tend to follow Arab prototypes. The collections of horse trappings I was able to document in the field were extraordinarily diverse in age, provenance, and style of individual pieces. The horse owners had inherited some from their fathers, commissioned others from local leatherworkers, and acquired still others on their travels.

Thus leather objects identified in museum collections as Mande more often than not share certain decorative features, which, I suggest, constitute a regional Mande style. These features include a preference for reddish brown and black hues, geometric design motifs, incised and peeled designs, a liberal use of fringe, and palm-fiber embroidery (Plates 36-38). This is not the only style in which Mande craftsmen work, but it is the most salient.[20] For example, the consistent clustering of these stylistic features on imported object types is significant. It suggests that it may have been important for leatherworkers to give these objects a distinctively indigenous look.

Patrons presumably supported and may have requested this aesthetic coherence in their commissioning of such objects. A cavalry warrior fully equipped with Mande-style sword and dagger, shot pouch, and powder horn, his own person and his horse draped with embroidered amulets and fringe, must have cut quite a figure riding across the savanna.

FIGURE 70. Horse neckpiece with amulets and palm-fiber embroidered tassel. Mandingo. Museum für Völkerkunde, Hamburg (27.124.1124).

REGIONAL STYLES OF LEATHERWORK

Mande style leatherwork on the objects described above stands in contrast to that of other objects that are part of a more general Islamic style. The simplest of amulets described above are such items. Similarly, slippers *(mukew),* for example, are associated with Islamic and prestige dress throughout the Sudanic region (Figures 71, 72). Barth (1857, 1:513-14) was surprised to find that in nineteenth-century Kano, slippers were made by "Arab" craftsmen for export north.[21] In Timbuktu and Djenné, slippers are the special domain of Arma leatherworkers, who claim that the origin of their craft is Moroccan. The tools these craftsmen use, and the Arabic names by which they are known, are identical to those recorded in Morocco and elsewhere in North Africa, and they are quite different from those used by other craftsmen in West Africa. Although the best quality continue to be produced by Arma craftsmen, such slippers are among the items now made by some Mande leatherworkers. Rather than incorporating their own stylistic elements, Mande craftsmen follow as closely as possible the style of North African or Arma prototypes. This includes techniques and materials not commonly employed in other types of Mande objects, in particular, embroidery with cotton or silk and the use of yellow leather. Some Mande leatherworkers also make boots *(coronw),* but these too tend to follow Arma or European prototypes. Thus, slippers and boots, whether made by Arma, Hausa, or Mande craftsmen, have retained stylistic features that continue to link them in both style and form to the North African tradition.

However, most types of objects made by Mande craftsmen are distinguishable from those made by leatherworkers in other parts of West and North Africa. For example, sandals for which the Hausa are so famous are quite different in style from Mande ones described above (Figures 73-75).[22] In contrast to the thick peanut-shaped sole of Mande sandals, Hausa ones have wide, thin soles, rounded on top and bottom and flared on either side of the heel. The Mande preference for simple black painted and impressed designs on the strap and sole contrasts with the more highly decorated Hausa sandals, with different colors of leather (especially green), and embroidered, painted,

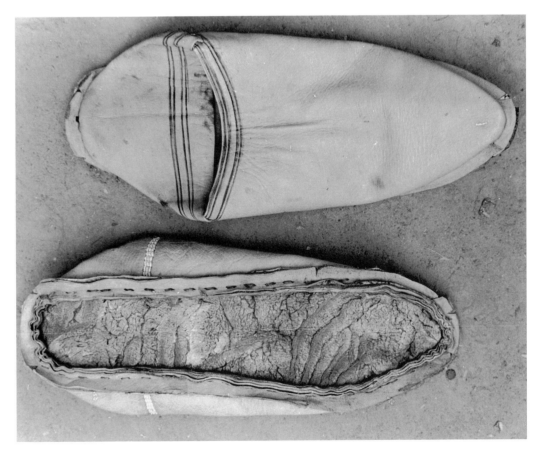

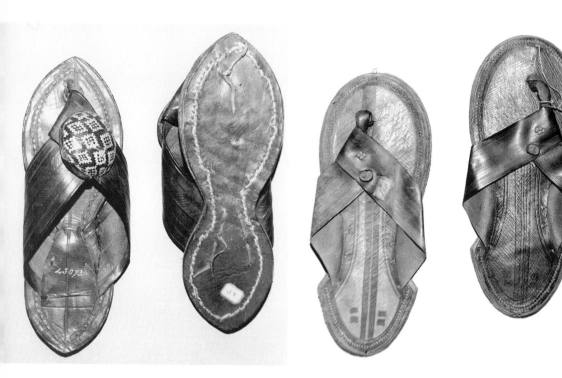

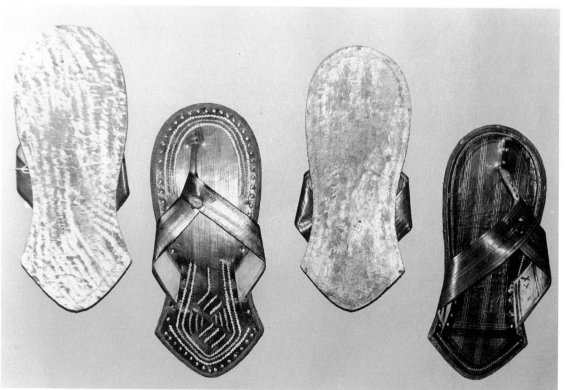

FIGURE 73. Pair of Mande-style sandals *(sabaraw),* with palm-fiber embroidered buttons. Collected by John H. Smyth, United States Minister to Liberia. Department of Anthropology, National Museum of Natural History, Smithsonian Institution, Washington, D.C. (E43073).

FIGURE 74. Pair of Tuareg sandals. Department of Anthropology, National Museum of Natural History, Smithsonian Institution, Washington, D.C. (E423867 and E423868).

FIGURE 75. Hausa-style sandals collected in 1900 by Diehl in Togo. Acquired in 1908 as part of an exchange with the Leipzig Museum of Ethnology. Department of Anthropology, National Museum of Natural History, Smithsonian Institution, Washington, D.C. (E249855).

FIGURE 76. Detail of a bag with leather and cotton embroidery, leather appliqué, and painted and incised and peeled designs, typical of Tuareg leatherwork. Department of Anthropology, National Museum of Natural History, Smithsonian Institution, Washington, D.C. (E422947).

FIGURE 77. Cushion cover with painted designs, typical of Moor leatherwork. Purchased in 1988 from Moor women in the market at Mourdiah, Mali. Collection of Barbara E. Frank.

impressed, and stamped designs. In place of a large button, Hausa sandals often are decorated with a small circle of fringe or, on more luxurious versions, with a large rosette of ostrich feathers.

Tuareg leatherwork (Figure 76) shares with that of the Hausa a tendency to employ elaborate combinations of appliqué, reverse appliqué, embroidery, and stamped designs, quite different from the more restrained colors and textures of Mande leatherwork. Moor leatherwork (Figure 77), with its characteristic intricate geometric and curvilinear patterns incised into or painted on the surface, is equally distinctive. That each of these traditions—Mande, Hausa, Tuareg, and Moor—shares a repertoire of forms disseminated by means of trade, travel, and Islam is undeniable. The distribution throughout this region of the wallet form described above is evidence enough of such common ground. However, the diversity of ways in which these forms are made distinctive precludes describing Sudanic cultures as homogeneous.

In fairness to William Fagg (and indeed to anyone attempting to assign attributions to museum objects long removed from the field), one of the problems is a lack of published information on West African leatherworking traditions. Thanks to Lhote (1950, 1952, 1955), Gabus (1958), Nicholaisen (1963), and others, there was at the time Fagg was writing a body of literature on Tuareg leatherwork, backed up by decent and fairly well documented collections. Gabus's collections of material culture among the Moors of Mauritania are astonishingly comprehensive, and the sections in his publications devoted to leatherwork are not insignificant. However, the best sources on Hausa leatherwork to date remain two brief articles from the mid-1970s by David Heathcote (1974). What little information there is on other West African traditions is much less accessible, a few pages buried in the arts and industries sections of monographs of individual ethnic groups.[23] Yet museum collections are loaded with leatherwork from all over West Africa. While some of it lacks detailed collection data, there are enough well-documented pieces that certain patterns begin to emerge.

For example, one of the pieces identified by Fagg (1971) as "Hausa-Manding" is a particular style of saddlebag (Figure 78), of which there are perhaps hundreds in museum collections. These bags are trapezoidal in shape, usually with a semicircular or more rarely triangular flap. Five to seven appliqué circles, usually white leather and red cloth, are stitched on the front surface of the body of the bag and the flap. Often intricate leather-embroidered designs arranged in rows are stitched across the bottom of the bag and up the sides, occasionally filling in the area around the appliqué circles. The back side is usually plain. Hanging from the bottom is a row of fringe, including three or four wide panels decorated with incised and peeled designs. Similar panels and fringe often are attached to the top corners of the bag.

Focusing only on museum identification of those bags for which there is specific collection data, the Hausa-Manding label quickly loses its viability. In 1933 Franz Olbrechts collected two pairs of bags, one purchased in a market in San, Mali, and the other presented to him by the Mobo Naba (the Mossi ruler) in Ouagadougou (Wagadugu; present-day Burkina Faso). Other museum documentation suggests that bags such as these were made or used by various Voltaic peoples, including Dogon, Mossi, Bobo, Bwa, Fula, Kassena, and Gurma, primarily in the Voltaic region of northern Togo, northern Ghana, and into northern Côte d'Ivoire, throughout Burkina Faso, and into east central Mali.[24] I photographed several pairs of this style and type belonging to horsemen of Dogon, Soninke, and Bamana origins in a number of Sudanic towns, including a pair at the compound of a Fula leatherworker in Fatoma that belonged to a Dogon horseman en route home to Bandiagara.

FIGURE 78. Voltaic-syle trapezoidal saddlebag with cloth and leather appliqué, embroidery with leather and palm fiber, and incised and peeled designs on the wide bands hanging with fringe from the bottom. When it was purchased in Bamako in 1983, it was identified as Dogon, as was almost any old looking object in the antiquaire's section of the Grand Marché. Collection of Barbara E. Frank.

FIGURE 79. Drawing (after Tautain 1887, 229) of a bag collected by Dr. Louis Tautain and identified by him as a saddlebag for a Bobo horseman or groom.

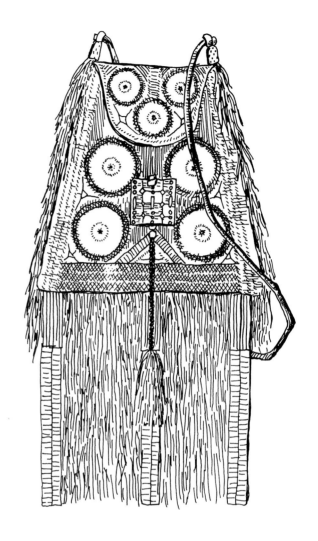

In the late nineteenth century, the colonial officer Dr. Louis Tautain acquired a bag of this type, which he identified as a Bobo horseman's bag (Figure 79). He commented on its unusual qualities: "The work is very original and absolutely special. I have never seen its analogue either in form or process of ornamentation, or color of leather (white) among the Moors, the Mandingka [Mandinka], the Soninka [Soninke], the Bamana, or the Foulbe [Fula]" (1887, 233, fig. 30).[25]

In agreement with Tautain, I suggest that this style is original, even though it exhibits appliqué and embroidery techniques common to Hausa leatherwork and cut and peeled designs typical of Mande leatherwork. But these are combined in a way that is neither Hausa nor Mande. Whether a more precise attribution within the Voltaic region is possible must await further study. In my survey of West African leatherwork in museum collections, my focus has been on distinguishing Mande leatherwork from others; nevertheless, my sense is that much more could be done in the way of sorting out regional styles by working with existing documentation and objects, should someone have the tenacity to undertake such a task. In the meantime, these leatherworking traditions continue to be subsumed under a generic Sudanic label at best, or misidentified as Hausa, Tuareg, or even Mande.

This survey of Mande leatherwork has revealed that the range of types of objects suggests a

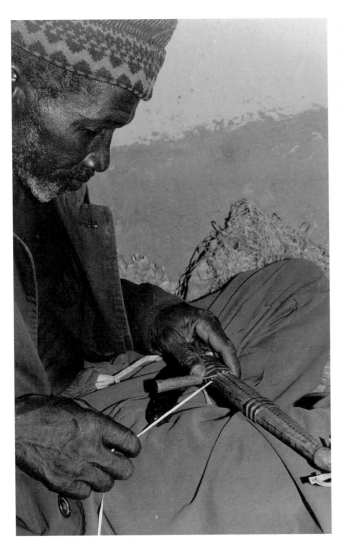

FIGURE 80. Maninka leatherworker Souleymane Kouyaté
embroidering a knife sheath
(murutan) with thin plastic
strips in emulation of palm-
fiber embroidery. The surface
of the leather is scored in narrow, parallel lines and an awl
(binyè) is used to open a passage for the plastic strips.
Kangaba, Mali, 1988.

FIGURE 81. Maninka leatherworker Souleymane Kouyaté,
having completed the
embroidered part of a knife
sheath *(murutan),* uses a blunt
awl *(binyè)* to impress a pattern in another section of the
sheath. Kangaba, Mali, 1988.

significant amount of contact and exchange between West
and North Africa as well as within West Africa. However,
certain stylistic features allow one to distinguish Mande
leatherwork from that of other major leatherworking traditions in West and North Africa. The differences among these
traditions lie primarily in style, especially in the combination
of particular materials, design patterns, and decorative techniques, rather than in type of object made.

Mande-style leatherwork is characterized by the use of
primarily reddish brown or maroon leather, in contrast to the
wider range of colors and materials (cloth, green leather, and
thin sheet metal) employed in Tuareg, Hausa, and other traditions. Black geometric painted designs stand in contrast to the
scrolls and other curvilinear patterns typical of Moor leather-

FIGURE 82. Objects with
palm-fiber embroidery made
by Mandingo leatherworker
Sini Mansaray, including
leather-covered bottles, powder horn, and Western-style
purses and trays. Several of his
tools are in the foreground.
Freetown, Sierra Leone, 1988

work. The technique of incising the surface of the leather and peeling off portions of the upper layer is used primarily on the wide panels that hang from various objects, forming a major element of Mande design. This technique is employed by other leatherworkers but is usually combined with other techniques that seem to dominate the object's appearance. Similarly, stamped and impressed designs tend to be more prominent on objects from the Mande region because they are not obscured or overpowered by the appliqué and embroidery patterns typical of Hausa and especially Tuareg leatherwork. Another common feature of Mande leatherwork is the technique of molding the leather over raised parallel ridges around the shafts of sword and knife sheaths, quivers, and powder horns. Finally, perhaps the most distinctive element of Mande leatherwork is the use of palm-fiber embroidery, in contrast to embroidery with leather, cotton, wool, or silk employed by Hausa and Tuareg leatherworkers (Figures 80–82).

This combination of design techniques appears on a wide range of objects most consistently associated with warfare, such as sword sheaths and shot pouches, but also on sandals and small bags. It is perhaps best understood as a broad regional style, useful in distinguishing Mande leatherwork from that of Moor, Tuareg, and Hausa craftsmen, and from North African traditions. However, while I maintain that this is a Mande style, it is not limited exclusively to either Mande craftsmen or Mande patrons. Craftsmen of other ethnic origins within the Mande region compete to produce objects similar, if not identical, in style to their Mande counterparts. For example, it would be difficult to distinguish the knife sheaths made by Mande Bamana and Soninke craftsmen from those made by non-Mande Dogon and Fula craftsmen. In fact, as with pottery, object types and styles are perhaps the least distinctive element of the leatherworking traditions of these ethnic groups. It is by exploring the technology by which these objects were made that Mande traditions may be more closely defined.

4

THE TECHNOLOGY OF MANDE POTTERY

The technology of African pottery production is deceptively simple. The best potters manipulate the clay with ease into amazingly symmetrical forms, without benefit of sophisticated potter's wheels or kilns with carefully controlled temperatures (Plates 12, 15, 17; Figure 83). And yet there is a surprising diversity in the techniques these potters use. The ways potters make pots reveal more about the origins of different traditions than the styles of the finished products. Pottery production reflects specialized knowledge transmitted from one generation to the next and augmented by individual experience. Each step of the process is surrounded by prescriptions for success and proscriptions against failure. Although potters may attempt new forms upon the commission of a client, they are much less likely to experiment with the process itself. The style of their technology, how and why they make pots the way they do, is more culture specific than the style of the objects they produce (cf. Gosselain 1992). Subtle differences between the way Bamana and Maninka potters form and fire may be compared with major differences in the technological styles of other ceramic traditions in the region. In fact, it is the combination of sophistication, conservatism, and variation that provides evidence of independent origins and makes the study of ceramic technology such an effective tool in reconstructing history.

FROM THE CLAY PIT

The first task the potters undertake is to gather the raw materials. Digging the clay pit is the only part of the production process for which the women have the assistance of their husbands. It is the single most important and most dangerous part of their enterprise. Mande potters say that raw clay has *nyama*, a kind of vital energy or "heat" *(funteni)* that pervades all things.[1] If not handled properly, the clay has the capacity to destroy one's health and well-being. They claim it can cause barrenness, sterility, miscarriage, blindness, illness, and even death. This power in clay is most intense at its source, the clay pit. One potter described the effect as a kind of gas emitted when the clay is

FIGURE 83. Bamana potter
Seban Fané finishing the rim
of a large water jar *(jifinye)*.
Kunògò, Mali, 1991.

PLATE 1 (previous page). Maninka potter Nansa Doumbia with her brother and his wife. She is one of the best and most respected potters of Kangaba, the one to whom others often come for advice and assistance. Gouala, Mali, 1992.

PLATE 2. Maninka potter Nakani Kanté. She is an excellent potter; however, without daughters or daughters-in-law to assist with daily chores, she has little time for pottery making. Kangaba, Mali, 1992.

PLATE 3. Maninka potter Koloko Kanté is a *nègètigi,* "master of the iron (knife)," one of the few remaining *numumusow* in the region to perform excision. Kangaba, Mali, 1992.

PLATE 4. Maninka potter Nakan Kanté with her twin daughters and a daughter-in-law, selling pots at the weekly market. These include a brazier *(singon),* several cooking pots *(dagaw),* and water jars *(jidagaw).* Kangaba, Mali, 1992.

PLATE 5. Pots for sale at the weekly market, including incense burners *(wusulan-bèlèw)* and small mortars and pestles in the left foreground, cooking pots *(dagaw),* and water storage jars *(jidagaw).* Banamba, Mali, 1988.

PLATE 6. Water jar *(jidaga)* made by Maninka potter Nansa Doumbia in emulation of the large water jars made by Somono and Fula potters in the Inland Niger Delta region. Gouala, Mali, 1992.

PLATE 7. Bamana water jar *(jidaga)* with molded lizards alternating with nodules suggestive of breasts and navels. The narrow neck is common on these older vessels, which often have figurative designs. Collection of Lon and Richard Behr. (Photo: courtesy Douglas Dawson)

PLATE 8. Water jars *(jidagaw and jifinyew),* basins *(fagaw),* and cooking pots *(dagaw)* ready to be fired. Kangaba, Mali, 1991.

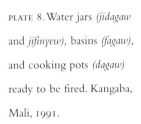

PLATE 9. Potters at a weekly market in Fatoma. In the foreground are, left to right, pot lids, a brazier, cooking pots, rainspouts, and couscous steamers. In the left background are water storage jars and more cooking pots. The range of ceramic wares is similar to those made by Somono potters in Djenné. However, Fula potters in the region produce pots of a similar style. Fatoma, Mali, 1984.

PLATE 10. Pots for sale in the Koutiala market. In the foreground are Mande-style blackened cooking pots with several enamel-painted water jars. In the background are the red and white Mopti-style water jars from the Inland Niger Delta region. Koutiala, Mali, 1991.

PLATE 11. Maninka potter
Nakani Kanté forming the bot-
tom of a vessel over a mold.
Bangaba, Mali, 1992.

PLATE 12. Maninka potter Nansa Doumbia finishing the surfaces of three water jars *(jidagaw)*. The wooden platter *(kurun)* that serves as a turntable is in the foreground, and an old washbasin *(faga)* holds water in which the potter's tools soak, ready for use. Kangaba, Mali, 1992.

PLATE 13. Maninka potter Nakani Kanté scoring the bottom of a pot still on the mold in order to add a foot. Kangaba, Mali, 1988.

PLATE 14. Maninka potter Nakani Kanté adding the foot to a pot still on the mold. The wooden palette *(kurun)* serves as a turntable. In the foreground are the bottom parts of two vessels under construction, a cooking pot *(daga)* and a couscous steamer *(nyintin)* with holes pierced. Kangaba, Mali, 1988.

PLATE 15. Bamana potter Assa Coulibaly adding the rim to a water jar *(jidaga)*. The vessel is placed on the broken base of a large water jar filled with sand, which functions similar to the wooden palette *(kurun)* used by Maninka potters. Banamba, Mali, 1988.

PLATE 16. Bamana potter
Assitan Ballo rolling a
twisted-string roulette
around the belly of a cooking pot *(daga),* imparting
the characteristic impressed
diagonal lines. Kunògò,
Mali, 1991.

PLATE 17. Bamana potter Seban Fané working on a small water jar *(jidaga)*. The bottom of a broken water jar filled with gravel serves as the turntable. In the background are two large water jars *(jifinyew)* ready to be fired. The rough surfaces of the bases of the pots are from the netted-fiber tamper used when the vessels were still on the mold. Kunògò, Mali, 1991.

PLATE 18. Bamana potters stack large pots upright on a circular bed of wood, with smaller vessels upside down around them. The pile is then covered with wood, carefully placed to prevent the pots from touching each other. On this occasion, because of our presence and our cameras, the husband of the women began to help them place the wood until he realized in frustration that his wives were quietly repositioning each piece he had laid. Kunògò, Mali, 1988.

PLATE 19. Maninka potter Nakani Kanté preparing the red slip paint for a water jar. She grinds a stone high in iron oxide against a stone mortar, adding water as needed. Kangaba, Mali, 1988.

PLATE 20. Bamana potter Assa Coulibaly adds wood to a small firing. Some of the vessels fired on this morning were available in the afternoon market (PLATE 5). Banamba, Mali, 1988.

PLATE 21. Bamana potter Seban Fané dipping a cooking pot hot from the fire in a vegetal solution to blacken the surface. Kunògò, Mali, 1988.

PLATE 22. Bamana potter Assitan Ballo sealing small cracks in the surface of a large water jar *(jifinye)* with clay. Kunògò, Mali, 1988.

PLATE 23. Bamana potter Diarrasou Traoré using leafy branches to splash a large water jar *(jifinye)* with a vegetal solution while it is still hot from the fire. Kunògò, Mali, 1988.

PLATE 24. Maninka potters
Hawa Kanté and Minata
Doumbia smothering a pot
with sawdust to blacken the
surface. In the foreground
are pots holding a solution
of tree bark and water that
is used to splash the surfaces
of larger pots, making them
a rich, shiny black. Kangaba,
Mali, 1991.

being dug, a gas that makes one dizzy if the person is not properly protected. Men and women each prepare their own special solutions in which to bathe prior to the expedition. This medicine is strong enough to protect the women on subsequent trips to the clay pit and during their work with the clay for the remainder of the season.

Because the best sources of clay are often out in the bush far from the village, the potters and their husbands must also contend with the various spirit forces, or *jinèw*, of the chosen place. In some instances, these *jinèw* have specific identities; greetings and prayers are offered by name.[2] According to tradition, special sacrifices must be performed to ensure the safety of all who participate in the digging and the success of the potters work in the coming months.[3] I was told that people do not venture near the clay pit because of the control potters are believed to have over the spirits, which might be directed toward them with ill effects.[4] Others cite the importance of protecting the clay from contamination by an unsanctioned presence. It is especially taboo for a menstruating woman to enter the clay pit.[5]

After the fall harvest and before the beginning of the dry season, a day is chosen by mutual consensus among the men and women, sometimes with the aid of a diviner. The only restriction is that it cannot be a Monday or a Friday, a proscription that is also observed for later trips to the clay pit and in some cases for firing. The sacrifice that is prepared may include a special meal of white creamed rice. Red, or more commonly, white kola also may be offered. In some cases a pure white chicken must be sacrificed at the spot. It is then sent home with one of the women to be prepared for the midday meal eaten at the clay pit. The sacrifice is performed by the men after the location has been determined. Selecting the particular spot seems to be a joint enterprise between the women and the men. They recognize by telltale cracks in the landscape where the best quality clay is to be dug and they rely on the experience of years past. The men take up pick axes and hoes and remove the surface layer of mud until they reach the purest deposits of clay, generally between one and two meters down. Then they begin to dig the clay. As huge basins are filled and passed to the surface, the women distribute the clay into stock piles, one for each of the participating potters. Either the clay is transported back to the compound and stored there, or, during the course of the dry season, the potters return to the site as needed to replenish their supply of clay. If their stock is depleted before the end of the season, women either negotiate with other potters for some of their remaining stock or return to the clay pit and dig as much as they need and are able to carry.

The women of Kangaba have access to clay deposits about a mile or two outside the village, but the best quality clay is on the other side of the Niger River in the floodplain. Most of the clay tends to range from a light yellow gray to a darker charcoal gray, and generally it has relatively few impurities. By contrast, the potters of the Kolokani region face smaller deposits, greater difficulties in getting to the various locations, and considerable variation in the quality and color of the clay they eventually garner.

After the women return to their compounds, the clay is broken up and spread in the sun to dry. Any obvious impurities are removed, and the clay is then stored in large ceramic vessels. At least one day before the potters intend to use it, the clay is covered with water and allowed to soak overnight.

The prepared clay mixture has a high percentage of temper or grog to prevent excessive shrinkage during firing, which would result in cracks and fissures.[6] The women make the grog by pounding sherds of broken pots into a fine grain. The fastest way to do this is in a mortar, in the

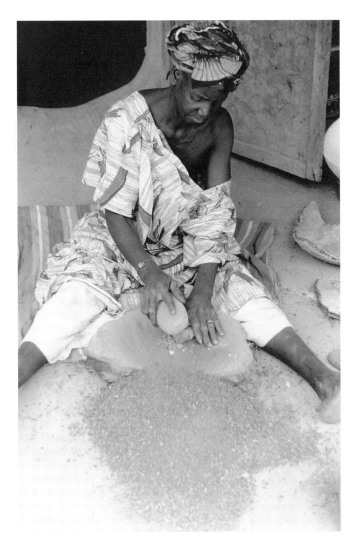

FIGURE 84. Bamana potter
Assitan Ballo gently pounding
old pots for grog. Kunògò,
Mali, 1991.

FIGURE 85. Maninka potter
Nansa Doumbia sifting temper ground in a mortar to
remove the fine dust particles.
Kangaba, Mali, 1991.

FIGURE 86. Bamana potter
Sunkoro Sissoko mixing clay
and temper with her right
foot. Kolokani, Mali, 1991.

same way that food grain is prepared. However, hand grinding is recognized to be better because, though more time-consuming, it produces particles of more even size and less goes to waste as dust (Figures 84, 85). The women begin mixing by clearing a space on the ground or on a mat and dumping a basin of the wet clay onto a circle of temper. They then add additional measures of temper. With their right foot extended, they begin a kind of dance, rocking back and forth around in a circle, compressing the clay beneath their soles and gradually incorporating more and more into the mixture (Figure 86). The verb *ka dòn kè,* "to dance," is used to describe this part of the process. Temper is added as needed. In the Kolokani region, straw is often added to the mixture. The final proportions are approximately 30 to 40 percent temper to clay. If the mixture becomes too dry, the women may sprinkle it with a little water. The dance continues. When the proper consistency is reached, the mass of clay is wedged briefly with the hands and divided into balls sized according to the molds to be used. Despite the apparent casualness of the mixing process, there is not a great deal of latitude in the proportions. The women know by feel if they have it right. Too much temper and the vessel will crack during construction, too little and it will burst during the heat of the firing.

THE FORMING PROCESS

None of the procedures outlined above are significantly different from those employed by potters throughout the larger region. It is in the next stage of pottery production that the most tangible evidence of distinct pottery traditions begins to take shape. For the initial forming process, Bamana and Maninka potters rely on convex molds (Plate 11; Figures 87, 88). Damaged pots that are cracked or have chipped rims and are therefore no longer suitable for cooking, but with particularly nice shapes and of appropriate sizes, are saved as molds rather than being broken up for grog. The potters begin by flattening out a pancake of clay sized according to the type of pot to be made and the mold they have prepared with a dusting of ash or fine grog. The circle of clay is shaped with the right foot and then placed on the mold. It is gently but firmly pounded evenly over the surface, working from the top center down and around. This compresses the clay and reduces the chances of air bubbles or foreign matter remaining. The clay is left to sit on the mold until it is somewhat firm and able to support the addition of the side walls. Depending on the type of vessel being made, a foot may be added at this time (Plates 13, 14; Figures 89, 90).

Once the pot has dried just enough to support itself, it is removed so the mold can be used again. There is no particular length of time for drying, as the process is affected by variables such as moisture in the air, time of day, and whether the potter has chosen to speed things up by placing the mold in the sun, or slow the process down by placing it in the shade. Also, either the entire mold or the edges may be covered with a damp cloth. The women know by touch whether a pot is dry enough to stand on its own. This part of the process also requires skill and attention, because while the potters do not want the pots to collapse, neither can they let them get too dry because the new clay will not adhere properly.

The vessel is then turned upright and placed on a device that allows the potter to turn the vessel as she works. Maninka potters use a wooden platter *(kurun* or *kurunmuso),* which they identify as one of the most important of the potters' tools (Figure 91).[7] The *kurun* is commissioned from a blacksmith-sculptor, but according to some of the potters, not just any blacksmith can successfully

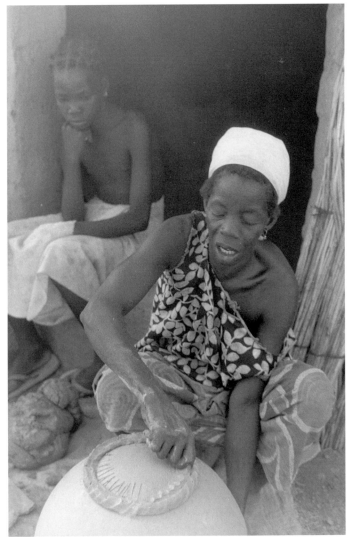

FIGURE 87. Bamana potter Sunkoro Sissoko forming the bottom of a pot over a mold. Kolokani, Mali, 1991.

FIGURE 88. Maninka potter Assetu Doumbia forming the bottom of a pot, with several others in various stages around her. Bamako, Mali, 1991.

FIGURE 89. Maninka potter Nakani Kanté forming the foot of a pot. Kangaba, Mali, 1988.

FIGURE 90. Maninka potter
Nakani Kanté forming the
foot of a pot. Several partially
formed pots surround her.
Kangaba, Mali, 1988.

complete the task. Because of the *nyama* of the wood best suited for this purpose,[8] it is said that the turntable must be made by a man who has already lost his first wife, as she would certainly die should he attempt such an assignment. In contrast, Bamana women make their turntables without danger from the bottoms of large broken water jars, which are filled with sandy gravel and placed into a slight depression in the ground for support (Figure 92). Whether wooden *kurun* or pottery basin, the device becomes the equivalent of the potter's wheel for the remainder of the forming process, turned with the hand.

The inner surfaces of the vessel are scraped and smoothed, a process that removes any traces of the rough outer surface of the mold. The edges are trimmed with a knife and scraped with a piece of broken calabash or a large seed pod. Coils are added, compressed on either side of the edge to ensure a tight bond between new and old clay. The remaining walls are built up with coils and the surface is smoothed (Figure 93, 94). In many instances, crosshatched patterns remain from the impression of a fiber net held over a stone or fired clay tamper during the initial forming process on the mold. These patterns may be enhanced with corncob or twisted-string roulettes (Plate 16;

FIGURE 91. Maninka potter Nansa Doumbia scraping the interior of a brazier *(singon),* which has just been removed from a textured mold. The bowl rests on a wooden platter *(kurun),* which serves as a turntable. Kangaba, Mali, 1991.

FIGURE 92. Bamana potter Assa Coulibaly adding coils to a water jar *(jidaga).* The bottom of a broken water jar filled with sand serves as a turntable (see Plate 15 and Figure 8). Banamba, Mali, 1988.

FIGURE 93 (above left). Bamana potter Seban Fané adding coils to the sides of a large water jar *(jifinye)*. Kunògò, Mali, 1991.

FIGURE 94 (above right). Bamana potter Seban Fané scraping and consolidating the sides of a water jar *(jidaga)* with a corncob. Kunògò, Mali, 1991.

FIGURE 95 (left). Bamana potter Assa Coulibaly making a water jar *(jidaga)*. While a rough pattern remains on the lower surface of the pot, the textured surface of the belly of the jar has been enhanced with a twisted-string roulette. The potter turns the pot, turntable and all, with one hand while shaping the rim with the other (see Plate 15 and Figures 8 and 92). Banamba, Mali, 1988.

FIGURE 96. Potter Nansa Doumbia smoothing the rim of a water jar *(jidaga)* (see Plate 12). Kangaba, Mali, 1992.

FIGURE 97. Potter Nansa Doumbia using a piece of cloth to smooth the surface and a bit of straw to impart an impressed line around the belly of a water jar *(jidaga)*. Kangaba, Mali, 1992.

FIGURE 98. Bamana potter Assitan Ballo painting a red slip design on a water jar *(jidaga)*. She uses her finger or a chiffon of cloth to paint the design. Kunògò, Mali, 1991.

FIGURE 99. Pots made by
Maninka potters ready to be
fired. They include water jars
(jidagaw) with slip-painted
designs on the shoulders; several low, wide bowl forms
(fagaw) used for washing
(center right); and large water
storage jars *(jifinyew)*.
Kangaba, Mali, 1991.

Figure 95). The resulting texture also serves a functional purpose by breaking up the surface, creating more resiliency to withstand the thermal shock of the firing and later cooking processes.

The potter uses one hand to form the rim and the other to turn the palette in a motion similar
to that of a potter's wheel (Figure 96). Occasionally, for larger vessels, the potter moves around the
pot to form the rim. A piece of cloth or a sheath of baobab leaves is used to smooth the surface.
On many of the vessels, a small piece of straw or bamboo is used to impress lines in the rim and
sides (Figure 97). While the vessels are firm but not completely dry, the upper surfaces are burnished with smooth pebbles or strings of baobab seeds. Ideally, they are allowed to dry completely
before the firing process. However, prefiring by putting hot embers into the interiors of the vessels
is not unknown. Water jars, incense burners, and other small pots destined for public display are
painted with red slip designs before firing (Plates 4, 5, 6, 8, 19; Figures 98, 99). These vessels will
become a rusty peach color upon firing, with the slip designs appearing as a darker red. The large
water jars, braziers, and cooking pots will be turned a rich, shiny black during the firing process.
Variations in design patterns and in shape are subtle to the untrained eye, but the potters can easily
distinguish their work from that of others.

TO THE FIRE

Bamana and Maninka potters use the same basic principles and practices for firing, with minor variations. While ritual precautions once surrounded the firing, few are adhered to today. In the past, it
was said to be dangerous for a menstruating woman to approach the firing, though opinion seemed

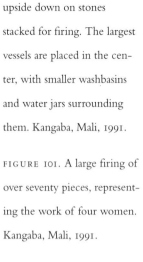

FIGURE 100. Pots turned upside down on stones stacked for firing. The largest vessels are placed in the center, with smaller washbasins and water jars surrounding them. Kangaba, Mali, 1991.

FIGURE 101. A large firing of over seventy pieces, representing the work of four women. Kangaba, Mali, 1991.

FIGURE 102. Lighting the fire. Kunògò, Mali, 1988.

FIGURE 103. Pottery jars (*jifinyew* and *jidagaw*) stacked upright on a bed of wood for firing. The slip-painted jars will be pulled from the fire and allowed to cool, while the others will be turned black at the end of the firing. Kunògò, Mali, 1988.

divided over whether the greater danger was to the pots or to the woman. Aside from the need for a pregnant woman to protect herself from the heat of the fire, no other restrictions applied. The only proscription that continues to be observed is not firing on Friday, though at present this has as much to do with honoring the sanctity of the Muslim holy day as with maintaining a pre-Islamic tradition.

Firings take place regularly throughout the height of the dry season from January to May, especially in towns like Kangaba, with a population of some fifteen to twenty active potters. Women often fire together with others of the same household. Most firings average about twenty-five to thirty-five pieces.[9]

There are some variations in the firing process that are only partially attributable to differences in the environment. In Kangaba the vessels are stacked upside down, raised a few inches off the ground by small stones (Figures 100, 101). Bamana potters place the large pots upright on a bed of wood (Plate 18; Figures 102, 103). In both settings smaller pots encircle larger ones in a symmetrical fash-

FIGURE 104 (below). Maninka potter Nansa Doumbia pulling a pot from the fire with a *wòlòsò*. Kangaba, Mali, 1991.

FIGURE 105 (opposite, top left). Bamana potter Assa Coulibaly dipping a pot in a vegetal solution while the pot is still hot from the fire. Banamba, Mali, 1988.

FIGURE 106 (opposite, top right). Maninka potter Nansa Doumbia smothering a pot hot from the fire with millet chaff and sawdust to blacken the surface. Kangaba, Mali, 1991.

FIGURE 107 (opposite below). Bamana potter Assitan Ballo maneuvering a large water jar (*jifinye*) from the burning embers with the *wòlòsò*. Kunògò, Mali, 1991.

ion, with rarely more than one layer on top. The pile is then carefully covered with wood, the first branches positioned to secure and separate the vessels. The best kinds of wood are the hard woods that burn hot and long.[10] The women complain that today they have to walk farther and farther to get sufficient amounts for the firing, often settling for less desirable woods. Straw and cow dung occasionally provide additional fuel, but they are not common.

Once the fire is lit it burns rapidly (Plate 20). Within an hour the women take up long wooden poles fitted with iron hooks called wòlòsòw (Plate 21; Figures 104, 107).[11] Like the wooden palette (kurun), this piece of equipment is acquired from the blacksmith, and it too is infused with nyama. This critical tool allows the potter to approach, ducking under the most intense heat waves, and hook or maneuver the pots from the fire.

The women begin by lifting the smaller vessels red hot from the outskirts of the fire. The pots are plunged into a special bath that seals and blackens the surface (Figure 105). The most common liquor is made from the fresh bark of one of a number of trees, a reddish solution that is freshly prepared for each firing.[12] There is another liquid that in Kangaba is sometimes used in combination with or in place of the reddish mixture. It is the waxy residue from the making of karite butter, which has been allowed to ferment and is said to be especially effective for sealing the pores of the fired clay. The blackness of the surface is often enhanced by a kind of raku-like process of smothering the vessels in sawdust, peanut shells, or millet and rice chaff (Plate 24; Figure 106). As they work their way to the vessels too large to dip, the potters use handfuls of leafy branches from cangèrèbilen (Combretum glutinosum) or kunjè (Guiera senegalensis) trees to splash the surfaces with the liquid (Plate 23). The process can be quite dramatic, as the women, draped in extra layers of old clothing to shield their skin from the intensity of the fire's heat, move in to retrieve each piece, then skillfully manipulate it to the edge of the firing ground as steam and smoke rise around them (Figure 107).

When the last vessel has been pulled from the fire after perhaps an hour or two of intense activity, an assessment of the results is possible. The literature leads one to expect a high rate of breakage during the firing process. In fact, obvious failures (pots blown apart or with large sections missing) are relatively rare. When they do happen, it is invariably the work of a young potter, who will be criticized for failing to achieve the proper mixture of temper and clay or for allowing a stone or millet seed to remain in the clay body. More common is the appearance of small fissures in the rims and bodies of the vessels. These are often treated immediately upon removal from the fire with one of a number of techniques. In Kangaba, the women rub the cracks while the pots are quite hot with a locally available fruit known as zaban (Saba senegalensis). In the Kolokani region, they use a mixture of dried acacia powder and wet clay (Plate 22).

A COMPARISON OF TECHNOLOGICAL STYLES

The forming technique used by Bamana and Maninka potters is perhaps the most commonly employed across West Africa (Drost 1967; Roy 1975, 1987a), and Mande potters may well have been responsible for some of its dissemination. Convex molds (Figure 108) are used by most Mande potter groups, including Bamana and Maninka, as well as by Soninke and Soninke-related potters to the north and east (de Zeltner 1915; Saint-Père 1925; Boyer 1953; Gallay 1970; LaViolette 1987,

FIGURE 108. Somono potter Niamoye Nientao forming a water jar (jidaga) over a convex mold. Djenné, Mali, 1983. (Photo: Adria LaViolette)

FIGURE 109. Senufo kpeene (Kpeenbele) potter Mawa Koné using a convex mold to begin a pot. Katiali, Côte d'Ivoire, 1982. (Photo: Carol Spindel)

FIGURE 110. Fula potter Fanta Guro Kassé using a paddle and anvil technique to form a water jar. Djenné, Mali, 1983. (Photo: Adria LaViolette)

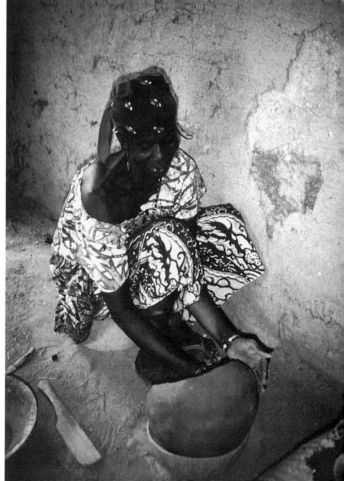

FIGURE 111 (above left). Jula potter Fatoumata Kouyaté in the initial forming stages of a pot. The potter is seated on a wooden plank, with a cylinder of clay placed on a large broken pottery sherd in front of her. Using the heel of her hand, she pounds out the center and pulls up the sides before shaping the vessel into a hemispherical shape. Sissingué, Mali, 1991.

FIGURE 112 (above right). Jula potter Aramatou Kouyaté mounting the sides of a large water jar *(jifinye)* with coils. Doguélédougou, Mali, 1991.

FIGURE 113 (left). Jula potter Aramatou Kouyaté shaping a large water jar *(jifinye).* The rim will be completed and surface decoration added to the belly while the pot remains on the palette. Only then will the vessel be removed and the bottom scraped and rouletted. Doguélédougou, Mali, 1991.

1995). They also are employed by the two major Senufo pottery-producing groups in northern Côte d'Ivoire (Spindel 1988, 1989): the wives of brass casters, known as *kpeene* (Kpeene, Kpeenbele), who are the most important potters in the region in terms of scale of production (Figure 109); and the wives of blacksmiths, known as *tyeduno* (Tyeduno, Tyedunbele, Cedumbele). It is significant that Mande origins have been suggested for both of these groups, both of which are now well integrated into Senufo society.[13] Convex molds also are used by some Bwa and Mossi potters in Burkina Faso, who also may be of Mande origin.[14] In the village of Sarnyéré, Gallay (1981) documented the use of a convex mold technique by male Dogon potters, an apparent departure from the more common use of a paddle and anvil technique employed by female Dogon potters and also documented in the archaeological context (Bedaux 1983, 26-29). A convex mold is used for large vessels by some Fula potters, along with a paddle and anvil technique more common to concave mold techniques (LaViolette 1987, 1995).[15]

The significance of the distribution of the convex mold technique among Mande and Mande-related groups becomes apparent when the technique is compared with the forming technologies of other potter groups. At least two other quite distinct technologies are employed in the region, and these differences suggest the independent origin of several ceramic traditions.

A concave mold with variations on a paddle and anvil technique is used by Sonrhaï potters as well as by most other Mossi, Fula, and Dogon potters (Figure 110). Some Somono potters of Mopti and Djenné combine the use of a concave mold with a coiling technique in the initial phases of construction (LaViolette 1987, 1995; Gardi 1985, 224-62). The concave mold also is used among various groups south and east of the Mande region, in the Mono region of Benin (Adandé and Metinhoué 1981), among the Moba of northern Togo (Kreamer 1989), among the Gurma (Gulmance, Gulmantche) of Burkina Faso (Geis-Tronich 1989), and others.

Christopher Roy (1975, 1987a) has identified a third technique found east and south of the Mande region, which he calls "direct pull" since it does not involve the use of a mold. I first encountered this technique among Jula potters of the Kadiolo region (Figures 111, 112). Although they share a similar repertoire of pottery types with their Mande counterparts in the north, they use a completely different process to make these pots. The clay mixture they prepare is wetter and more elastic than that used by Bamana and Maninka potters in the Mande heartland. They form the clay into cylinders, which they place on small pieces of broken pottery that serve as turntables. The women position themselves on a long, wooden plank with the cylinder of clay and turntable in front of them and begin by pounding a depression in the center of the clay with the heel of their right hand, turning it with their left. They then switch to pounding out the center with the tips of their fingers. When the desired depth is nearly reached, they combine pounding with pulling the clay upward, very quickly forming it into a vaguely hemispherical shape. The interior of the vessel is then smoothed and shaped with a large seed pod while the clay is still quite loose and pliable. They then set the pot aside, while starting two or three others, before adding coils to complete the sides and rim (Figure 113).

Once the rim is completed and the pot has been allowed to become leather-hard, the exterior surface is scraped and smoothed with a variety of tools. Decorative patterning is added by means of wooden and plaited-fiber roulettes. Once the rim has been polished and designs added to the shoulder and neck of the vessel, the pot is removed from the ceramic turntable and excess clay on the bottom is scraped off to form the appropriate shape (Figure 114). The surface is smoothed and

decoration is added, as well as a foot, if desired. Just before the firing, the vessels may have a red slip rubbed into the smooth upper surfaces. In both the directness of the initial forming method and the extent of excess clay scraped off, this process is fundamentally different from that employed by Mande potters in the heartland, a difference that cannot be ascribed solely to variations in the quality or character of the available clays. Even though these potters identify themselves as Jula and speak a Mande language, their pot-forming technology suggests a non-Mande origin. While the issue of their identity will be addressed in chapter 6, examining where else a similar forming process is employed provides important clues to the distinct origins of this ceramic tradition.

Variations of the direct-pull technique are used by a broad spectrum of potter groups in Mali, Burkina Faso, Côte d'Ivoire, and Ghana. Bobo potters work directly with a lump of clay on a small wooden palette turned on a large circular grinding stone (Gallay 1991-92). Roy's description of a Lobi potter at work presents some parallels to the techniques of the Kadiolo potters:

> The potter begins by placing a small, fired-clay dish on the floor of her work area, which will serve
> as a support for the base of the new pot. She then forcefully slaps a large mass of kneaded clay into
> this dish. Using her right fist, she forces a hollow into the center of the mass. Then, bending over
> the clay, with her right hand inside the pot and her other hand outside, she begins to force the
> fresh clay upward, pulling the clay toward her chest, and simultaneously thinning and heightening

FIGURE 115. Jula women
stacking hundreds of pots for
a large firing. The women
begin by laying a huge circle
of wood. Even though it is a
communal firing, the women
are responsible for providing
the wood and straw for their
section and for properly
stacking their pots. Sissingué,
Mali, 1991.

the walls with the pressure of her fingers as they slide over the plastic material. Her back is parallel to the ground as she bends, and her elbows and arms do all of the work (Roy 1987a, 52).

Potters among the Mo peoples of Ghana also construct pots without the use of a mold. In one method, the potter commences by placing a large ring of clay onto the cleanly swept ground. She then proceeds to pull the walls of the pot up until the desired size and shape are achieved. As in the technique used by the Lobi potters, the vessel remains stationary, the potter moving around it as she works. In another method of constructing pots, the potter forces a depression with her fist in the center of a mass of clay before pulling up the sides.[16] The base is formed later in the process.

There are several potter groups in northern Côte d'Ivoire whose techniques in the beginning stages of forming a pot seem to correspond even more closely to those employed by the Jula women. Unlike the two main Senufo potter groups, the Nafanra potters use a small clay palette turned on a wooden plank. Carol Spindel (1988, 10–16) suggests a possible connection between

Nafanra and Baule potters through their use of what she refers to as a "pinch pot" technique in the beginning stages of forming a pot; she also identifies similar decorative techniques and certain parallels in their respective apprenticeship systems (see also Soppelsa forthcoming). Bernadine Biot (1991) describes a similar forming process among the Wan and Mono of the Mankono region of central Côte d'Ivoire.

While these potters share with the women of Kadiolo the lack of reliance on a mold and the technique of forcing the moist clay upward, there are subtle differences in the initial phases of constructing the pot—in the shape of the clay when starting (mass and ring versus cylinder), in the position of the vessel under construction (stationary versus rotating), and in the posture of the potter (bent over and working around the vessel versus seated with the vessel turning in front). Although a historical connection among these methods is possible, a conclusive link must await more detailed analyses of the techniques employed by these and other potter communities throughout the region.

At this point, however, it seems clear that these technologies—convex mold, concave mold with paddle and anvil, and direct pull—are different enough to argue that there are at least three distinct pottery traditions in the region. The use of a convex mold is particularly characteristic of Mande pottery technology. Outside the Mande heartland, it seems to be employed either by potters for whom Mande origins have been posited, or by non-Mande potters who could have adopted the technology from a Mande source. Furthermore, in the two instances where Mande potters use one of the other techniques, among the Somono of Djenné and among the Jula of the Kadiolo region, historical factors may explain their use of non-Mande technologies.[17]

When the firings of Mande potters are compared with those found elsewhere in the region, the differences that emerge are only partially attributable to variations in available materials. At first glance, the relatively small firings of the work of one or two Bamana or Maninka women contrasts dramatically with the large quantity of pots in the communal firings of the Kadiolo region, where as many as a thousand pots might be fired at one time (Figure 115). These large firings occur approximately once every three weeks during the height of the dry season. Smaller firings are done periodically by individuals and small groups. The Kadiolo potters create a thick bed of narrow sticks on which the pots are carefully placed. The large pots are placed upright in the center with smaller pots stacked around and on top of them. Carefully placed pieces of broken pots form a protective shield around some of the pots on the outer tiers. The pile is then covered with multiple layers of straw and lit. For the next several hours the women watch for openings in the burnt straw where the partially fired pots are exposed, onto which they toss additional armloads of straw. Even though the fire is subdued after the first few hours, the pots are allowed to continue baking until just before dawn of the following day. Although the women are familiar with the process of turning the pots black in the manner described above, the vast majority of what they produce remains the red color of fired clay.

Elsewhere potters adapt their methods to available sources of fuel. In the region of Djenné and Mopti, potters rely more heavily on straw, grasses, millet stalks, and dung, since wood is scarce. Straw is the primary fuel used farther south among the two major Senufo groups. Like the Jula potters, they too do large communal firings and have a similar manner of stacking the vessels. Combinations of wood, straw, grasses, and dung are employed by Soninke, Dogon, and Fula potters. The most significant exception to the commonalty of firing practices throughout the region is the use of low mud-walled kilns by some Mossi and Bwa potters in Burkina Faso (Roy 1987a, 56). Although the distribution of these kilns is limited, they do extend into Mali in the area between Koutiala and San.

Treating pots to a vegetal bath hot from the firing is one of the more dramatic aspects of pot firing throughout much of West Africa. In some cases the desired effect is a deep, shiny black surface, as among most Mande potters as well as among the Baule of Côte d'Ivoire and the Akan of Ghana. In other cases, the effect is one of subtle marbling or of tinting the surface, as among the Senufo as well as the Shai of Ghana. Oxidation of the surfaces with dry materials in a raku-like process is also not limited to Mande potters.

In addition to the more obvious elements of the physical process of pottery production, there is a broad range of prescriptive and proscriptive behaviors that ensure the success of the enterprise. Unfortunately, few studies have been concerned with the ritual behaviors of pottery production. As Eugenia Herbert (1993) reported in her review of beliefs and practices, perhaps the most universal taboo is that of restricting menstruating women from exposure to and contamination of the most critical moments in pottery production (digging clay and firing), just as in iron smelting and forging. Similar proscriptions exist among the Senufo (Spindel 1988), Asante (McLeod 1984), and Shai (Quarcoo and Johnson 1968). Several authors mention sexual taboos particularly around the process of digging clay, which, as mentioned above, is for the Bamana and Maninka the most spiritually charged undertaking of pottery production. One of my informants told me that were a *numumusow* to have sexual relations with someone other than a blacksmith and then enter the clay pit, the clay would certainly be contaminated. Likewise, the taboo would be broken if a blacksmith were to sleep with a *hòròn* (noble) woman and enter the clay pit.

Elsewhere in the region, there are some important parallels with the ritual practices of Bamana and Maninka potters. For example, like their northern counterparts, the Jula potters of Kadiolo prohibit digging clay and firing on Fridays and Mondays. Since both are generally daylong activities, the ban allows the women to participate fully in the Friday prayers, but most potters stated that this is a proscription from the pre-Islamic past.[18] The Senufo *kpeene* potters also avoid offending the spirits of the clay pit by not digging on Fridays or Mondays (Spindel 1988, 21–22; 1989, 68). They too perform a sacrifice at the beginning of the season and recognize the sacredness of the place by giving it a proper name and offering prayers to the spirits associated with the place. Among the Shai potters of southern Ghana, clay pits are presided over by priestesses responsible for their proper treatment and respect for taboos. Digging, for example, is not allowed on Thursdays and Fridays (Quarcoo and Johnson 1968, 69). Similarly, Asante women are forbidden to make pots on Fridays, according to McLeod (1984, 369), because it is designated as a "male" day. Other proscriptions seem to be more locally based. In the Kadiolo region, for example, eating peanuts or onions and wearing gold are forbidden at the clay pit. This is apparently due to an event in the distant past when gold was discovered in one of the pits.

Thus it is possible to define the technological style of Mande pottery and distinguish between Bamana and Maninka variants. Both mix a dry clay body, use a convex mold followed by coiling techniques in forming, and employ limited decorative techniques. While Bamana potters use a large basin filled with fine gravel as a turntable, Maninka potters use a wooden tray made especially for the purpose. Both potter groups fire primarily with wood, occasionally adding straw or other fuels, and blacken most of their pots hot from the fire with a vegetal bath and smothering process. While

Bamana potters stack their pots upright on a bed of wood, Maninka women set theirs upside down on stones, saving most of the wood to be used on top of the pile. Both Bamana and Maninka potters observe fewer proscriptions than their ancestors once did, but they continue to respect the sanctity of certain days and limit the participation of menstruating women in some stages of the production process. Of these characteristics, the initial stages of forming are the most distinctive by comparison with other traditions and the least dependent on external environmental or other factors. This is what constitutes the technological style of Mande pottery, a style that is more distinctive than that of the objects these potters make.

5

THE TECHNOLOGY OF MANDE LEATHERWORK

Implicit in the assumption that Mande leatherworking is an Islamic craft is the notion that the technology must have been introduced along with imported objects and design concepts. However, as with Mande pottery production, it is to the technological style that one must turn for a more complete story. Evidence for the indigenous origins of Mande leatherwork lies in the materials, tools, and techniques these craftsmen use to make objects that otherwise reflect centuries of contact and trade throughout West and North Africa. While objects and object styles may move easily across ethnic and geographic boundaries, technology is more conservative. Although leatherworkers across the Sudanic region have access to the same materials for tanning and dyeing, the choices they make and the way they use these materials reflect different technologies. Unlike the potters, leatherworkers seem more willing to experiment with new devices and incorporate them into their ever expanding tool kits. However, the distinctive shape of the knife on which they rely most reflects the different origins of the leatherworkers' technologies (cf. Plates 39, 41). It is by sorting out the core elements of a leatherworker's tool kit that Mande leatherworkers may be distinguished from their competitors.

THE TANNING PROCESS

In the late eighteenth century, Mungo Park reported that leatherworkers, "are to be found in almost every town, and they frequently travel through the country in exercise of their calling. They tan and dress leather with great expedition" (1799, 282).[1] Among Bamana, Maninka, and Soninke peoples today, where leatherworking remains the exclusive domain of men, the wives and children of leatherworkers often assist with tanning, drawing the water and pounding the acacia pods and other vegetal materials used in the tanning process.[2] Although most craftsmen say they used to do their own tanning, many of them now purchase already tanned skins in the market. Some leatherworkers no longer do leatherworking, preferring to tan skins for sale to other craftsmen who are still active, or to traders who buy the skins and take them to sell in Bamako or elsewhere.

Goats and sheep are the primary source of skins used for tanning in the Western Sudan.[3] Cowhides, as well as the skins of other large animals, are used untanned for the soles of sandals and slippers. Tanners usually acquire these skins from butchers. Sometimes they are fresh, or they may have been dried for later sale and transport. Tanners sometimes work the skins of antelopes, leopards, monkeys, and other wild animals acquired from hunters, treating them in such a way as to preserve the pelt with the hair. Today, snake, crocodile, and lizard skins are tanned for use on Western-style belts, handbags, and sandals, but it is rare to see these skins on traditional objects such as amulets and knife sheaths.

Animal skins must undergo a series of procedures in preparation for the actual tanning process. Untanned hides and skins are highly susceptible to attack by molds and bacteria, part of the natural process of the decomposition of organic materials (Morfit 1853, 146–52; Forbes 1966, 1). If they are not to be tanned directly, skins may be dried and held in this state for a limited period of time prior to processing. Skins are first soaked in fresh water to relax and soften them. Then they are thor-

FIGURE 116. Soninke leather-worker Salim Soumanou and two of his grandsons scraping the hairs from skins that have been removed from the lye solution. Sirakorola, Mali, 1983.

oughly washed to remove any excess dirt, blood, and loose tissue that has adhered to the surface.

The hairs are usually removed prior to tanning (Figure 116).[4] This is accomplished by means of soaking in a caustic alkaline solution. In the past, a lye solution of water and ash was prepared.[5] Now that imported caustic soda is available, it is used in preference to the more traditional lye solution because it is more potent and works faster. This part of the process plumps up the skin, loosens the fiber structure, and dissolves or softens the roots of the hairs so that they may be scraped easily from the epidermis. The soaking takes from one to five days, depending on a variety of factors—the strength of the solution, the time of year (it takes less time during the hot season), and the number, type, and thickness of the skins. The skin is removed from the lye solution, rinsed in clear water, and then draped over a mortar or a wooden beam laid on the ground. The hairs are easily scraped away with a wooden baton or a dull knife.

The next step is to remove any remaining hair follicles from the outer surface and the dark, fleshy material that adheres to the inner side. Mande tanners immerse the skins in a bate of chicken manure and water and allow them to steep for several hours or overnight, occasionally rubbing them.[6] This part of the process renders the skins particularly soft and flexible.

Bating may be combined with or followed by drenching, a process that cleanses by removing all traces of the lye and relaxes the swollen state of the skins (Forbes 1966, 4). Mande leatherworkers generally use a solution made with an infusion of millet bran and water that has been allowed to sour or ferment. This liquid may be mixed with the skins and chicken droppings or treated as a separate bath. Both of these processes (bating and drenching) prepare the skin to accept and absorb the tannin. The skins are then scudded by carefully scraping the blackened fleshy material from the inner surface with a sharp knife. The hair side is given another scraping at this time. The skins are rendered white and ready to be tanned.

Tanning is the process by which raw animal skins are transformed into a stable, durable material, known as leather (Morfit 1853; Waterer 1956; Forbes 1966, 1–67; Reed 1972; Plenderleith and Werner 1971). Vegetable tanning promotes the union of tannin with the gelatinous tissue of the skin, permanently changing its protein structure, making it water resistant, and preserving it from decay. At the same time, the strength and durability of the fibrous structure is maintained. Although there are a variety of vegetable substances available in the Western Sudan that are high in tannin, the principal source for Mande tanners is the fruit of the acacia tree, called *bagana* or *baanan* in Bamana (Figure 117). The seed pods are pounded to separate the hard seeds, and the remaining shells are reduced to powder and rubbed into the skins. The skins are allowed to soak in a solution of macerated acacia pods and water. While they are soaking, the skins must be frequently rubbed and kneaded. The strength of the solution is gradually increased by the addition of more powdered acacia. If the pods are not available or are considered too expensive, the bark of the acacia, which also contains tannin, may be used, as well as a variety of other vegetal materials locally available. The tanning process itself takes anywhere from one to four days. When the skins are sufficiently tanned, they are washed and allowed to dry. They are then scraped, stretched, and beaten to make them smooth and pliable, ready for sale.

While all of the materials used are widely known, it is the tanner's art to know the proper proportions to yield the right strength of the solutions and to know by feel and appearance the proper timing of each phase of the procedure. Every stage requires careful attention; too long in any one of the solutions can ruin the skins, yet neither can the process be rushed with success. The tanner must adjust his technique to the climate of the season and know how to take advantage of available materials. Care must be taken as well during the rubbing and scraping processes not to tear or cut the skin. Tanning requires expertise and experience.

DYEING MATERIALS AND TECHNIQUES

Prior to the introduction of commercial chemical pigments and dyes, the most common colors used by Mande leatherworkers were black, reddish brown, and occasionally yellow. Although variations in the tanning process yield a subtle range of hues from almost ivory white to a light golden brown, the skins are dyed neither as part of the tanning process nor in a separate process using the entire skin. Instead, Mande leatherworkers paint the surface of the natural skin with color as needed when creating an object.

FIGURE 117. Seed pods of the acacia used in tanning. Sirakorola, Mali, 1983.

Mande leatherworkers continue to mix their own black dye in the traditional manner rather than using imported inks. The principal ingredients are a sour liquid, scrap iron residue obtained from the blacksmith, and sugar or honey. The sour liquid might be the juice or pulp of acacia or tamarind pods, citron, or any of a number of acidic fruits mixed with water. The solution is left to ferment for as long as a week, although faster results may be obtained by bringing the mixture to a boil and then allowing it to sit for several days. The consistency of the solution varies from a thick brownish substance to a translucent charcoal gray. When it is applied to the surface of the object, the leather appears simply to be wet, but within seconds the surface oxidizes to a rich black. Black is usually applied in fine lines as part of the design, using a small blunt-edged knife, or larger areas may be painted with a cloth swab. If the leatherworker is working on a small item, such as an amulet, he may put it into the pot containing the liquid for several minutes after it has been sewn. It will be a solid black when it is retrieved.

Traditionally, a deep maroon red was produced from a special kind of millet known as *farawòrò* (*Sorghum caudatum* var. *colorans*). The outer sheaths that have the deepest red color were removed from the stalk and pounded in a mortar to a fine powder. This was mixed with a solution of ash and water. The grains are said to be inedible; *farawòrò* was cultivated in small plots by leatherworkers specifically for its color. This red millet was documented as early as the late eighteenth century by Mungo Park (1799, 283). In the late nineteenth century Georges Tellier made special note of the cultivation of this kind of millet by leatherworkers in Kita, who otherwise, he noted, did not do agricultural work. Tellier wrote:

> On this subject, one must note an exception to the rule that states that the "dialli" [*jeli*] do not
> farm; it is the following. The "dialli-karangués" [*jeli-garanke*] cultivate a sort of special millet that is
> not eaten, but from which the ears yield, by maceration in hot water, a red-brick dye that they
> employ for their leather and which is regarded highly. It is sufficient for them, moreover, to raise

each year [about] twenty stalks in a corner of their courtyard. It is work that is consistent with their courage. This millet is cultivated exclusively by them and, each harvest, they put aside one or two ears for sowing the coming year (1898, 214).[7]

Other sources confirm its restricted use exclusively for dyeing leather (Raffenel 1856, 1: 408-9; de Zeltner 1915, 224; Saint-Père 1925, 50-51). While most Mande leatherworkers mentioned millet as a traditional source for red dye and praised the rich color it yielded, few take the trouble to use it today.

Some leatherworkers insisted that the only colors they had before the imported pigments became available were red and black, and indeed these colors predominate in museum collections of Mande leatherwork. Others report that yellow was among the colors they produced using one of a variety of natural materials and methods. *Ntiriba (Cochlosperum tinctorium)* was among the botanical specimens collected by Mungo Park on his second expedition in the Western Sudan in 1805. He recorded that it was "called Tribo, a root with which the natives dye their leather of a yellow colour" (Park 1815, 61). *Ntiriba* was also noted in Djenné by Charles Monteil ([1932] 1971, 239) as one of several means of dyeing leather yellow. The roots were harvested and allowed to dry, reduced to powder, and mixed with hot water or a potash solution. The mixture was ready immediately. Some said the roots could even be cut and applied directly to a moistened skin.

The roots of *nyamaku (Curcuma longa)* are also identified by leatherworkers today as a traditional source of a yellow-red dye. Like the process for *ntiriba,* the roots were cut and the pulp was pounded into a paste that could be rubbed directly into the surface of the leather to impart the color. *Nyamaku* is a kind of turmeric, similar to ginger; it was cultivated in the savanna and forest regions as a leather dye (Ben Sai 1944b, 21). According to Monteil ([1932] 1971, 239), it was imported into Djenné from the Bobo Dioulasso region especially for the leatherworkers.[8]

Traditionally, Mande leatherworkers did not use a green dye for leather. However, skins already dyed green were occasionally imported from the Hausa region, and a few leatherworkers did have some knowledge about how the color was obtained, even though they themselves had never dyed skins in that way.[9]

Outside of black, reddish brown, and, in some cases, yellow and green, other colors were not available in the Western Sudan until the introduction of commercial dyes and paints. According to Tellier (1898, 213), leatherworkers in Kita were using both European pigments and vegetal dyes in the late nineteenth century. Similarly, Fernand Daniel (1910, 42) noted Soninke leatherworkers using both European colors and traditional vegetable dyes. J.-H. Saint-Père (1925, 51) reported in the 1920s that Soninke patrons complained about the imported colors used by leatherworkers, saying that the colors ran when it rained and ruined their clothing. They much preferred the traditional dyeing methods, which were more durable and colorfast. Monteil ([1932] 1971, 239) found that dyes imported from Europe were being used in Djenné in the 1930s.

The use of traditional vegetable dyes seems to have coexisted with the use of commercial pigments for much of the past century. Most leatherworkers are familiar with the traditional sources and methods even though chemical pigments were available when they were children first learning the trade. While black continues to be made in the traditional manner, most craftsmen today use commercial pigments. What is especially important, however, is that despite the availability of a wider range of potential colors, leatherworkers and their patrons continue to prefer the traditional colors of black, reddish brown, and yellow.

The processes performed by Mande leatherworkers require only a rather limited basic tool kit (Plates 40, 41; Figures 118-21). Essential tools are sharp-edged knives for cutting and scraping the leather; awls for piercing and sewing; wooden forms for smoothing, creasing, and polishing; containers of homemade paste, black dye, and water; and something to provide a flat, smooth surface on which to work.

The most distinctive element in the tool kit of a Mande leatherworker is the knife that he uses more than any other tool. In fact, the shape of the blade is an important indicator of the ethnic identity and regional origin of the leatherworker.[10] The knives used by Soninke leatherworkers, especially in the west, tend to have single-edged, long, and relatively straight blades. Bamana and Maninka leatherworkers, in contrast, use knives with single-edged, curved, or hooked blades, not as long as those used by their Soninke counterparts. These particular shapes are so important that European-style knives are taken to the blacksmith to have their blades reworked into the appropriate shape (Figure 122). There is no specialized terminology that accompanies these tools. The Bamana/Maninka term is *muru,* while the Soninke term is *labo,* both generic terms for knives used in domestic and other contexts as well.

Most Mande leatherworkers have several awls (*binyèw* or *binyènw; bune* in Soninke) of various sizes and thicknesses and a ball of beeswax to facilitate piercing holes in the leather or hide (Figure 123). Whatever the size, the blade is usually round in cross section, with a cylindrical or tapered wooden handle. Another essential tool in the leatherworker's kit is a wooden implement that serves a variety of functions, including molding the leather, polishing surfaces, sealing seams, and creasing edges (Figure 124). It is also used to impress lines into the surface or draw them on with the black dye. The Bamana term for this tool is *nugulan,* derived from the verb *ka nugu,* which means "to polish" or "to smooth." The term in Soninke is *naxaade,* also derived from the Soninke term for the action undertaken with it. This term is similar to the Fulfulde *(nakhade* or *nirkirde),* reflecting the close correspondences between these two languages.

Mande leatherworkers used wooden slate as a work surface (Figure 125). They are of very hard wood, oblong in shape. Most are rounded at one or both ends, rarely with a handle or knob at the top. These boards are constantly being scraped in order to clean them and smooth the surface, and thus over time the edges become rounded and the surface may even be worn entirely through (Figure 119). The most common term for the slate is *wala* or *walaha,* the same term used for the wooden slates that serve as writing boards for Muslim scholars and students of the Koran. They have the same shape, but the latter tend to be thinner and lighter than the leatherworkers' slates.

Aside from these essential tools, Mande leatherworkers have adopted tools from other leatherworking traditions. Most important in this category are the Arab-style scissors that appear in some Mande tool kits (Figure 118). These are used primarily to clip loose threads and rarely to cut leather, a task for which the leatherworkers rely on their knives. Scissors are called *masu* or *kemesu* in the different Mande languages, clearly derived from the Arabic *miqass* (plural, *maqāss*).

Another tool adopted from Arab tradition by some Mande leatherworkers is the wooden shoe last used for making Arab-style slippers (Figures 71, 118, 119, 126). A typical set consists of one piece in the shape of the slipper; a long, thin piece that slides in on top; and a small wedge driven

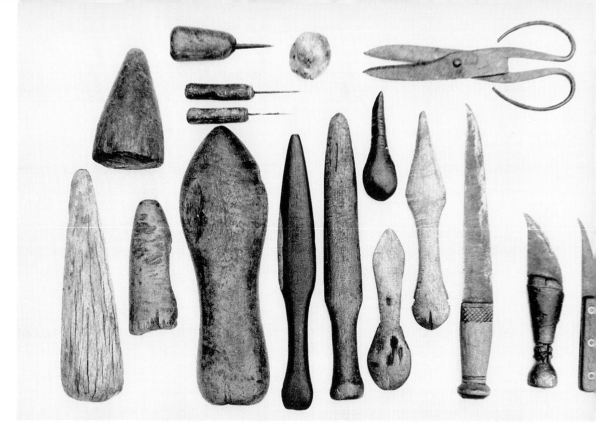

FIGURE 118. Tools purchased from Soninke leatherworker Makan Yafa in Kayes, representing about a third of the original kit, including at least one example of each of the principal types of tools. The small knife on the far right is for making impressed and painted designs; it is not sharp enough to cut. The three wooden forms at the lower left are for making slippers. Collection of Barbara E. Frank.

FIGURE 119. A typical though rather worn Soninke tool kit belonging to Boubou Soumanou. It includes knives (muruw); awls (binyèw); wooden forms for polishing and pounding (nugulanw); wooden forms for making slippers (mukeyiri), top center; and a wooden slate (wala), which is completely worn through. The small knife below the slate is blunt and is used to draw designs with black dye. The tool next to it is a metal stamp. Bamako, Mali, 1983.

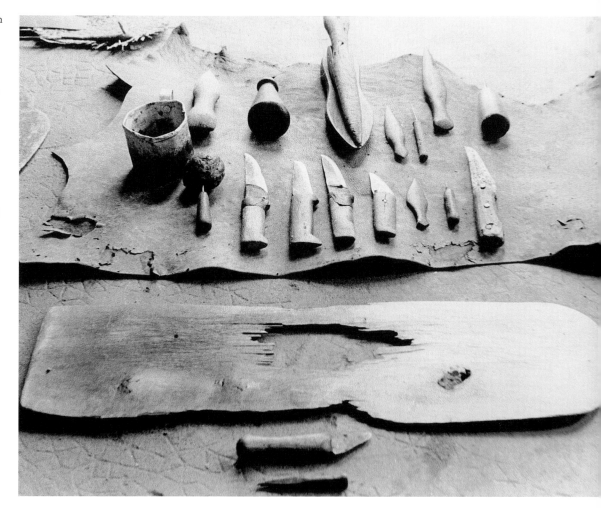

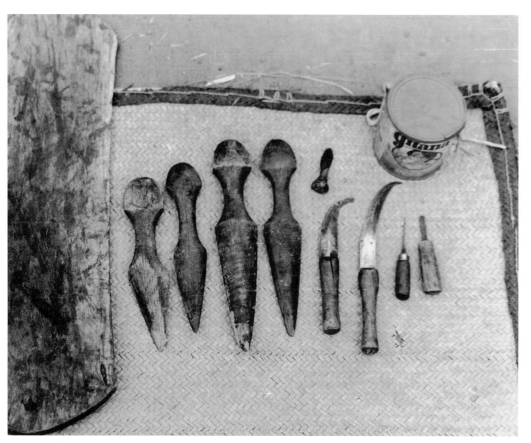

FIGURE 120. The tool kit of Soninke leatherworker Kalidou Ousmane Sylla, with only the most essential tools. Ti (near Fatoma), Mali, 1984.

FIGURE 121. The tool kit of Bamana leatherworker Bandjoukou Cissoko including knives with curved, hooked blades *(muruw)*. Segou, Mali, 1983.

FIGURE 122. Knives *(muruw)* belonging to Bamana leatherworker Bo Traoré. The one on the left was made locally, while the other two were imported and taken to the blacksmith to have the blades reworked into the appropriate shape. Banamba, Mali, 1984.

FIGURE 123. A selection of awls *(binyèw)* and beeswax from the tool kit of Soninke leatherworker Makan Yafa. Kayes, Mali, 1983.

FIGURE 124. A selection of wooden polishers *(nugulanw)* from the tool kit of Soninke leatherworker Makan Yafa. Kayes, Mali, 1983.

between the two. The upper surface of the bottom form is relatively flat unless worn down from use, while the lower surface against which the leather or hide of the sole will be shaped is slightly rounded. The size of the last varies according to whether the slippers are intended for men or women. Because of the association of slippers with Muslim dress, it seems likely that the forms used in their manufacture were introduced into the Western Sudan from North Africa, possibly via the Arma leatherworkers of Djenné and Timbuktu. In fact, these forms, of the same design and three-part configuration, are virtually identical to those recognized as indigenous in Morocco (Brunot 1946, 243-45; Guyot, LeTourneau, and Paye 1936, 22, pl. 2).

There are some indications that European-style wooden lasts for shoes and boots were adopted by some local leatherworkers during the colonial period (Figure 127). Various authors from the first part of this century have noted the use of wooden forms, including Saint-Père (1925, 48), who distinguished between a locally made version (probably the Arab one) and the imported European style (see also de Zeltner 1915, 223). European shoe lasts come in a variety of forms, from single block to broken or split lasts, but all have the full shape of the back of the heel of the foot up to the ankle. In contrast, the forms used to make slippers are inserted from the back and have no heels (Salaman 1986, 144-45, fig. 2:6 from Diderot's eighteenth-century encyclopedia). Monteil ([1932] 1971, 238) described the wooden forms used by the leatherworkers and then remarked on the skill of these craftsmen in creating, repairing, and copying anything that one might show or explain to them, including shoes for Europeans using these forms. Although Monteil's published account does not indicate whether the forms were acquired from Europeans, a colonial report—based in part on Monteil's earlier 1903 monograph—noted that the leatherworkers of Djenné deserved encourage-

PLATE 25. Soninke leatherworker Bakhodoré Sylla
contemplating the purchase
of a leopard skin. Bamako,
Mali, 1988.

PLATE 26. Blind leather-worker Shekna Diakité. He identified himself as a *garanke;* however, his father's family was originally Fula from Bankass (southeastern Mali). They emigrated to the north several genera-tions ago and intermarried with local *garanke* families. Nara, Mali, 1988.

PLATE 27. Soninke leather-worker Seydou Sylla with his grandchildren. The Sylla family (including several sons and nephews) is the most prominent *garanke* leatherworker clan of Sansanding. They compete with Fula, Bwa, Arma, and Bamana leatherworkers in regional markets. Sansanding, Mali, 1984.

PLATE 28. Bamana griot-
leatherworker Mambi
Kouyaté. Although he was
willing to allow me to take
pictures of him while he
was doing leatherwork, it
was his identity as a griot
and musician that mattered
most. This is the way he
most wanted to be photo-
graphed. Kangaba, Mali,
1992.

PLATE 29. Mande-style pouch *(bòrò)* with stamped, painted, incised, and peeled designs on the flaps; palm-fiber embroidered beads; and an abundance of fringe. Formerly Civic Center Museum, Philadelphia; now housed at the Atwater Kent Museum, Philadelphia.

PLATE 30. Rather crudely
made Mande-style sword
sheaths *(npanmurutanw)*
among the items for sale in
a tourist market. Dakar,
Senegal, 1983.

PLATE 31. Bamana leatherworker Nejon Kouyaté with his horse and trappings. The saddletree is small with a vertical pommel ending in a round, flat disk and a rounded cantle, both more or less perpendicular to the side-boards. The neck amulet is woven with palm fibers. Somba, Mali, 1983.

PLATE 32. Horse and Mande-style saddle *(kerike* or *gale)* with arked back belonging to griot-horseman Djigi Kouyaté. anamba, Mali, 1984.

PLATE 33. Saddle *(kerike)* belonging to a Soninke horse owner. The saddletree has a vertical pommel and flared cantle covered with yellow leather and painted designs. Touba, Mali, 1984.

PLATE 34. Griot-horseman Masiri Koita with his horse and an eclectic mix of trappings. He has a Masina-type saddle, a cord-appliqué and embroidered saddle blanket from Dioro (Mali), a metal-covered Tuareg-style halter with reins made by Tuareg women, a Mande-style embroidered neck amulet (also acquired from Tuareg women), and brass stirrups purchased in Ouagadougou, Burkina Faso. Sansanding, Mali, 1984.

PLATE 35 (previous page). Horse with several layers of headstalls, neck ornaments, bridle, and forehead fringe. Some of these are Tuareg style, covered with thin sheets of gold-colored metal punched with holes. The Mande-style neck amulets are embroidered with thin strips of white plastic. Touba. Mali, 1984.

PLATE 36. Detail of a shot pouch *(kisèbòrò* or *nègèden-bòrò)* with fringe and palm-fiber embroidered tassels. Collected before World War I in Sierra Leone. Ethnography Department, Berne Historical Museum, Berne, Switzerland (Sie Leo 482).

PLATE 37. Soninke leather-worker Moriba Soumanou demonstrating the technique of carefully incising the surface of the leather and then peeling off selected pieces to reveal the undyed, suedelike surface underneath. Sirakorola, Mali, 1983.

PLATE 38. Detail of Figure 69: belt (?) with palm-fiber embroidered buttons, fringe, and wide panels with cut and peeled designs. Staatliche Museen, Preussischer Kulturbesitz, Museum für Völkerkunde, Berlin (IIIC 5668).

PLATE 39. Soninke leather-worker Sogoro Soumanou cutting a strip of leather with a straight-bladed knife *(muru* or *labo).* Garanké-bougou, Mali, 1983.

PLATE 40. A painting on the door of a leatherworker's shop in Segou depicts the craftsman with the essential tools of the trade. Across his lap he holds a wooden slate *(wala)* that serves as a work surface, and in his hand is a knife *(muru)* for cutting and scraping the leather. By his side are an awl *(binyè)* for stitching, a wooden tool for polishing and creasing *(nugulan)*, and a pot *(daga)* that could be for either water or the traditional black dye. Segou, Mali, 1984.

PLATE 41. Tool kit of Bamana leatherworker Bo Traoré, including hook-bladed and straight-bladed knives *(muruw),* wooden polishers *(nugulanw),* awls *(binyèw),* and beeswax. Banamba, Mali, 1988.

PLATE 42. Tool kit of Fula leatherworker Nouhoum Boubou Sango, including a horn containing paste, shells for mixing small amounts of imported powdered pigments, two locally forged knives and two imported ones, wooden polishers, a pair of scissors, awls, and beeswax. Djenné, Mali, 1983.

PLATE 43. Dogon leather-worker Adama Gana cutting leather with a crescent-shaped knife *(kana)*. Sevaré, Mali, 1983.

PLATE 44. Arma leather-
worker Baba Touré cutting
leather with a pair of scissors. Djenné, Mali, 1983.

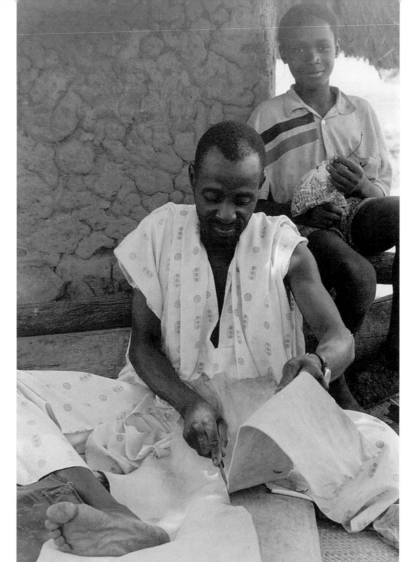

FIGURE 125. Soninke leatherworker Moriba Soumanou
cutting leather against a
wooden slate *(wala)*.
Garankébougou, Mali, 1983.

FIGURE 126. The tool kit of
Soninke leatherworker
Mohamadou Simaga, includ-
ing wooden shoe lasts and
European pliers and hammer.
Kita, Mali, 1983.

ment and that they had already received from the Europeans wooden forms enabling them to make shoes and boots in the European fashion.[11]

I documented a variety of other tools in the assemblages of Mande leatherworkers, some of which have specialized uses, others that serve a wide range of functions. A tool that is associated with leatherworkers who make slippers is a conical-shaped wooden mallet used especially to pound the rawhide soles. Although most use a wooden form for tooling the leather, some leatherworkers have adopted a metal creaser or die for making indented lines, usually down the center of the slipper upper. This is an iron tool with a curved, grooved edge, which would be either dipped into the black dye or heated and impressed onto the surface. Some leatherworkers also have iron stamps with simple cross and circle patterns, which are used to imprint the surface of the leather with a tap of the hammer or mallet. Another tool whose marks are evident on some museum objects from this region is a compass used to draw fine circular designs. However, early ethnographic accounts do not mention compasses among the leatherworkers' tools, and only rarely does one see them in Mande tool kits today.

Some Mande leatherworkers have acquired European tools designed for leatherwork such as leather punch pliers and an occasional iron cobbler's foot. More often, however, they have adopted general tools to serve a variety of functions — hammers, pliers, files, screwdrivers turned into awls, and toothbrushes and other brushes for applying color (Figure 126).

A COMPARISON OF TECHNOLOGICAL STYLES

Elsewhere in West Africa, the materials used in the preparation of the skins and in the tanning process itself are similar to those used by Mande tanners — from dehairing with ashes, bating with chicken dung, drenching with fermented bran solution, and finally, tanning with the pods of the acacia.

Among the Hausa of northern Nigeria, for example, acacia pods are the principal source of tannin, as well as among the Yoruba, who claim to have learned techniques of leatherworking and tanning from the Hausa (Dalziel 1948, 202-3; Lamb 1981; Dodwell 1953, 129; Bray 1976, 129; see also Hodge 1982, 47, for use of other materials). The materials and techniques used by Moor women for tanning goat and sheep skins are virtually identical to those described above. The process they employ for heavier skins, such as cow or oxen hides, employs primarily the same materials but is a bit more involved and time consuming (Caillie [1830] 1968, 1: 103-4). Acacia pods are known as a tanning agent among various other Saharan groups (Lyon 1821, 234-35, 249). Among the Tuareg, a variety of materials and techniques are used for different parts of the tanning process, but the most common material is a type of acacia.[12]

In North Africa and Egypt, acacia pods are but one of a wide variety of vegetal materials and oils employed in tanning. Acacia pods were among the materials excavated at a predynastic tannery in Egypt, a find yielding the oldest known extant examples of tanned leather (Lucas 1948, 47-48; Gansser 1950, 2943; Forbes 1966, 5-7, 23). However, while acacia might be among the oldest sources, it is far from being the most common, at least in recent times. Although some of the steps of the tanning process used in the famous large-scale tanneries of Morocco parallel those used in West Africa, the primary source of tannin is the gall of *takkut (Tamarix articulata)* (Jemma 1971, 39-44, see also tables 1 and 2; Brunot 1923, 89, 91-92; see also Hardy 1938b). Another important source of tannin in North Africa is oak bark (Brunot 1923, 88; Jemma 1971, 39). Other vegetable tannins employed include sumac and pomegranate rinds. In any case, what is important is that the tanning processes employed in North Africa and Egypt rely primarily on substances other than acacia pods.

One of the most important features of production that distinguishes different tanning techniques is whether pots or pits are used for the process. This aspect of the technology seems to correlate directly with the scale of the operation and the degree to which the craft has become specialized. Traditionally, Mande leatherworkers tanned whatever they needed in the way of skins in large pottery vessels above ground. This method has the advantage of being easily transportable and is appropriate for a small-scale operation within the family compound.[13]

In contrast, in Sassolo, not far from Mopti, tanning is done on a large scale in pottery vessels sunk into the ground in an open area of the village (Gardi 1985). The work is done by men who are professional tanners, not leatherworkers (Figure 128); they take advantage of the availability of skins from the large animal market in nearby Fatoma. They sell individual skins to local leatherworkers and also ship large quantities off to Bamako for sale and export. Similarly, in northern Nigeria, at least since the nineteenth century, Hausa tanners have done tanning on a sizable scale in large pits sunk into the ground (Lamb 1981). Here too, tanning and leatherworking are quite separate occupations.

In Morocco, the tanning of sheep and goat skins is done on a large scale in tanneries with as many as a hundred workers; there may be as many as thirty rectangular pits for liming and forty or fifty circular pits for the tanning process itself (Figure 129). In Marrakesh, according to Jemma (1971, 65, passim), the tanning of cow and camel hides is done on a much smaller scale than in the large government cooperatives for tanning sheep and goat skins, but even these smaller operations use sunken pits. The industry in Morocco has become even more specialized such that different parts of the tanning process itself, as well as the tanning of different kinds of skins, are carried on by different groups of craftsmen.

It may be useful to compare some of these aspects of tanning with indigo dyeing because of a number of parallels between the two industries, including some shared technology and similar distribution patterns (see Boser-Sarivaxevanis 1969). Some of the same materials are used; ashes, lye solutions of ash water, and more recently, imported caustic soda are employed for depilating the skins in tanning and as a mordant in indigo dyeing. Where indigo dyeing is done in pots above ground, as in the Western Sudan, the same is true for tanning. Where the large-scale indigo dyeing industries use pits, one finds tanning done in the same manner. In Oyo, pots used for tanning are obtained by the tanners from indigo dyers (Bray 1976, 131). In addition, tanners in northern Nigeria purchase dye pit sediment from indigo dyers for

FIGURE 127. Bamoye Maiga, an Arma leatherworker in Djenné, with a European-style wooden boot tree. Djenné, Mali, 1983.

use in making the cement that lines the tanning pits (Shea 1975, 142, 176, n. 1). There is evidence to suggest that in northern Nigeria indigo dyeing was done originally in pottery vessels above ground, then in large vessels sunk into the ground, and finally in large pits dug into the ground. According to Philip Shea, this series of innovations had a major impact on the development of the Hausa indigo-dyed cloth industry in the nineteenth century (1975, 74-75, 176, n. 1). It may be that the tanning industry in Nigeria underwent a similar development and that pottery vessels buried in the ground such as can be seen at Sassolo represent a transitional phase between pot and pit tanning. The distribution of indigo dyeing in pits from northern Nigeria across the northern edge of the forest regions in Benin, Togo, southern Burkina Faso, northern Ghana, and northern Côte d'Ivoire corresponds to the kola trade routes dominated by Hausa traders (Adamu 1978). It is not surprising that as a result there is a strong Hausa influence on the styles of leatherworking, dress, and indigo dyeing throughout the region. In any case, while indigo dyeing developed to an industrial level in the Western Sudan, such was never the case for tanning.

As with tanning materials, Mande leatherworkers share with their counterparts elsewhere in West Africa knowledge of a variety of ingredients used to obtain leather dyes. A concoction similar to that prepared by Mande leatherworkers for black is used by Hausa, Yoruba, and Tuareg craftspersons. According to Dalziel (1926, 237-38; 1948, 202-3), the Hausa use acacia pods, or other ingredients that contain tannin, mixed with iron slag refuse and honey or sugar. The Yoruba of Oyo make black with iron dust and a cold maize mixture, or with starch, old iron, and ashes obtained from the

FIGURE 128. Bwa tanners working skins in a tanning solution in large pottery vessels sunk into the ground. Sassolo, Mali, 1984.

FIGURE 129. A large-scale tannery in Fez, Morocco, 1984.

blacksmith (Bray 1976, 129; Dodwell 1953, 129). Stones rich in iron oxide, water, and dates, or sugar if dates are not available, are used by the Tuareg to make black (Lhote 1950, 519).[14]

Similarly, the use of varieties of sorghum for dyeing leather red was at one time widespread in West Africa. Barth noted that in Kano "tanned hides ('kulábu') and red sheep-skins, dyed with a juice extracted from the stalks of the holcus, are not unimportant [as items of local manufacture for trade], being sent in great quantities even as far as Tripoli" (1857, 1:514). According to Dalziel (1926), a variety of *Sorghum guineense* was one of the two major sources of red dye in this region, the other being aniline dyes. Although the latter have been available at least since the turn of the century, the red millet dye has continued to be employed among the Hausa and among various peoples who may have learned the technology from the Hausa, including the Yoruba (Bray 1976, 129), the Bariba of northern Benin (Lombard 1957, 24), and various ethnic groups in Togo, Ghana, and Bornu (Lamb 1981, 62; Dalziel 1926, 226-30).[15] In addition, red sorghum was used by both northern and southern Tuareg groups (Lhote 1950, 519; Nicolaisen 1963, 282).

Although sorghum as a source of red dye was not unknown in North Africa, it was not widely used. In Algeria, sorghum was used for dyeing both leather and wool red (Dalziel 1926, 230). In Morocco, by contrast, prior to the adoption of commercial dyes, the most common sources for a maroon red color for both wool and leather were madder and cochineal. According to Jemma (1971), in Marrakesh the only color skins were dyed as part of the tanning process was yellow, made with pomegranate rind. However, sheepskins were treated to one of two different tanning

processes; one yielded "red" sheepskins tanned with mimosa (acacia) bark, and the other, "white" sheepskins tanned with *takkut*.

Some of the same materials used by Mande leatherworkers to achieve a yellow dye are known elsewhere in West Africa. Turmeric *(Curcuma longa)* was used in northern Nigeria, in Bornu, and among the Tuareg (Dalziel 1926, 232; Lhote 1950, 519). However, there are several other sources of yellow dye of which Mande leatherworkers do not seem to have been aware. These include the roots of *Cryptolepis sanguineolenta,* made with a paste of the fruit of the tamarind, used to dye leather in Sokoto (Dalziel 1926, 231). Dodwell (1953, 129) noted the use of crushed ginger and lime juice by Yoruba leatherworkers of Oyo in 1953 (see also Bray 1976, 129). Among the northern Tuareg and in the tanneries of Morocco, the ripe fruit of the pomegranate *(Punica granatum)* was used with a mordant to achieve a yellow color (Nicolaisen 1963, 282; Jemma 1971, 44). The Hausa also used *Anogeissus schimperi* as a leather dye (Dalziel 1926, 232-33).[16]

As with tanning techniques, variations in the materials traditionally used to obtain particular colors throughout West Africa are minor. Although various substances are used to create a black dye, the principle underlying the process is basically the same throughout West Africa. Like tanning, perhaps the most important distinction that can be made between Mande dyeing practices and those employed elsewhere has more to do with the method and scale of production than the particular materials used. In the Western Sudan, with the exception of the occasional use of imported green skins, leatherworkers dye skins themselves as part of the process of creating an object. In contrast, Hausa tanners dye skins on a large scale comparable to that of tanning. These skins are then sold already dyed to leatherworkers. This makes sense given the Hausa preference for appliqué techniques. Although Yoruba leatherworkers traditionally did both tanning and dyeing, the former is now done by goat traders and the latter by the leatherworkers themselves (Bray 1976, 129-31).

The introduction of commercial dyes has not radically changed these distinctions. Mande leatherworkers keep small containers of powdered pigments to mix with water as needed to apply to the surfaces of the objects they have made. In contrast, Hausa tanners dye leather skins in large pits with a variety of aniline dyes before they are sold to leatherworkers. Color preferences based on traditional vegetable dyes have not been greatly affected by the availability of commercial pigments. Red, yellow, and black continue to be preferred in the Western Sudan, in contrast to the wider range of colors used in northern Nigeria and among the Tuareg.

The types of tools used by Mande leatherworkers are, in general, similar to those of leather craftsmen elsewhere in West and North Africa, and many have parallels in the Western world (Plate 42; Figures 130, 131). Where differences exist they may in some cases be attributed to specialized work. For example, a wide-bladed awl for stitching the thick saddle pad is found only in the tools kits of those leatherworkers who specialize in saddle making, whether they be Bamana, Soninke, Fula, or Dogon (Figure 131). Wooden shoe lasts are found only in the tool kits of those leatherworkers who have taken up making Arab-style slippers, regardless of their ethnic origin.

However, when different tools are used to perform essentially the same function in the hands of leatherworkers of different ethnic origins, this reflects the continuity of technologies that are culturally specific (see Gardi 1985, 303-18, table 12). The correspondence between ethnic identity and tool form is most apparent when the tool with which the leatherworker most often cuts the leather is singled out (Figure 132). The distinction between the long, straight-bladed knives of Soninke leatherworkers and the short, curved knives of Bamana leatherworkers becomes more sig-

FIGURE 130. The tool kit of Fula leatherworker Ali Sango, including scrapers, metal stamps purchased from a Tuareg blacksmith, a hammer, toothbrushes, and two pairs of scissors—one locally forged, the other imported. Fatoma, Mali, 1984.

FIGURE 131. The tool kit of Bwa leatherworker-saddle-maker Mamadou Issa Koné, including both sickle-shaped and crescent-shaped knives, a pair of scissors purchased from an Arma leatherworker, several awls for stitching the saddle pad, and a compass (above the slate) used to "make the eyes of the saddle." Sassolo, Mali, 1984.

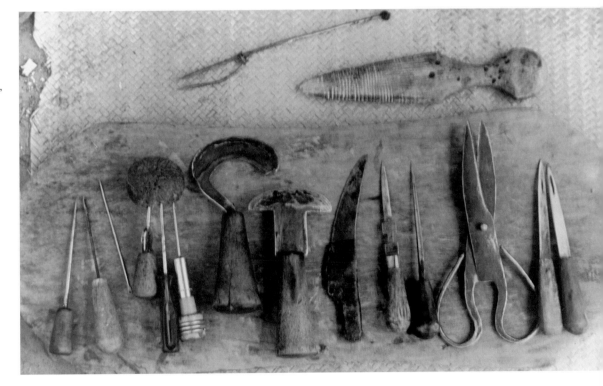

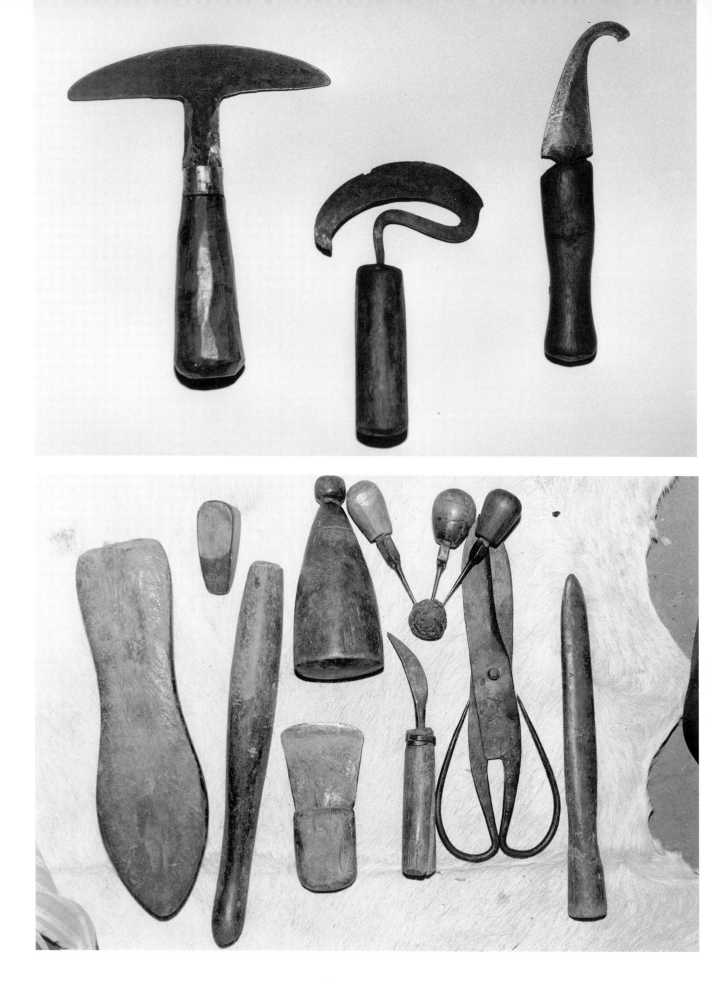

FIGURE 132. Leatherworker's
knives, including a crescent-
shaped knife *(kana)* with a
central stem acquired in 1983
from Adama Gana, a Dogon
leatherworker in Sevaré; a
sickle-shaped knife (also
called *kana*) acquired in 1984
from Seydou Sylla, a Soninke
leatherworker from San-
sanding, typical of Bwa tool
kits, but not usually found in
Soninke ones; and a knife
with a short hook blade
(muru) purchased in 1984 from
Bamana leatherworker Bo
Traoré in Banamba. Collection
of Barbara E. Frank.

FIGURE 133. The tool kit of
Arma leatherworker Almaden
Touré, with a metal creaser
(between the scissors and the
scraper). Djenné, Mali, 1983.

FIGURE 134. Tools purchased
from Arma leatherworker
Baba Tawati that had
belonged to his father, including a cardboard pattern for
the soles of slippers. Collection of Barbara E. Frank.

nificant when compared to the principal cutting tools of other leatherworkers in the region. For example, Bwa leatherworkers use short, sickle-shaped knives to cut and scrape leather, while Dogon leatherworkers use either a half-moon or crescent-shaped knife with a central stem (Plate 43). The consistent appearance of these knives in the tool kits of Bwa and Dogon leatherworkers, their occasional appearance in those of eastern Bamana and Soninke from the same region, and their absence in Bamana and Soninke tool kits to the west, all suggest a Voltaic rather than Mande origin. Similarly, the short, spatula-shaped tool used by Arma leatherworkers for scraping sometimes appears in the tool kits of other leatherworkers in the Inland Niger Delta region, but not in those farther west. Arma leatherworkers use scissors to cut leather (Plate 44; Figures 133, 134). Because of the distinctiveness of the cutting tool, it is often possible to identify the origins of leatherworkers simply by examining their tool kits.[17]

Exceptions exist to these rules. Leatherworkers from different ethnic origins often sit side by side in the marketplace; they borrow tools from one another, they purchase or commission new ones, and they do not hesitate to incorporate other tools such as Arabic scissors and European hammers or pliers into their tool kits (Figure 135). Indeed, the frequent presence of scissors bearing an Arabic-related name may lead one to presume a strong Arab influence on local leatherworking traditions. However, with the exception of their primary use by Arma slipper makers of Djenné and Timbuktu, scissors simply form a useful addition to the tool kit of Mande and other leatherworkers; they are not part of its core (Figures 118, 130, 131, 133, 134). They have not supplanted the knife as the single most essential tool.

So far as other tools are concerned — wooden slate, awl, and wooden polisher — these do not vary significantly in form from one region to another or between leatherworkers of different ethnic

origins working in the same region. Flat wooden slates are employed across West Africa by Bwa, Fula, Dogon, Moor, Hausa, and Yoruba leatherworkers (Figure 136). Boards equipped with feet to raise the surface about six inches off the ground have been documented in use by Bella and Tuareg women of Niger.[18] In contrast, the Arma of Timbuktu and Djenné rely on a smooth stone (Figure 137), along with those Hausa, Tuareg, or Sonrhaï craftsmen who work untanned hide into small containers known as *bata* (Balfour 1934, 6-7, figs. 1, 3; Dudot 1969, 56).[19] Although some leatherworkers in North Africa work on stone, the most common surface is a large, circular wooden bench quite different from the slate forms common across West Africa (Brunot 1946, 240-41; Guyot, LeTourneau, and Paye 1936, pl. 3; Hardy 1938a).

Awls are used by leatherworkers throughout West and North Africa. Like those in the Western Sudan, they range from being small and delicate to being rather large and imposing. Wooden tools similar to the *nugulan* are used by Hausa, Tuareg, and Moor leatherworkers (Idiens 1981, 41, fig. 37; Heathcote 1974, 25, pl. 6; Gabus 1958, 321-22; Nicolaisen 1963, 275, fig. 219b). While this tool serves the dual function of polisher and creaser in West African tool kits, these functions are generally performed by two different tools in North Africa. Some North African leatherworkers use a small wooden tool with grooved edges for making indented lines, but a metal tool like that used by the Arma appears to be more common, while polishing is done with a large wooden or brass mallet (Guyot, LeTourneau, and Paye 1936, pl. 2; Hardy 1938a, 257-58, 264; Brunot 1946, 240-47; Louis 1968, 47-50).

Although wooden forms for slippers are used by leatherworkers in North Africa, there is no documentation of their use in northern Nigeria. One of the tools described above, a large rounded wooden form used both as a polisher and a hammer or mallet in the Western Sudan, is not among the tools of Hausa leatherworkers documented by Heathcote (1974), nor is it mentioned in other sources for Hausa, Yoruba, or Bariba. It may have been replaced by a European-style hammer in these tool kits. The form does appear in Niger, but according to Nicolaisen (1963, 275, fig. 219c), the Tuareg of Ahaggar prefer to use a smooth stone. Leatherworkers in North Africa (Hardy 1938a, 257-58, 264; Brunot 1946, 241; Louis 1968, 48-49) use a large wooden mallet turned on a lathe, giving it a shape somewhat different than the hand-carved conical ones found in the Western Sudan.

Knives are especially varied in form. Jean Gabus collected various tools from Moor women in Mederdra, western Mauritania, including a number of knives with straight, single-edged blades (Gabus 1958, figs. 270-73). Leatherworking knives with a straight cutting edge and a tapered point have been documented among both southern and northern Tuareg (Musée d'Ethnographie, Neuchâtel, collected by Gabus; Nicolaisen 1963, fig. 219d). A leatherworking knife with a double-

FIGURE 135. Leatherworkers in the weekly market in Sirakorola. Those in the foreground are all from the same extended family of Soninke leatherworkers, many of them from the town called Garankébougou, just outside Sirakorola. The leatherworkers in the background are from two Bamana griot families (Kouyaté and Diabaté) living in the area. Sirakorola, Mali, 1983.

FIGURE 136. Fula leather-worker Ali Sango with his wooden slate positioned so that it tilts slightly toward him. Fatoma, Mali, 1983.

FIGURE 137. Arma leather-worker Baba Maiga with the smooth stone slab that serves as a work surface. Djenné, Mali, 1983.

edged, leaf-shaped blade was acquired by Gabus in Tahoua, Niger, where it was identified as being the work of a Hausa blacksmith (Neuchâtel 49.3.168; see Gabus 1958, fig. 277). According to Lhote (1950, figs. 1, 2), sandal makers of Hausa origin established in Agades use this type of knife as well as a spatula-shaped scraper. Lhote (1952, 919-55) illustrates a similar knife used to shape the clay mold to make the rawhide container known as *bata,* the finest quality of which are made in Agades by Hausa craftsmen.[20] Among the Bariba of northern Togo, knives with wide, single-edged curved blades are used by leatherworkers who are said to be of Hausa origin (Lombard 1957, 47). The Yoruba, who also trace the origins of their leatherworking traditions to the Hausa, use short, single-edged rounded blades (Sieber 1973; Dodwell 1953, 127). A similar knife form is used by royal leatherworkers in Benin (Dark 1973, pl. 75, fig. 188). Yet the Hausa tool kits published by Heathcote and Idiens do not include knives. In these tool kits, like their North African counter-parts, scissors are the principal cutting tool (Heathcote 1974, pl. 6; Idiens 1981, fig. 37; cf. Guyot, LeTourneau, and Paye 1936, pl. 2; Hardy 1938a, 257, 264; Brunot 1946, 241-42; Louis 1968, 48-49).

This comparison of materials and techniques employed in tanning and dyeing, as well as of the makeup of tool kits, reveals the many features Mande leatherworking shares with other traditions in

North and West Africa, as well as some that are distinctive. With the exception of the Arma tradition, the technology of tanning and leatherworking in the Western Sudan is quite different from that in North Africa. Materials used in tanning and dyeing skins in Morocco are not the same as those used in West Africa. Scissors are the only tool whose origin can be traced across the Sahara with any certainty due to the distinctive shape and Arabic-derived terminology. Otherwise, the vocabulary associated with Sudanic tool kits tends to be nonspecialized and non-Arabic.

The use of similar materials for tanning and dyeing throughout West Africa reflects a shared ecology and perhaps some exchange of expertise. However, significant distinctions between Mande technology and that of the Moors, Tuareg, and Hausa suggest a different course of development, if not different origins for these traditions. Most important among these differences are the division of labor by gender, degree of specialization, and scale of production. Although women may assist their husbands with certain aspects, tanning and leatherworking are primarily the domain of men among Mande groups and others in the Western Sudan, in contrast to the Tuareg and Moors, where it is women who do both tanning and leatherworking. While Mande leatherworkers tan skins on a small scale for their own leatherworking needs, tanning is a separate profession among the Hausa, where it is practiced on a large scale.

Finally, the relationship between Mande leatherworking and that of their immediate neighbors—especially Fula, Dogon, and Bwa—reflects to some extent a common environment. With the exception of the Bwa tanners of Sassolo, neither materials nor techniques employed for tanning can be associated exclusively with any one of these ethnic groups. It is difficult to say whether similarities in these aspects of the technology reflect shared expertise or whether they arrived at similar solutions as a result of independent experimentation. However, while the basic tool kits of Bamana, Soninke, Fula, Dogon, and Bwa leatherworkers are similar, the distinctive character of the principal cutting tool suggests that even these traditions have different origins. By continuing to use different knives to make objects that are otherwise indistinguishable, these leatherworkers have chosen to preserve that aspect of the technology of leatherworking learned from their fathers.

As noted above, leatherworkers have been more willing to experiment with new tools and techniques than potters. It is only when one concentrates on the most critical aspect of the technological style that the parallel between pottery and leatherworking becomes apparent. In the case of pottery, it is the initial forming that distinguishes Mande technology from that of others. For leatherwork, it is the shape of the cutting tool. Study of the technology of these craft traditions has brought us closer to defining an art history of Mande leatherwork and pottery than was possible by looking just at objects. Exploring the identity of craftsmen and women will provide an even richer portrait of Mande artistic heritage.

6

MANDE POTTERS
Numumusow

Mande potters see themselves as a separate social category from the Mande majority. While the literature often presents *numuw* as a "caste" ranked hierarchically within Bamana and Maninka ethnic categories, these women argue that their origins are quite distinct. Restrictive marriage practices have allowed them to preserve this sense of difference and maintain a near monopoly on their domains of expertise. The endogamy Mande ideology requires of blacksmiths and potters continues to be observed to this day with few exceptions, regardless of whether individual members take up the crafts of ironworking and ceramic production.

When asked to define the term *numuya* (literally, the state of being a *numu*), Mande people (including blacksmiths, potters, and nobles alike) refer most immediately to the act of beating iron *(nègè gosi),* in other words, blacksmithing. It is only when further elaboration of other culturally assigned tasks and domains is requested that a full sense of how *numu* identity is perceived emerges. Thus, wood carving and pottery, circumcision and excision, as well as healing, midwifery, hairdressing, and sorcery, are inextricably part of Mande perceptions of what it means to be a *numu*. Translating *numu* simply as "blacksmith" (or in French, *forgeron*) clearly restricts our understanding of the essential roles the *numuw* play in society (McNaughton 1988, 1995; Brett-Smith 1994). The limitations of such labels become even more evident when attention is turned to the identity of *numumusow,* too often simply translated as "blacksmith women" (Plates 1-3; Figures 138, 139).[1]

BLACKSMITHS, WOMEN, AND ORAL TRADITIONS

In Mande cosmology, the blacksmith plays a major role as culture hero and bringer of civilization (see especially McNaughton 1988, 1995). Blacksmiths are said to have *barika*—spiritual power or force. The first child in the world was a blacksmith who collected wood, gathered the first ore, built the first smelting furnace, smelted the first iron, and created the first hoe. The blacksmith then cleared the bush with the new tools he had created. Only after these acts of creation did the *hòròn*

FIGURE 138. Maninka potter Sayo Kanté learned both pottery making and basketry from her mother. When she was a child they did not farm, but received grain in exchange for the pots and baskets they produced. Gouala, Mali, 1992.

(the farmer "nobility") arrive on earth. Mythical smiths are also credited with such civilizing acts as inventing Mande initiation societies and creating the first wooden mask for the boy's Ntomo association. Their exclusive rights to leadership of Komo, the powerful men's association, supports their claims to its creation. In describing these well-known series of cosmological acts, potters add that pots of clay made by blacksmiths' wives were the first utensils in which humankind cooked food. In this way, they create a place for themselves alongside their fathers and husbands in Mande oral traditions.

In an apparently dichotomous role, it is the blacksmith who emerges in other tales as a powerful sorcerer capable of the most horrific acts. First and foremost of these epic characters is that of Sumanguru (Sumaworo) Kanté, legendary Blacksmith King of Yesteryear, who wages an occult battle with the Lion King, Sunjata Keita. But Mande peoples do not distinguish between good and evil as mutually exclusive categories or character traits. As McNaughton (1995) notes, despite acts of cruelty and barbarism, Sumanguru Kanté is praised and respected for his extraordinary powers. To this day the spot where he is said to have disappeared into the rocks near Kulikoro is the destination of pilgrimages by those seeking supernatural guidance and assurance for their futures. Mande blacksmiths of the Kanté and Sumaworo clans claim descent from this powerful figure, invoking his memory in songs and praises.

In fact, when I asked a potter of the Kanté clan how her patronymic was praised, she responded with the following lines:

> Sumaworo donna Manden
> Ani mògògolo kulusi donna Mande
> Sumaworo donna Manden
> Ani mògògolo dulòki donna Mande
> [Sumaworo entered Mande
> (wearing) pants of human skin
> Sumaworo entered Mande
> (wearing) a shirt of human skin]
> (Koloko Kanté, Kangaba, 1992)[2]

Once heard, who can forget the stark visual image created by this text. The potter went on to characterize her (in)famous ancestor as an essentially good person *(mògò nyuman)* with a devastating temper and the capacity for destructive acts when provoked. She called him *cefarin*. The term *farin(ya)* means strong, audacious, and courageous, but it can also mean wicked, brutal, and cruel (Bailleul 1981, 58).[3] Thus, despite his ultimate defeat at the hands of Sunjata, Sumanguru is honored as a powerful sorcerer whose awesome powers are a source of pride for his descendants.

Members of Doumbia, Koroma, and Sissoko blacksmith lineages are among those who trace their ancestry to the larger-than-life figure of Fakoli, also a central character in the Sunjata epic (Conrad 1992). In most variants Fakoli is identified as Sumanguru Kanté's nephew. When his wife, Keleya Konko, is seduced and stolen away by the blacksmith king, Fakoli transfers his allegiance to his uncle's archenemy, Sunjata, thereby assuring the latter's success. He too is credited with mysterious acts indicative of his supernatural powers.

By contrast, references in Mande oral tradition to women generally, and to blacksmith women in particular, are comparatively scarce.[4] The amount of attention given to women in the Sunjata epic, for example, depends greatly on the particular variant consulted. Even though the very name

Sunjata, or Sonjara, is a contraction of the hero's name and that of his mother, Sogolon (i.e., Sogolon's lion) (Conrad forthcoming), some versions barely mention her or her female counterparts. This is not the case in a series of oral texts recently collected by David Conrad in Guinea, in which Sogolon and other women renowned for their mystical powers figure prominently.[5] As well as providing more information than was previously available on several female heroines, these texts introduce a host of other women by name to a larger audience.

It is primarily as powerful but duplicitous wives, sisters, and lovers that women make an appearance on the stage of these epic tales. It was Sunjata's sister who seduced Sumanguru and revealed to her brother the secret of her husband's powers. And as recalled above, it was the seduction of Fakoli's wife that led him to abandon his blood relative to join the forces of Sunjata. Women as treacherous femmes fatales are perhaps the most conspicuous of female characters in Mande oral history (Conrad 1992).[6]

Women also play a role as "mothers" who are either the source of, or provide access for, the male hero's occult powers.[7] Principal among these in the Sunjata epic are Do Kamissa, the Buffalo Woman; Sunjata's mother, Sogolon; and Fakoli's foster mother, Ma Tenenba.[8] According to Johnson (1986, 9), Do Kamissa's disruptive power is so strong that it upsets the cosmos, causing *fadenya* principles of competition and aggression to reign supreme until she can be subdued and the cooperative, communal spirit of *badenya* returns.[9] She is identified as the source of Sunjata's occult powers, although the means of transmission are not especially clear. She takes responsibility for arranging the marriage of her ugly and deformed younger sister, ultimately sacrificing herself in order for Sogolon to fulfill her destiny as Sunjata's mother.

Sogolon herself commands extraordinary supernatural powers that are continually put to the test. She uses sorcery to protect herself from unwanted suitors prior to the man who would sire Sunjata. She demonstrates her sorcery in an occult battle against her husband-to-be and proves herself worthy of becoming mother to the ruler's heir. She must then defend her privileged position and protect her son against the treachery of her jealous cowives.

Similarly, Fakoli's destiny rests on his foster mother's determination to properly prepare the child for the role he will play in adulthood. Ma Tenenba takes him on a ritual journey to the most sacred sources of spiritual power and makes sure he undergoes a series of ritual initiations that ultimately will protect him and ensure his future success.

Women, often sisters, who are sacrificed in order for the male hero to succeed, make up another category of female characters. Most prominent among these is Kosiya (or Diouma) Kanté, Sumanguru's sister and Fakoli's birth mother. Kosiya consults with her cowife Ma Tenenba and, reassured that her son will be well cared for, offers herself in exchange for the spiritual resources her brother will need to bring all of the ancient state of Soso under his command.

It is unlikely that any of these women were *numumusow*. And though blacksmiths today claim descent from Sumanguru and Fakoli, it has been argued that they were probably not themselves blacksmiths. Rather, they represent rulers of noble status whose positions of power were due in part to their control over vast iron-producing regions and presumably over their blacksmith subjects (see esp. Conrad 1992, 180-87; Herbert 1993). If social mores forbidding the intermarriage of blacksmiths with members of the ruling nobility were already in place at the time of Sunjata and Sumanguru, then these women probably were from nonblacksmith ruling families. While this may clarify the ambiguity of identity and status in the oral sources, it does little to dissuade Mande potters of their claims to such distinguished heritage. Their sense of kinship is direct and indisputable, and it provides a point of departure to explore just how important clan identity has become.

FATHERS' DAUGHTERS

As in most patrilineal societies, Mande children are considered the property and responsibility of their father and his kin group. For a young woman, it is her father's clan, or *siya,* that determines what options the family elders may exercise with regard to marriage alliances. Even as she marries and becomes a productive and reproductive member of her husband's household, she retains her father's patronymic.

Although Kanté is one of the most widespread of blacksmith-potter patronymics, it is not the purest of blacksmith clans, as there are some Kanté who maintain *hòròn* status. Most blacksmiths and potters identify Fané as the most pure of blacksmith identities, as those who have *always* been blacksmiths. They say that the Fané were the first blacksmiths and that they are the ones who taught others the trade. By contrast, none of the other common blacksmith patronymics are exclusively *numu* clans. Like Kanté, Coulibaly (Kulibali), Koné, and Traoré (Tarawele) can be either blacksmith or noble. Ballo, Bagayoko, Sinayogo, and Sumaworo are usually but not exclusively blacksmith names. Camara (Kamara) is the one patronymic most consistently identified as *fune* (the class of bards most closely associated with Islamic traditions); however, Camara blacksmith and noble clans also exist.[10] Depending on the setting, the Doumbia name may be recognized as griot, noble, or blacksmith.

This patchwork of different identities within blacksmith-potter clans suggests a flexibility to the system that contrasts dramatically with contemporary ideology. Mande people stress repeatedly that *hòrònw* marry only *hòrònw, numuw* marry only *numuw, garankew* marry only *garankew,* and *jeliw* marry only *jeliw.* This is not simply a matter of the divide between ideology and practice. Genealogical information on potters and blacksmiths reveals the extent to which these social restrictions are upheld. Even in the late twentieth century, after decades of social upheaval and change wrought by colonialism, independence, and modernization, marriage patterns remain conservative.[11]

An alternative explanation is to suggest that there was a transitional period in the past when blacksmithing, pottery, leatherworking, and oral artistry were in the process of becoming the exclusive domain of certain branches of particular clans. Inconsistencies in the present system of clan identity and profession are often attributed to times of hardship in the distant past. For example, according to one blacksmith elder (interview with Boundiali Doumbia, Goula, 1992), all Doumbia were originally *hòrònw.* During a time of famine and hunger when farming became too difficult and *hòrònw* were unable to feed their kin, some children were given to griot families while others became blacksmiths. They left to their descendants both their fathers' *hòròn* patronymic and their foster family's identities as *jeliw* and *numuw.* The complexities of the relationship between clan identity and profession today are not attributable to any degree of flexibility in marriage patterns or in career choices, but to a period in the distant past when the social system seems to have simultaneously expanded and become codified.

Even within certain patronymic clans, there are important differences dependent on a person's particular line of descent. There are, for example, several blacksmith lineages represented in the town of Kangaba. One traces its descent to Noiballa Kanté, while the founding father of another was Faraba Kanté from Balandugu. Although both are "Kanté," there is very little interaction between these two families on either formal or informal levels. They live and work separately and do not intermarry. Each has its marriage partners in different neighboring villages, but while they too may have the same patronymics, they are not from the same lineages. The particular lineage into which a potter is born has significant implications for her future as wife and mother. It also determines which of these women have the right to become exceptional in other domains.

NUMUMUSOW: EXCEPTIONAL WOMEN

Mande potters clearly see themselves as much more than simply the wives of blacksmiths. Ask a Mande potter to define *numuya,* and she will present beating iron and making pottery (*dagalo, dagajo;* literally, raising pottery, making it stand) as equivalent, gender-specific categories. Like their male counterparts, these women have a strength of character they believe derives from their identity as *numumusow.* Theirs is an exceptional heritage, and they do not hesitate to say so. They are proud of their birthright. While the strength required for women generally to draw water, prepare food, plant, and harvest is considerable, the potters claim that *hòròn* women lack the capacity to endure the demanding physical stress of pottery production.

Furthermore, *numumusow* say that it takes more than training, skill, and strength to be a potter. Even if a Maninka or Bamana woman were to sit next to them (i.e., apprentice themselves) for months, they would quite simply not succeed when they tried on their own. As soon as they returned to their own families and tried to repeat all of the various steps, they would forget some critical stage in the process. Away from the presence of their teachers, their pots would either collapse during forming or explode during firing. Knowledge of pottery production and the capacity to successfully carry it out are among the qualities that set *numumusow* apart from other women.

The sense of distinctive identity these women share extends beyond notions about their exclusive rights to the technology of pottery production into the social and ritual arena. They take on special responsibilities at critical moments in people's lives. Perhaps most important is the role *numumusow* have long played in the excision of young Mande girls.[12] According to tradition, it is the *siya,* or clan identity, of a woman's father that determines whether she has the courage to take up the knife to perform excision. It is not a choice any *numumuso* could make on her own, nor is it determined by her marriage; rather, it is a right based on her particular genealogy.[13] According to the only potter in Kangaba (Plate 3) who still performs excision:

> As for me, I did not take my knife because of something else, but because of my *siya.* I took it because of my wisdom. I took it because of my origin. My father, my mother, my grandfather, my grandmother, they were all *nègètigiw.* I took it because of this. . . . Since then I have met with only good things and respect. What causes this? It is because I know what I am doing. I will continue until God calls me, God willing (Koloko Kanté, Kangaba, 1992).[14]

To become a *nègètigi* (master/owner of the knife), a *numumuso,* generally past the age of menopause, apprentices herself to a woman renowned for her skill and success at excision. It would be extraordinarily dangerous for a Maninka woman to perform excision and equally hazardous for a potter who is not properly prepared. The *nyama* (spiritual energy or force) of the operation is powerful, and only those with the proper training and teaching know the medicines to protect both exciser and patient. It is a time when the danger of sorcery is at its height:

When you go to do an excision in another village, you take three pebbles. . . . You say the names of *subaga* [sorcerers], you throw one before, one behind, and one that way [to the left]. When you arrive at the place, you take a handful of sand, you speak into it, you divide it and scatter it around the place where you will do the excision. There are some who go to dig a small hole [and insert dangerous substances] and cover it with the mat [on which the newly excised will be seated]. Someone who is very observant can see easily a place where the ground has been broken and something put in it. When they place the mat, you say, "No, my mat is not placed that way"; you take it and you look around for a good place (Koloko Kanté, Kangaba, 1992).

Blacksmith women who are *nègètigiw* must have tremendous courage and self-confidence to be able to meet the challenges of their particular expertise.

The role of blacksmith men as leaders of the powerful men's association Komo is well known (McNaughton 1979, 1988; Zahan 1974). By contrast, very little is known of parallel organizations for women. In the late 1940s Germaine Dieterlen recorded the existence of a special association of women potters responsible for the maintenance of special altars dedicated to their trade (1951, 124-27).[15] Most important of these altars was a carved wooden object representing the thumb of the potters. It was believed to have absorbed the souls of departed potters by being touched to the corpses as part of the burial process. It also played a critical role in the initiation of new potters and in the resolution of broken taboos. Placed near or upon the ashes of the firing ground, *nyintin* (the type of vessel generally used for steaming couscous) also served as altars critical to the initiation of young women into the society, and to annual sacrifices and purification rites. Before they could become members of the society, *numu* girls underwent rites of consecration involving public acknowledgment of their excision and their virginity, and private instruction in the history of their craft, the dangers they will endure, and the importance of observing certain taboos. Their bodies were rubbed with karite oil, and they were required to seal an oath of allegiance by running their tongues over the ceramic altar. At the end of the initiation process, there was great feasting and the girls were given several pots by their elders to sell until they could make their own as full-fledged potters.

According to Dieterlen, every year, the same day their husbands made their own sacrifices, the potters made offerings of cowrie shells (formerly used as currency) to the forge. They then assembled at the firing ground, stripped, and presented their genitals to the *nyintin* in an act of submission to the spirit forces that guide successful pottery production. They rubbed themselves with a mixture of karite oil and the charred remains of birds attracted by the fire, which the women shot down and roasted. They then purified themselves by dancing through the flames and made offerings of pots on the fire.

Viviana Pâques also documented the symbolic basis of pottery production as part of a broader study of the philosophical consciousness of the Bamana (1956, 385).[16] She reported that Thursdays and Mondays were days of sacrifice when the potters went to dig clay from the clay pit at the edge of the river.[17] When they began a pot, they would move around the mold in the same direction as the stars moved. They perceived of pots with restricted rims used for cooking medicinal substances as male, while those without necks used for water were identified as female. Each type received different treatment during forming and firing according to its use and personality as masculine or feminine. The female water pots were decorated with the *jò (djo),* a netted fiber (held over a stone or pot sherd) impressed into the bottom of the newly formed pot while it was still on the mold, and the twisted-fiber roulette. These tools left either lozenge-shaped patterns or diagonal lines, which according to Pâques were interpreted as symbols of the feminine principles of earth and water. The water jars also received nodules and other marks corresponding to female breasts and scarification marks. The two types of vessels further were distinguished from one another by the number of stones upon which they were raised in preparation for the firing—four as a feminine number, three for the masculine ones—and by their placement—the feminine ones north and south, the masculine east and west. The fire could be lit only by two twin girls as yet unexcised.

So few traces of such beliefs remain that it may never be possible to judge their extent in time or space. Over the last twenty to thirty years, Islam has taken a strong hold, and people are reluctant to discuss animist practices of the past. Occasionally, in conversations with elder women about ritual, belief, and the past, fragments of information emerge. Such is the case for the women's society called Nyagwan, identified in the literature as the female equivalent of Komo. It apparently was not restricted to *numu* women, although in at least one instance the occult power of the Doumbia blacksmith clan was such that their women were recognized as its *tigiw* (owners/masters).[18] When a woman married and left her father's village she would be included in the Nyagwan of her husband's family but would never lose membership in that of her father's clan. The association was primarily for senior women, though younger women, especially those who had successfully borne several children, might be allowed to join.

As part of the preparations for Nyagwan celebrations, the faces of the women were washed with specially prepared medicinal liquids, not to protect the eyes but to allow them to see things they otherwise would not. Women in their late forties and fifties speak with awe and respect for the sorcery the elder women commanded during their performances. They say that Nyagwan elders would slap the ground and water would miraculously appear with which they would wash their faces. They were able to breathe fire from their mouths.[19] They say the elders were able to move mounds of earth miraculously to the site of the celebration. Similarly, they could attach a bit of string to a huge tree trunk and effortlessly transport it to the performance arena where they would set the wood afire. There also were displays of statuary, wooden figures draped in white cloth placed next to an elder woman who recited sacred phrases and kept guard over a basket of sacred objects. During the course of the celebrations, participants danced with figures and objects from the basket. The women elders, it is said, were capable of making their saliva flow like a river to douse the fire when it was time for the celebrations to be over.

Unfortunately, much of this storehouse of traditional knowledge has been lost with the passing of the elders. Many of the potters spoke of senior women, renowned for their knowledge of the occult, who have died in recent years without imparting this knowledge on to the next generation. One of the potters recalled with great respect and some trepidation the power her grandmother had at her disposal. When she was a young girl, she remembers on one occasion helping prepare for a firing. That day, the sky was black with rain clouds, but her grandmother insisted she carry the pots to the firing ground:

> When clouds came, she told us to take the pots to the firing place. And I said, don't you see the clouds? And she said take them anyway, and we brought all these pots to the firing place and covered them with wood and lit the fire and the wind blew and she asked me to return home [probably for embers with which to start the fire], and before I returned [to the firing ground] she had wrapped white thread around a small stick and planted it near the fire, and it rained all around us

without falling on the pots; the rain did not come where we were. We removed the pots from the fire, and she told me to be ready when we returned home because we would be soaked before we got there. She took the stick and there was a lot of fire. When she took the stick the rain started. Our pots were filled with water. But I couldn't ask her [for her secrets], and she died when I was there [i.e., before her marriage]. She had *dalilu* (Nansa Doumbia, Kangaba, 1991).[20]

Dalilu is a term difficult to translate easily. It may be interpreted as the means by which actions are carried out and the special knowledge required to accomplish them (see McNaughton 1982, 1988, 42-48, passim). It refers simultaneously to the occult resources upon which exceptional individuals draw to achieve desired results, to a wide variety of herbal and medicinal cures and effects, and to the spoken prayers that accompany such actions. The same potter remembered helping her father cut and transport wood from out in the bush, a task fraught with potential danger. Upon embarking, he would take three stones, throw one before him, one behind, and take the third in his left hand, all the while offering prayers and incantations (similar to the ritual precautions cited above for excision). She was too young and it was simply not her place to ask what he was doing or saying, but she knows they were protected from harm as a result. He too had *dalilu*.

Numumusow continue to perform other roles in the social lives of others. Their presence is often required at rites

FIGURE 139. Bamana potter Diarrasou Traoré dressing the hair of a young woman. Kunògò, Mali, 1991.

of passage such as childbirth, baptism, marriage, and death.[21] They are considered especially adept at hairdressing and may be the only ones to dress the hair for certain occasions (Figure 139). This is an avocation they traditionally share with other *nyamakalaw* women. In addition, they are often the ones to prepare and offer special sacrifices on behalf of the community. In the spring of 1992 I was fortunate to witness a series of sacrifices and dances performed prior to the annual fishing of a large pond not far from Kangaba. The event involved hundreds of people from Kangaba, Keyla, and other nearby villages. The preparatory sacrifices were directed by a representative of one of the founding families of Kangaba, as the traditional proprietor of the pond and its fishing rights. On this particular occasion, the sacrificial meal of creamed millet was transported by young *numu* women, and the dancing centered on two young blacksmith men performing various acrobatic maneuvers with two *numu* girls. If chosen, the children of griots and marabouts are also expected to participate.[22]

These are elements that continue to inform the identity of Mande blacksmith women. They have a sense of difference based on a proud heritage that provides them exclusive access to certain resources and domains of knowledge, from which they gain self-respect and confidence in their unique capacities.

Social and artistic domains are therefore not isolated from one another in the Mande context. Comparing shared and distinctive aspects of the social position of Bamana and Maninka potters to those of neighboring peoples provides useful clues to the histories of these traditions. The identity of potters as female, as members of an endogamous artisan class, and specifically as the wives of blacksmiths, is quite widespread in West Africa. The ceramic arts are generally recognized through-out West Africa and across the continent as a woman's art form (Berns 1993; Herbert 1993; Kreamer 1989).[23] Exceptions exist in the immediate region among the Dogon (Gallay 1981; Bedaux 1986) and the Mossi (Roy 1987a), where in certain locales men as well as women produce pottery. Similarly, among the mixed Fula (Peul) and Maninka (Malinké) populations of the Fouta Djallon region, both men and women produce pottery (Appia 1965). Among the Moba of northern Togo (Kreamer 1989), male and female potters are distinguished by the use of different technologies and by the gender-specific categories of activities for which their products will be used. Thus Moba male potters corner the market on beer pots, while female potters produce the greater variety and quantity of vessels essential to the domestic tasks of women. In each of these settings where men are identified as potters, pottery production is not their exclusive domain, nor do male potters pro-vide the full range of pots for the needs of society. Their roles as potters seem to be more special-ized than those of their female counterparts.

The identification of female potters with male blacksmiths is also widespread, from the Mande heartland to the mountains of Cameroon (Barley 1984; Drost 1968; Herbert 1993, 203; Sterner and David 1991), their monopoly on the artistic domains of pottery production and ironworking pro-tected by restrictive marriage practices. The role of blacksmith wives as excisers, midwives, and healers noted for sorcery or spiritual powers is frequent, though not as dominant as the basic potter-blacksmith paradigm. In the Western Sudan, these associations appear to be strongest among Mande peoples and those most clearly influenced by Mande tradition.

Like their Bamana and Maninka counterparts, Soninke potters are the wives of blacksmiths (Saint-Père 1925; Pollet and Winter 1971). They are collectively called *tago* (singular, *tage*).[24] Among the Jawara (Diawara) of the Soninke regions of Kingui and Bakounou, there are several categories of blacksmiths (Diawara 1990, 44–46). The *taganbinnu* are active as blacksmiths and their wives are the principal potters. The *kusantago* are blacksmiths who have left ironworking behind and have become oral historians and praise singers for their patrons. However, their wives continue to pro-duce pottery, and they practice excision and other activities more commonly associated with black-smith wives.[25] A third category is the *tagadinmanu,* primarily from the Soumbounou (Soumanou) clan, blacksmiths who play the lute and work leather but whose wives are apparently not potters.[26]

According to de Zeltner (1915), Soninke potters are known for their spiritual powers, espe-cially magical formulas to prevent others from practicing their trade. It is to a blacksmith-potter that Soninke women bring their daughters to be excised (Pollet and Winter 1971; Boyer 1953). As for the other tasks identified with Mande *numumusow,* Pollet and Winter (1971, 217) tell us that the pot-ter wives of Soninke blacksmiths are also renowned for their ability at hairdressing, and though they share this avocation with the wives of bards and leatherworkers, blacksmith women are acknowl-edged as masters of this skill.[27]

Similarly, most Senufo potters are the wives of metalworkers, including the *kpeene* whose husbands are known traditionally as brass casters, and the *tyeduno* whose husbands are identified as blacksmiths and gunsmiths (though both groups have more recently taken up weaving).[28] Attributes ascribed to Senufo blacksmiths and potters support the notion of historical ties between Mande and Senufo traditions. Like Mande *numuw,* Senufo blacksmiths are regarded with awe and cautious respect for the secret knowledge they are believed to possess, knowledge based in part on their close association with the earth and its special forces (Spindel 1989, 68-69). The Senufo blacksmith has at his command special formulas for creating protective charms and also provides council and offers solutions to combat all manner of ills, especially involving the occult. According to Holas, the unique position of the blacksmith in Senufo society is to some extent shared by his wife:

> The blacksmith's wife, the potteress, is his counterpart on the social level and, connected like him by marriage to telluric entities, assumes a parallel function in a field of the ritual practices centred round fertility and procreation. The sacerdotal position of the potteress is nonetheless not as marked as that of her blacksmith husband. Excisers, midwives, healers with a specialized knowledge of medicinal plants and fortune-tellers are preferably recruited from the potteress environment (1968, 125).[29]

Unfortunately, aside from these rather general statements, there is very little information available on the specific roles of Senufo potters in these sacred domains. Current research is hampered by the devastating effects of warfare and slave raiding in the region during the last part of the nineteenth and early twentieth centuries, and the extent to which Islam has taken hold in the region since colonization and especially since independence. Many communities have abandoned activities associated with the institution known as Poro, the men's society that regulated much of the spiritual, economic, and social life of the community in pre-Islamic times. They have destroyed (or sold) their ritual objects and burned the once sacred groves (Spindel 1989, 68).

Exceptions to these general rules for potter identity are significant because they signal the presence of different pottery traditions as suggested by the distinctive technologies discussed above. Thus among Fula populations of the Inland Niger Delta region, potters are more often the wives of griots and weavers than of *nyeenyBe* blacksmiths or jewelers (LaViolette 1987, 1995; Gardi 1985). The *nyeenyBe* are an artisan social class more or less comparable to the Mande *nyamakalaw.* They include blacksmiths, leatherworkers, and bards, as well as weavers, jewelers, and a separate category of woodworkers and saddle makers. Intermarriage among different artisans within the general class of *nyeenyBe* seems to be more common than that between different Mande *nyamakalaw* groups. However, the association of Fula potters with griots and weavers is far too widespread to dismiss as the relaxing of some previously held social rules inherited from Mande culture. It seems more logical to suggest that Mande and Fula social categories emerged within their own distinctive contexts. As further evidence of historical difference, among the Fula, excision and the delicate operation of gum and lip tattooing are generally performed by griot women, not by potters.[30] Among the Fula (Peul) of the Fouta Djallon region, potters are sometimes the wives of leatherworkers (Bah 1943-44).

Another setting in which potters are not aligned with blacksmiths is the Kadiolo region of southern Mali. That these potters are the wives of griots is especially significant because they represent an exception to the rule within what appears to be a Mande context (Frank 1993). The potters identify themselves as Jula, and though they may be able to converse with their Senufo patrons, they speak Jula among themselves. They are the wives of Mande griots who have left behind the practice of *jeliya* (praise singing) and now earn a modest income farming, trading, and occasionally leatherworking. The most common family name is Kouyaté, recognizable in the Mande heartland as a patronymic exclusive to griots. Despite the women's claims to a Mande origin, the technology they use springs from a quite different tradition, which suggests they have more in common with other potter groups south and east than those of the Mande heartland. Indeed, the Jula potters appear to have become Mande by virtue of the particular historical circumstances—slavery or intermarriage—their ancestors encountered, but they have preserved evidence of their non-Mande origins most clearly in the technology of their pottery production.

Ironworking in the region is the domain of a group called *fono* (or *vono*), and although they intermarry with the Mande *numuw* of the region and share certain Mande patronymics, the specializations of the two groups are seen as quite distinct. While *fono* blacksmiths produce iron tools essential for the majority Senufo-Bamana farming population, the *numuw* provide their skills primarily as woodcarvers, though they are said to have done iron smelting in the past. Most important, their wives are not potters. The wives of *fono* blacksmiths specialize in producing baskets, while *numu* women are known for the various traditional soap products they sell in local markets. Neither they nor their ancestors within living memory have ever done pottery. In this region, circumcision is now performed by the local imam in Muslim tradition, while excision generally is done by an experienced senior woman. It is not a responsibility associated with either griot-potter or blacksmith-potter identity. The extent to which identity, craft specialization, and social roles seem to diverge from both Mande and Senufo models suggests a complex history of interaction not only between the two dominant cultural centers, but among other populations especially east toward the Voltaic region.

Linking identity to the more tangible and visual domains of ceramic styles and technology allows us to more clearly distinguish Mande ceramic traditions from those of peoples with whom they have long interacted and exchanged objects and ideas. It also demonstrates the impact Mande artistry may have had on other West African traditions.

7

MANDE LEATHERWORKERS
Garankew and *Jeliw*

In most of the literature on Mande social organization, *garankew* are identified as "the" leatherwork-ers (cf. Delafosse 1912, 3:118; Dieterlen 1955, 40; Hopkins 1971; Labouret 1934, 106, Pâques 1954, 63). However, in the course of my fieldwork, various contradictions arose between this literature and my field observations concerning the identity of leatherworkers and the relationship between ethnicity, *nyamakala* status, and craft specialization. I was unable to locate a single leatherworker who identified himself as both *garanke* and either Bamana or Maninka. *Garankew*—even those working in predominantly Bamana or Maninka areas—consistently claimed Soninke origins (Plates 25, 27). Those leatherworkers who did identify themselves as Bamana or Maninka also stated that they were *jeliw,* not *garankew* (Plate 28). Thus *garankew* are not the only Mande *nyamakalaw* to provide their services as leatherworkers. In their absence, and often in competition with them, Bamana and Maninka griots do tanning and leatherwork in addition to their roles as bards.

Like Mande potters and blacksmiths, *jeliw* and *garankew* have preserved a sense of distinctive identity through oral traditions concerning their collective ancestral pasts and the place of particular clans in that heritage. Their identity rests in part on their status as *nyamakalaw* and in part on occu-pational specialization, as overlapping but not contiguous categories, enabling them as individuals to respond to changing political, economic, and religious circumstances. The widespread distribution of Mande leatherworkers beyond the heartland reflects the greater independence and mobility of leatherworkers as compared with their female counterparts.

FIRST ANCESTORS: WALA IBREHIMA AND SURAKATA

There are several layers to the oral traditions evoked by both *jeliw* and *garankew* concerning the ori-gin of leatherworking and of their own ancestry. Some of these traditions reflect the impact of Islam on shaping conceptions of history.[1] Leatherworkers often stated that the origin of leather-working goes back to the time of the prophet Muhammad. *Garankew* trace their ancestry to Wala

Ibrehima (the prophet Abraham), whose skills with leather served him well. He is often identified as the one to have made all of the horse trappings for Muhammad.[2] In one version of the origin of leatherworking, Wala Ibrehima's workers were said to have been clearing a field when the sun became hot and there were thorns on the ground. He was the first to cut leather and make shoes to protect the feet of his workers.

Surakata, the legendary ancestor of the *jeli*,[3] is identified as a pagan warrior whose efforts to capture Muhammad are repeatedly thwarted by the prophet's mysterious powers. He is so impressed that he converts to Islam and sings the praises of Muhammad, becoming the first griot. One of the versions of the Surakata legend collected by Hugo Zemp in Côte d'Ivoire is of particular interest because in it the role of the griot as leatherworker is sanctioned by Muhammad:

> Our ancestor is Surakata. He did not pray [i.e., He was not a Muslim]. At that time there was a great war. Surakata did not want to pray and Muhammad asked him, "Why aren't you praying?" Surakata responded, "I do not pray!" Later on in the war Surakata was stopped because he did not want to pray. When he was being tortured, he cried out and asked for forgiveness. Then Muhammad said, "Because he cries out well, do not kill him! He will remain with us and cry out. All of the children and grandchildren of Surakata will be griots."
>
> Muhammad gave Surakata an awl and said, "You must sew the tail of my horse." Then he said, "When marabouts write on pieces of paper, enclose them in small packets of leather and stitch the skin." And since that day, we have worked the skin (Zemp 1966, 616-17).[4]

Sewing the tail of the horse is a reference to horsehair fly whisks that are an emblem of status and prestige and often a symbol of power and authority throughout much of West Africa. The second task, the sewing of amulets in leather casings, is one of the most important the leatherworker performs. None of the other published versions of the Surakata legend make such explicit reference to leatherwork (e.g., Johnson 1986).

Other traditions concerning Surakata and Wala Ibrehima reflect the relationships among *garankew, jeliw,* and *numuw,* at least from the viewpoint of the teller. In one legend as told by a *jeli,* Surakata accepts for a high price the commission of announcing the names of the dead following one of Muhammad's battles, after each of the other *nyamakala* ancestors, including Wala Ibrehima, have refused. He and his fellow griots use drums to announce the deaths to avoid the stigma associated with being the bearer of bad news (Conrad 1985, 47-48; see also Conrad 1981, 2:805). In another legend, the focus is not on linking their origins with an Islamic past, but on the source of friction between *numuw* and *jeliw* that prevents the latter from participating in Komo, the men's power association, traditionally organized and controlled by blacksmiths. According to a blacksmith Conrad interviewed:

> The reason *jeliw* cannot be in Komo is explained by their treachery. If you see that the *numuw* and the *jeliw* do not intermarry, if you see that the *jeliw* are isolated from our secret things, it is because our ancestor Numu Fayiri was the friend of Surakata. Our ancestor Numu Fayiri was the intimate friend of Surakata, so he raised his daughter to give her in marriage to Surakata. When the daughter attained the age of marriage, he dressed her, gave her gold and many things, then he called Surakata and gave him his daughter. The daughter was named Noufatima. After the marriage of Noufatima and Surakata, the grandfather of the *garanke*[w], Walali Ibrahima went to praise Surakata. The *garanke*[w] praise the *jeliw.* Surakata made a vow to give all he possessed to Walali Ibrahima, even if he didn't ask for it.

When Surakata left Numu Fayiri to return home with his new wife, he had to cross a river. By chance, it was the same day that Walali Ibrahima was on his way to the home of Numu Fayiri. As they crossed the river, the canoes of Surakata and Walali Ibrahima met in the middle. Immediately, Walali Ibrahima began to give praise upon praise to Surakata. Surakata had nothing with him to give to the *garanke,* so in order to keep his vow, he gave to Walali Ibrahima the daughter of Numu Fayiri whom he had just married. Surakata said, "I give you this girl. I will go on across the river, and when you get to the home of her father, tell him I passed her on to you." When Walali Ibrahima arrived at the house of Numu Fayiri accompanied by Noufatima, he explained what had happened. Numu Fayiri accepted Walali Ibrahima as his son-in-law and vowed never to show his Komo altar to Surakata. He vowed to bar *jeliw* from all his ritual activities, and he swore that if ever a *jeli* saw the Komo, he would castrate him (Satigi Soumarouo, Kabaya, 1975, in Conrad 1981, 2:812–13).

While this is strong language that is perhaps as much bluster as symbolism, what is significant is the way the story links *garankew, jeliw,* and *numuw* through their Islamic ancestors. These traditions present an Islamic heritage shared by both *garanke* and *jeli* leatherworkers that telescopes time and transcends ethnic identity.

TRADITIONS OF ORIGIN: WAGADU AND MANDEN

Questions about the origins of the *nyamakalaw* and of leatherworking often evoked the memory of a more immediate heritage than the distant exploits of the companions of Muhammad. Although Wala Ibrehima and Surakata are considered as venerable ancestors to the *garankew* and *jeliw,* it is Wagadu (Ouagadou) and Manden that are glorified as their ancestral homes (see Monteil 1953).[5] These traditions of origin reflect the identification of these craftsmen not with separate histories, but with what might best be described as different phases of the same history.

Garankew would often ask if I had heard of Wagadu and the great empire of Ghana:

The origin of *garanke* is Manden, and before that Wagadu. When everyone left Wagadu and came to Manden, they all had a choice to do what they wanted. Those who were leatherworkers remained leatherworkers. . . . God did not make speech easy for everyone. Those for whom speech was easy, they became *jeliw;* those who could beat the iron became *numuw,* those who could work leather became *garankew* (Boubou Soumanou, Bamako, 1983).

Another identified the town of Diara (Jaara) as the village where *garankeya* was born, saying,

The origins of the *nyamakalaw* are at Wagadu. The origins of *garankew* are at Diara, a Wagadu village. They created something, they created a race, as people gathered together to create something, *garankew* came out of that, *numuw* came out of that, *finaw [funew]* came out of that, that formation became like an association [*ton*]. Leatherwork has existed since the time of the prophet. Some Arabs did leatherwork, some did ironwork . . . those that worked leather were called *garankew,* those that worked iron were called *numuw,* those who played the *ngoni* [a type of lute], they were called *jeliw.* (Bakhodoré Sylla, Bamako, 1983).[6]

These statements suggest an element of choice and opportunities for change in the shifting of peoples that occurred as a result of the fall of the empire of Ghana, when adjustments were made in adapting to the development of a new center of power.

In fact, one of the most consistent traditions concerning the *garankew* and their relationship to

Wagadu supports such an interpretation. Leatherworkers say that there were just 4 "pure" *garanke* families to come out of Wagadu; all others joined the profession later because it was "sweet," there was much work, and a profit could be made. In these traditions, although the number 4 is consistent, there are minor variations in the total number and particular identity of clans. The interpretation most often given is that there are now 144 *garanke* clans; thus 140 clans have "become" *garankew* by taking up the profession, but only the first 4 are considered to be "pure." This appears to be one of several variations on Soninke traditions that there were 144 clans to emigrate from Wagadu following the fall of the Ghana empire. Frantz de Zeltner (1908, 221) reported a similar tradition concerning blacksmiths, that Soninke blacksmiths identify their first ancestor as Doumpaila, whose descendants may be divided into three groups—one of the first 4 families, followed by a second group of 40 families, and a third of 100 families, to arrive at a total of 144 Soninke blacksmith families.

The number 44 also appears in oral traditions concerning Mande heritage (Dieterlen 1951, xiii). In her article on myth and social organization, based primarily on research among the Maninka (Malinké) of Bamako and Kangaba in the 1950s, Germaine Dieterlen reported that the *garankew,* along with the *jeliw (dyelu) , numuw,* and *funew (finaw),* were said to have been among the 44 clans to have "come out" of Manden (1955, 40, passim; 1959; see also 1957, 124, passim). However, the myths of origin and other traditions she presented do not mention *garankew* (or *funew*), while *numuw* and especially *jeliw* figure prominently. For Bamana and especially Maninka griots, Manden is the heartland where their special status was conferred. Since it is griots who preserve these traditions, their prominence should come as no surprise. However, I suggest that *garankew* are largely absent from these traditions because Bamana and Maninka society relied primarily on griots for leatherwork. *Garankew* have been incorporated into their social networks rather late as one of a number of foreign minority specialist groups.[7]

FAMILY DESCENT: THE (IM)PURITY OF PATRONYMICS

An examination of *garanke* and *jeli* patronymics reflects both continuity and change in identity over time. The clan names by far the most often identified as being among the first four *garankew* are Ganes (Ganesi), Kaloga, Mangasi, and Samabali. These four family names are known as *garanke* patronymics exclusively. These are the families who have "always been" *garankew.*[8] The counterpart to the four "pure" *garanke* families among the *jeliw* are the Kouyaté, long the principal griot lineage for the royal Keita line. Kouyaté is "always" a griot name.

Other patronymics are sometimes recognized as *garanke,* sometimes as *jeli,* and sometimes as noble. Darame (Drame), Sylla, and Touré, for example, are all associated with noble Soninke heritage (see Gardi 1985, 155–56; Person 1963). However, Darame is also the family name of the founding lineage of one of the leatherworker groups among the Tukulor (Toucouleur) of the Fouta Toro (Wane 1969, 54),[9] and it is known as a generic patronymic for Dogon leatherworkers in the Masina region (Gardi 1985, 155–56). Some say that Simaga (Simaka) is a noble patronymic and that *garankew* with the name Simaga must have taken the name of their patrons. Others explain simply that those Diaoune (Jawne) and Simaga who did not take up the guitar to become griots turned to leatherwork. Soumanou (Sumbounou) is recognized as a *garanke* patronymic in some areas and as *jeli* in others. It is one of the most common *jeli* patronymics in the Wasulu region (Amselle 1972, 10).[10] According to Bokar N'Diayé (1970, 86), leatherworkers with the Soumanou patronymic were originally noble and are the only *garanke* who also play the guitar (that is, perform as griots). A Soumanou leatherworker defined himself (and his clan) as a sort of *garanke's garanke*. He said: "The Soumanou are *garankew* in the same way that the Kouyaté are *jeliw;* the Soumanou are above all other *garankew*. [They are] stronger and more powerful than all other *garankew*. All other *garankew* must give to the Soumanou" (Boubou Soumanou, Bamako, 1983). Some say that because the Soumanou can "beg" from others, they are therefore of inferior status—a different way of interpreting the same relationship. Soumanou are also said to have a special relationship with *numuw,* as *garankew* who play the guitar and drums as griots for *numuw.*

Patronymics recognized primarily, if not exclusively, as *jeli* include Danté and Diabaté (Jabaté).[11] In the Masina region, Koita and Koné are patronymics for Bwa leatherworkers, while Koita is identified as both noble and griot by N'Diayé (1970, 87-88), and Koné is recognized as a noble Bamana patronymic in the Beledougou region. Doumbia (Doumbiya) is sometimes griot, but may also be blacksmith.

Various answers are given to explain how a noble family could become *garankew* or *jeliw.* Although a logical explanation might be through intermarriage, both *garankew* and *jeliw* continue to insist that *garankew* marry only *garankew, jeliw* marry only *jeliw,* and *hòrònw* marry only *hòrònw.* They clearly view endogamy as the ideal situation, regardless of what in practice may have occurred. Some suggest that there might be special circumstances resulting in a change of identity, such as an orphaned child raised by a *garanke* or a *jeli* family. Eric Pollet and Grace Winter (1971, 234) suggest that following defeat in warfare, a noble might pass himself off as a griot or leatherworker in order to save himself from certain death. One must also consider the economic advantage of becoming a leatherworker at a time when those skills were in great demand. These explanations are similar to those given to describe how a noble could become a blacksmith.

Thus, the consistency of some of the oral traditions concerning certain leatherworker clans and especially the exclusive identification of these families with a particular craft reflects the considerable age and continuity of leatherworking within those families. At the same time, the variations in the relationship between other families and *nyamakalaw* identity suggest that individuals were able to respond to changing demands and circumstances.

THE SONINKE HERITAGE OF *GARANKEW*

Despite what the literature may say about the *garankew* as a Bamana or Maninka "caste," *garankew* themselves are quite clear on their Soninke heritage (Plates 25, 27; Figures 140, 141). Time and again during discussions of identity, they impressed upon me the difference between their birthright (or *siya*) as *garankew* and the occupational specialization that is but one part of that heritage. One *garanke* explained: "Anyone can learn to be a *garanke,* even if you are not of *garanke* origin. In Djenné, anyone can do it, even Bambara do it, even *jeliw.* But *garanke* is our race [*siya*], not just a profession" (Tamba Soumanou, Garankébougou, 1983).

They are quite adamant about the distinction between themselves as a particular social category and other leatherworkers, especially *jeliw.* For example, when asked whether *garankew* could be included among the *nyamakalaw,* another *garanke* said: "If you were our neighbor, we would lower ourselves, and cut a shoe, and go and give it to you, and you would take something out and give it to us, but we don't beg, [and] we don't dance" (Boubou Soumanou, Bamako, 1983). He then indicated that if by *nyamakalaw* we did not mean simply *jeliw,* then *garankew* could be included. Another asserted that *garankew* are the "true" *nyamakalaw,* while *jeliw* are nothing more than beggars (Amadou Laye Sylla, Bamako, 1983).

In fact, *garankew* figure far more prominently in Soninke oral traditions than they do in Bamana or Maninka ones. These traditions tend to focus on special relationships between certain *garanke* clans and certain noble families, relationships said to date back to the time of Wagadu (Pollet and Winter 1971, 187-265, esp. 223-24). In the legends collected by Adam (1903, 234-35) in the Nioro region concerning the founding of the Diawara kingdom, it was a leatherworker by the name of Diawara who was the first to meet the legendary founder Dama N'Guilli and his comrades upon their arrival in the Mande region, by tradition becoming their host. When Sunjata, the ruler of Mali, discovered that Dama had no given name, he requested him to take that of his host Diawara, as was the custom. Because of the critical role they played in the Dama N'Guilli legend, Diawara leatherworkers have always occupied an important position among the noble Diawara; the latter are even sometimes referred to as the "slaves" of the *garanke* Diawara (Adam 1903, 235). Upon their arrival in the region that was destined to become the Diawara kingdom, once again it was a leatherworker that Dama N'Guilli and his companions encountered. He informed them of where they were and presented them to the ruler of the country (Adam 1903, 238).

Other roles played by *garankew* in Soninke oral traditions are equally visible but not always pre-

FIGURE 140. Soninke leather-worker Tiefassan Khorkhoss came as a young man to Kolokani, where he settled and raised his family. Kolokani, Mali, 1983.

FIGURE 141. Soninke leather-worker Kalidou Ousmane Sylla. His grandfather left the Soninke heartland for the Guimballa region (between Mopti and Timbuktu) before settling in Ti (near Fatoma). Ti, Mali, 1984.

sented in such favorable light. One such tale was recorded by de Zeltner (1908, 218) around the turn of the century. According to the tradition, a member of the Simaga *garanke* clan came upon a member of the noble Soninke Kaga family stranded in the countryside in the heat of day without water. The *garanke* offered him a vessel full of water, but no sooner had the man taken a drink than he fell dead. Since that time, de Zeltner reported, if a member of one of these families offers a drink to a member of the other, he must place the vessel on the ground rather than hand it directly; the procedure is the same for returning the vessel. De Zeltner noted that there is also a special relationship between *garankew* and the noble Soninke Touré family. If one of the latter needs to have a cover made for an amulet, he commissions the work from a *garanke* but has someone else wear the amulet for a period of time before wearing it himself (de Zeltner 1908, 218-19). These traditions suggest a certain cautious respect for the potentially dangerous powers of the *garankew*.

In another Soninke tradition, the destruction of a town was credited to be the result of the deception of a *garanke* (Pollet and Winter 1971, 65). As the story goes, a leatherworker of the Dembaga family had been sent on a mission by the chief of one of the capital cities to another town. En route he apparently took a nap and managed to tear his clothing. Upon his return the chief asked who had done this to him. The *garanke* replied that he had been beaten by the people of the other town. Without verification of the leatherworker's story, the chief called on his people to take revenge against the other town. Thus, whether rendered as untrustworthy and perhaps dangerous individuals, or as hosts and intermediaries, it is significant that among the Soninke these roles went to *garankew*, not to blacksmiths or bards.

Garankew dominate the craft of leatherworking across the northern Sudanic region west of the Niger River, into Senegambia, Guinea, Sierra Leone, and Liberia.[12] I interviewed *garanke* leatherworkers as far east as Fatoma (east of Mopti); in Segou, Sansanding, and Niono; in the Maraka (Soninke) towns of Banamba (including Garankébougou, a small village of *garanke* families just outside of Sirakorola); in Kolokani, Bamako, Kangaba, and Kita; and as far west as Kayes. I also interviewed Mande leatherworkers of Soninke origin in Sierra Leone, in Freetown, Makenie, and Kabala. In many of these towns and especially on market days, these craftsmen competed with leatherworkers of other origins—Arma, Bamana, Bobo, Fula, Dogon, Maninka, and even Tukulor.

In addition to the widespread use of the Mande term (*garanke* or *karanké*) for leatherworkers throughout this region, there are several other factors linking their identity to a Soninke heritage.[13] Especially important is the close association of the *garankew* with other groups of Soninke origin and the predominance of common Soninke patronymics among these leatherworkers. In Guinea, *garankew* are closely linked to the Jakhanke (Diakhanké), specialized groups of Muslim clerics and traders, dispersed throughout the Senegambia region and into Guinea, who have maintained a sense of distinctive identity (Curtin 1972; Prussin 1995; Sanneh 1976, 1979). Like the Jakhanke, these leatherworkers are perceived to be particularly devout Muslims and often are identified as being of Jakhanke or Soninke origin (e.g., Durand 1932, 62-64). In a study of one of the suburbs of Conakry (Dixinn-Port), Claude Rivière (1967, 1969, 610-11) reported that a colony of Jakhanke (Diakanké) lived in a quarter officially called Dar es Salaam, a name attributed recently to replace that of Garankéla, or "place of the *garanke*." The founders of the colony arrived in 1905 and requested land to settle and presumably practice the trade of leatherworking. They were followed by several Soninke (Sarakole) leatherworker families. At the time of the study (the 1960s), the primary occupation of these people continued to be leatherworking, although some had become clerks, chauffeurs, and mechanics. Furthermore, many of these leatherworkers had family names recognizable as Soninke *garanke* patronymics, including Djoura (Diawara), Diakité, Kaloga, and Tounkara.

In the late eighteenth century, Thomas Winterbottom was traveling in the interior of Sierra Leone. Like his contemporary Mungo Park, Winterbottom was impressed by the skills of the leatherworkers, comparing their industriousness to what he perceived to be the indolence of most African men. He reported:

> Among the Foolas, however, and other nations beyond them, some progress has been made in forming distinct occupations or trades. One set of men, called garrankees or shoemakers, are exclusively employed in manufacturing leather, and converting it into a variety of useful articles, as sandals, quivers for arrows, bridles, saddles, &c. (Winterbottom [1803] 1969, 1:91).

Although Winterbottom associates these leatherworkers with the Fula, it is significant that he uses the Mande term to identify them. To this day there is a perception in Sierra Leone that the *garankew* are of Fula, not Mande, origin. Temne paramount chiefs report that they send for "Fula" leather-workers from Guinea to commission the elaborate regalia of chieftaincy.[14] I suspect that at least some, if not the majority, of these leatherworkers were of Mande origin, working for Fula patrons. In fact, the leatherworkers Prussin (1995, 45) interviewed in the Fouta Djallon region of Guinea spoke Maninka (Malinke) and identified themselves as Jakhanke (Diakhankhe) or Soninke (Sarakolle), with the family names Tunkara (or Tundara) and Sylla. Although my sample was limited, every one of the fifteen or so leatherworkers with whom I spoke in Sierra Leone identified themselves as Mandingo or Soninke.[15] Some traced their family histories back to Guinea where their fathers or grandfathers had worked for Fula patrons, suggesting a possible explanation for the perception of them as Fula. Several referred to the Soninke region of Diafounou in northwestern Mali as their ancestral homeland. Like their counterparts in Guinea as well as Mali, many of their family names, such as Diawara, Kalon (or Kaloga), Sylla, and Tounkara, are recognizable as Soninke *garanke* patronymics.

BAMANA *JELIW* AS LEATHERWORKERS

During my fieldwork, Bamana and Maninka leatherworkers consistently identified themselves as *jeliw* and did not view their occupation as leatherworkers as an exception to the rule, let alone a usurpation of *garanke* specialization (Plate 28; Figure 142). For example, Abdoulaye Diabaté, a Bamana leatherworker in Segou, stated that prior to his family coming to the city from a village in southeastern Mali, he did not know of *garankew* since there were none in his home country. He said they were *jeliw,* and that his father, grandfather, and great-grandfather before had always done leatherwork. In fact, "Jeliba," in addition to being an honorific title for masters of oral history throughout the Mande world, is a common term of address for leatherworkers in Segou, whether or not they are Bamana. For example, a Fula leatherworker who identified himself as a *sakke* (the Fulfulde term for leatherworker; plural, *sakkeeBe*) said that even he was called Jeliba, and that people in Segou do not distinguish among *jeli, garanke,* and *sakke* leatherworkers (Shekou Amadu Gakou, Segou, 1983).[16] Although the general population may use these terms interchangeably, preferring to view differences among these identities as insignificant, that is not the case for the leatherworkers themselves. *Jeli* leatherworkers are explicit about the distinction between their identity and that of the *garankew,* saying that only *jeliw* are "true" *nyamakalaw.*

In the literature there are references to bards as leatherworkers that have been either overlooked or considered an exception to the rule. In 1898, for example, Georges Tellier described the *jeliw* of Kita by what are now accepted as standard roles—as bards, praise singers, genealogists, messengers, and so forth. He added, however, that,

> . . . some of them are *karangués* [*garankew*], those who understand all the work of the currier, the tanner, the saddle maker, the shoemaker, etc., in a word, the manufacture of all leather objects. . . . Certain songs, certain dances, and the making of certain musical instruments, even the profession of the *karangué* is theirs exclusively (Tellier 1898, 83).[17]

Thus while Tellier recognized the term *karangué* as referring to the profession of leatherworking, perhaps drawing from earlier written accounts, it appears that in Kita these services were provided by *jeliw.* By the time of my own visit there in 1983, several *garanke* families were well established in the community. Most of them traced their origins to the Soninke region of Nioro or Kayes. They were now working side by side with *jeli* leatherworkers as well as one or more Tukulor leatherworkers from Senegal.

FIGURE 142. Maninka griot-leatherworker Souleymane Kouyaté, who divides his time and energies between leatherworking and praise singing. Kangaba, Mali, 1988.

Louis Tauxier provides additional evidence of the role of *jeliw* as leatherworkers in the Mande heartland (1908, 38-40). He describes the importance of the craft of the leatherworker in Guinea as second only to that of the blacksmith, cautioning that the word *cordonnier* (French for shoemaker) is really too narrow for all the items made by these leatherworkers. Although he does not discuss their identity, he does provide the names of several of his leatherworker informants, including Dieli Mori Kourouma, Manké Kamara, and Fanfodé Doumbouya. Since the practice of using *nyamakala* identity as part of a proper name is rather common, it seems likely that Dieli Mori Kourouma was a *jeli.* In addition, Kamara, Kourouma, and Doumbouya (or Doumbia) are sometimes identified as Mande bard clan names.[18]

In a later publication, Tauxier contrasted the position of Mande leatherworkers with those among the Mossi of Yatenga. He said that *dieli* (i.e., *jeli*) was the only term known for leatherworkers among Maninka (Malinké) and Wasulunke (Ouassoulounké, the people of the Wasulu region in southwestern Mali), while Bamana use the term *garanke.* He added: "*Dieli* accurately means griot, but since among the Maninka and Wasulunke only griots exercise the profession of leatherworker, there is no other name for them" (Tauxier 1917, 213).[19]

More recently, Jean-Loup Amselle (1972, 10) reported that the bards of Wasulu earn a significant part of their livelihood from leatherwork. Although Dominique Zahan (1963, 127-28, 131-32) identifies the *garankew* as a Bamana caste of leatherworkers, he also mentions in a footnote (147 n. 1) that Bamana *jeliw* often do leatherwork in addition to their own profession as bards.[20]

There are references in the literature to Mande bards doing leatherwork for non-Mande patrons outside the core Mande region, too easily dismissed as the result of isolated responses to a lack of demand for their oral skills. In his research among the Dan of western Côte d'Ivoire, Hugo Zemp found that in addition to Dan musicians, there were also bards of Maninka (Malinké) origin, some itinerant, others attached to the courts of chiefs. He noted that while it is usually assumed that Mande bards are professional musicians, earning their livelihood from their musical skills and oral artistry,

> this is not the case for the *yoebo* [the Dan word for *jeli*] among the Dan . . . whose revenues come primarily from their occupation as leatherworkers . . . they do not sing or drum any more frequently than the Dan musicians who are farmers . . . the *yoemi* [plural] among the Dan exercise above all the second profession of leatherworkers (Zemp 1964, 378).[21]

Like my informants in Mali, these Maninka bards perceive themselves as quite separate from the *garankew*. According to Zemp:

> The *yeli* [*jeli*] guard their distance from the *garanke[w]*, who are, among the Mande peoples, the true leatherworkers, and they consider them with contempt: [quoting one of his informants, who said] "If the *garanke[w]* request a gift from someone and he refuses them, they piss on him or dirty his household with their excrements. But we, we don't do that, we sing!" (Zemp 1964, 379).[22]

Apparently many of these Maninka bard families no longer work as musicians but are settled, earning part of their income from farming on land requested from their Dan hosts and part from leatherwork.

Among the artisan groups of the Senufo of northern Côte d'Ivoire, there are several that are almost certainly of Mande origin, including the blacksmiths and woodworkers known locally as Numu, and the wood carvers and calabash workers known as Kule (Kulebele), names clearly derived from the Mande terms *numu* and *kule*. Leatherworkers in this region are called Dieli (Tyele, Jelebele, Tyelibele), a term that appears to be derived from the Mande term *jeli*. However, their origins are a topic of debate (see Launay 1995); although Bohumil Holas (1966) and Yves Person (1964, 328) have identified them as being of Mande origin, Gilbert Bochet (1959, 61-101), Anita Glaze (1981, 40-42), Delores Richter (1980, 15), and others have argued for a Senufo heritage, despite the similarity of the name.

Glaze, for example, suggests that the Dieli may be a Senufo group that acquired artisan status at a relatively recent time, after having taken up the trade of leatherworking from economic necessity (1981, 40-42). She argues:

> There is no evidence that the Senufo Tyelibele have any relationship with the caste-linked groups called the "Dieli" and reported widely in Manding cultures throughout the Western Sudan. . . . In all the Manding cultures where the Dieli are reported, the occupation of leatherworking is specific to a quite different group, the "Garanké" (1981, 228 n. 33).

Part of her assessment is based on similarities between elements of the Dieli Poro and those of other Senufo Poro initiation societies. However, if the respective roles and occupational specialization of the *garankew* and *jeliw* within heartland Mande society have been misrepresented in the literature, as argued above, then the evidence concerning Dieli origins needs to be reevaluated.

As Robert Launay reveals (1995), the identity of these leatherworkers is only further confused by questions concerning their original language. According to Glaze (1981, 41) and Richter (1980, 15), they speak a language that appears to be unique, neither a Senari dialect of the Senufo language, nor Gur related, nor Mande. Person (1964, 328) argues that the language spoken by these leatherworkers is related to an archaic form of the Mande language spoken not only by several other groups of the Bondoukou region but also by the Vai and Kono of Sierra Leone. He suggests that the language was carried to these regions, first south and then west, during the fifteenth, sixteenth, and seventeenth centuries from the upper Niger region of Guinea among the Jalonke (Dyalonké), and that this early Mande influence was superseded during the seventeenth and eighteenth centuries by a new wave of Mande speakers, primarily Jula (Dyula). Launay has suggested that if the Dieli are of Mande origin, then they probably would have preceded other Mande immigrants to the area, including Jula traders and clerics. He reports that there are some local traditions in Korhogo that identify the Dieli as the original inhabitants.[23]

According to Kathryn Green, Dieli leatherworkers in the region of Kong identify themselves and are identified by others as Mande. Her informants clearly viewed this as common knowledge. In addition, descendants of one of the Dieli clans, now known as Watara, say that they were once Diabagaté (equivalent to the Mande *jeli* name Diabaté). Their oral traditions state that their ancestors were invited by the Watara warriors to accompany them from the Mande heartland to Kong, to be their bards and to provide services as leatherworkers. The other griot-leatherworking clans in Kong are the Baro, said to be from Sikasso, and the Kouyaté, also of Mande heritage.[24]

In my own more recent research on ceramic traditions in the Kadiolo region, I was therefore not surprised to find that the Kouyaté and Diabaté griots of the region once specialized in leatherwork.[25] They shared with other griots elsewhere in Mali a sense of heritage emanating from the Mande heartland, even though they claimed to have long since abandoned the practice of *jeliya*. Most had also given up the trade of leatherwork. Many had turned to farming and livestock and to the marketing of their wives' ceramic wares.

The broad distribution of *jeliw* as leatherworkers throughout and beyond the Mande region suggests that this is neither an isolated nor particularly recent phenomenon. It is simply too widespread to be explained as something a few griots adopted out of economic necessity or opportunism. Leatherworking may well have been central to the livelihood of griot families even as they were building their reputations as oral artists in the expansion and glorification of the empire of Mali.

THE COMPETITION

Today Mande leatherworkers often compete with craftsmen of other ethnic origins for clients in regional markets. On one occasion, on a weekly market day in Niono, for example, I interviewed three leatherworkers seated side by side, one Dogon, one Bwa, and the third Soninke. Of five leatherworkers interviewed in Kolokani, two were Bamana *jeliw*, two were Soninke *garankew*, and one was of Fula origin. The pattern is similar not only in the major cities of Segou and Bamako, but in the smaller towns of Djenné, Sansanding, Kangaba, Fatoma, Kayes, and Kita, among others.[26] In fact, during the course of my research, I interviewed leatherworkers from no less than eight distinct ethnic traditions. In addition to *garankew* and *jeliw*, these included Fula, Dogon, and Bwa leatherworkers in towns primarily east of the capital, Tukulor craftsmen in Kita, Arma slipper makers not only in Djenné, but in Banamba and Fatoma, as well as a female Moor tanner from Kayes.[27]

In the same manner that *garankew* and *jeliw* are quick to distinguish themselves from each other, these other leatherworkers similarly maintain their own identities as minorities working for a pluralistic patronage. As my interviews tended to be conducted in Bamana (or French), my interpreters and I often used the Mande term *garankeya* to speak of the craft of leatherworking. With the exception of the Arma, most leatherworkers had no objection to being referred to as *garankew,* but only if we were using the term in a generic sense, to mean "leatherworker." Similarly, as noted above, leatherworkers of various origins in Segou do not protest being called Jeliba, especially if a commission might be forthcoming. Invariably, however, when questions shift to family origins, ancestry, and ethnicity, leatherworkers are quite specific about their particular heritage.

The Fula leatherworkers *(sakke)* are part of an artisan class known as *nyeenyo* (plural, *nyeenyBe*), in many ways parallel to Mande *nyamakalaw.*[28] Among the most common *sakke* patronymics I encountered were Djonkoumba (Jonkumba), Gaaku, and Sango. These overlap with those recorded by Bernhard Gardi (1985) in the Masina region, including Siissaw and Yaatara (Yattara, Yaatera) as well as Jonnkummba (Jonkumba) and Gaaku (Gaakoy). Gardi lists the patronymic Sango (Sanngo) among Fula weavers known as *maabuuBe,* and indeed there are weavers among the family of a Sango leatherworker I interviewed in Djenné. The origin of the patronymic Yaatara is of interest because though today firmly rooted among the Fula, it appears to be associated with the Guimballa region where Tuareg, Fula, and Sonrhaï ethnicities overlap.

One Dogon leatherworker interviewed identified his "caste" as *gòòn* and his family name as Gana. He had come to Sevaré (near Mopti) from the Bandiagara region. Gardi (1985) identifies *jambu (jam)* and *gòòn* as the terms by which Dogon leatherworkers identify themselves, but notes that they are called *hossoBe* (singular, *kossojo*) in the Fulfulde language. The Fula place them between the noble and *nyeenyBe* classes within the social hierarchy, equivalent to the *jaawamBe,* a specialized class of warriors believed to be of Soninke origin. Gardi reports that Dogon people say that the *jambu/gòòn* were originally of noble Dogon families who in the distant past transgressed social rules, and having broken taboos, destined their descendants to an ambiguous but definitely low class status. Gardi identifies Drame and Darame as the most common *jambu* clan names but laments that this only further confuses questions of their origin. The patronymic Darame is associated with a "subcaste" among the Tukulor known as *sakkeeBe alawbe (galabo)* and is also known as a noble Soninke marabout clan name. Curiously, one of the strongest links the *hossoBe/jambu* have with Soninke heritage is that their wives specialize in indigo dyeing, a craft that to this day remains the particular domain of noble Soninke women. They are also, like the *jaawamBe,* apt to be involved in long-distance trade, an aspect that links both groups to a Soninke heritage.

Similarly, the identity of Bwa leatherworkers is not well understood. Those with whom I spoke use the Bamana term *jeli,* even when pressed for a Bwa term. Gardi encountered several Bwa leatherworkers from San and Sofara in the Mopti antiquities market who identified their "caste" as *hanu* and bore patronymics of Daabu, Dembele, and Debèrè. He notes that Koné is another common *hanu* patronymic, and indeed Koné and Koita were the family names I encountered most often. As noted above, among the Bamana, Koné is a noble patronymic, but it also appears among Mande griots.

Arma leatherworkers are the exception to all of these social rules and expectations. They are of noble status and claim direct descent from the Moroccan conquerors of the Sonrhaï in the late sixteenth century (Abitbol 1979; Rouch 1954). They are intermarried primarily with the Sonrhaï elite of Djenné and Timbuktu. The term *Arma* is believed to derive from the Arabic term for warrior, a reference to their military past. However, today they are identified as Islamic scholars and artisans of specifically those crafts most closely associated with North African and Islamic heritage. Prominent among these crafts are the exquisite hand embroidery of gowns and hats, fine jewelry work in gold and silver, and the crafting of elaborate Moroccan-style windows and doors. Arma leatherworkers specialize primarily in one type of object — slippers — usually of brilliant yellow leather, either plain or with bright silk embroidery. Some also produce embroidered boots, Koran covers, and wallets. They do not provide amulet covers, nor are they particularly eager to take on commissions for anything else.

By contrast, most leatherworkers are prepared to serve their clientele in whatever style or type of object requested. Virtually all of these craftsmen, with the exception of the Arma, cover amulets, make knife sheaths, and offer a variety of styles and sizes of wallets, pouches, and bags. Most are willing to produce sandals and to repair, strengthen, or decorate basketry hats and containers upon request. Some take on more specialized tasks, such as the creation of slippers, boots, or horse trappings, including the covering of the wooden saddletree and the stitching of the heavy saddle pad.

In this pluralistic setting, the ethnic identity of the artist does not necessarily correspond to that of the patron. Thus the association of certain types of objects with different ethnic groups has as much to do with the profession of the patron as the particular artist who produced it. The broad-brimmed fiber hats, for example, usually identified in museum records as Fulani and worn by Fula and other herdsmen out in the hot sun, may just as easily have been adorned by a Dogon or Bamana leatherworker as a Fula one.

For the leatherworkers with whom I worked, their identities as *garankew* and *jeliw* were not something they had chosen but part of their birthright. In the late nineteenth century, Tautain noted:

> Numu, Garanke, or Jeli born, Numu, Garanke, or Jeli you remain until your last day, even if you never exercise the profession designated by one of these names, and you will be the father, grandfather, great-grandfather, etc. . . . of children who perhaps will never be blacksmiths, leatherworkers, or musicians, but nevertheless each will remain Jeli, Numu, Garanke (1885, 346).[29]

Even as they lament the current lack of demand for their skills, the leatherworkers, like the potters, value their social position as distinct minorities. They are proud of their heritage and of the contributions they and their ancestors have made to Mande culture. They deserve a place in that history.

ARTISTRY, CULTURAL CHOICES, AND HERITAGE

Heritage and artistry are closely intertwined in the Mande world. This does not mean that the one is an inevitable consequence of the other. While qualities inherent in the different media and their attendant technologies have affected the paths these traditions have taken, the richness and diversity of Mande artistic forms are due in large measure to cultural choices made by individuals. It takes more than objects to make artistic traditions, and unraveling their past requires broader definitions of art, art history, and artist identity.

A comparison of object types and styles within a regional framework allows us to begin to see different patterns in the historical record. Leatherwork especially reflects the opportunities provided by long-distance trade, Islam, and warfare. Horse trappings provide the clearest example of objects that continue to echo their Arabic origins in both type and associated terminology. Evidence of their introduction into West Africa is confirmed by Arabic and European accounts. Mande leather-workers presumably were called upon to repair and ultimately to reproduce these objects for their equestrian patrons. However, whether the objects were horse trappings, sword sheaths, or sandals, these craftsmen gave them a decorative treatment—a look—that is distinctly Mande in style. The consistency and widespread distribution of this style suggests that this was the result of conscious aesthetic collaboration between leatherworkers and their clients.

By contrast, pottery production benefited little from these major themes in Mande history. In fact, the introduction of Islam must have lessened the demand for ritual vessels and probably contributed to the demise of figurative terra-cotta traditions. We may never know what these objects may have meant to those who employed them in ritual practices, nor who their makers were. However, because the notion of working with clay as a gender-specific craft is so firmly embedded in Mande ideology, it is at least possible that women were the makers of these important objects of the art historical past. Most of the products made by potters today continue to serve the basic domestic needs of the population—for cooling water, storing grain, cooking and serving foods.

There are several complex ceramic forms clearly based on foreign prototypes. Double-spouted water pitchers *(garigulètiw)* and braziers *(furunow)* are of more recent introduction than horse trappings, but the process by which they were incorporated into the repertoire was probably similar. A potter was commissioned to create such an object, having been provided with an example by a patron or having seen one in local markets. When the effort met with success, the potter added the form to her repertoire, even as she focused most of her energy on the more common cooking, cooling, and storage vessels.

While an analysis of objects demonstrates how imported forms become an integral part of Mande cultural traditions, a study of the technology of leatherworking and pottery reveals the long history of these crafts in the region. Materials and tools most often used are acquired or produced locally. The terms employed are generally indigenous and nonspecialized. Those tools that are not—such as the leatherworker's scissors or a Western-style pottery banding wheel—are clearly exceptions to the rule and are recognized as foreign imports, useful but not indispensable additions to their tool kits.

Craft technologies are essentially conservative. On the one hand, the way pots are made and the way leather is tanned follow patterns of behavior that have stood the test of time. Because they work, there has been little incentive to experiment with the process. This is especially true during periods of hardship when there is little time or energy and few resources to explore variations in the means of production. Because these activities are so labor intensive, not one branch for the fire nor one measure of caustic soda is one too many.

However, there are clear cultural choices revealed in the decision to continue certain features that are not absolutely necessary for the making or functioning of the object. For ceramics, cooking pots are dipped in a vegetal solution that renders their surfaces black and shiny, but only until the first time on the fire. While the treatment serves the function of sealing the pores and providing a bit more resilience to the vessel, the blackened surfaces are just as much a matter of stylistic choice and patron expectations as intended use. Similarly, the choice of what designs to paint onto the surfaces of water jars, or in fact, whether to paint those designs as opposed to modeling imagery in low relief, reflects conscious decisions on the part of the potter to satisfy current customer demands.

In leatherworking, a continued preference for the black and reddish brown colors once achieved by natural dyes, despite the availability of a wide range of commercial pigments, is another indication of cultural choices. The replacement of palm fiber with thin plastic strips in embroidery designs is clearly intended to produce a similar visual effect of a light pattern against a dark background. These new materials are physically handled in very much the same manner as the natural ones once were. Powdered aniline dyes are mixed only as needed and painted onto the surface of the object. The plastic strips are soaked in water and scraped with a knife before being threaded into the object. In these cases even the adoption of a new material has not significantly changed the visual outcome nor has it required the artist to modify the familiar steps of the technological process.

Identification of leatherworking and pottery as time-honored indigenous crafts is also reflected in the particular character of Mande society that accords these artists a special social status apart from the majority of the population. This is a system of such consistency, complexity, and wide distribution among Mande peoples that it must be of considerable antiquity. While the precise origins of this unusual cultural framework may never be determined, it is worth considering evidence of its development in time and space.

Pottery has been present in the Western Sudan for several millennia, but as yet there is no clear indication from the archaeological record of at what point pottery production may have become a specialized, gender-specific craft. It is with the appearance of ironworking that evidence for a blacksmith-potter nexus emerges. In a study of blacksmiths and potters in the Mandara mountain region of Cameroon, Sterner and David (1991, 363) suggest that if we can assume that it was the technology of iron production that necessitated the social and ideological separation of smiths from the rest of society, then it makes sense for their wives to have specialized in pottery production. The two crafts share parallel technologies of using fire to transform earthly materials (iron ore and clay). In addition, for both the busiest time of year is the end of the dry season, a time when those who rely on farming for a livelihood are spending long days clearing the fields. Thus it is not surprising that pottery and blacksmithing would become interrelated specialized crafts apart from farming.

Aside from these practical and economic concerns, there are plausible reasons to associate Mande smiths, potters, and leatherworkers with spiritual powers capable of controlling the *nyama* generated by their particular activities. Anyone who has witnessed blacksmiths at the forge cannot but be impressed by their mastery over their materials and their apparent stamina to withstand the heat and energy of forging. Smelting must have been an even more awesome process. Similarly, pottery firings are equally demanding for the potters, even though the real skill is in the making of the vessel, and the greater danger (according to the potters) lies in working with the clay itself. Leatherworking too involves an astonishing transformation of raw animal skins, though the process of turning putrefying flesh into a pliable, endurable material is visually less dramatic.

Evidence in the archaeological record to date of the link between technological and social or spiritual domains is circumstantial. The physical placement of blacksmith compounds apart from others has been interpreted simultaneously as one of social exclusion by the majority population, or as conscious protection of the secrets of the forge by the smiths (McIntosh n.d.). The discovery of a forge at Djenné-djeno with what appears to be a ritual offering just outside the door of stone axes, grinders, snake pots, terra-cotta figures, and iron rods seems to link blacksmiths with spiritual concerns as early as the tenth or eleventh centuries A.D. Roderick McIntosh (1993) argues that the visual symbols of this particular discovery and others constitute an ancient wellspring of images upon which different cultures have drawn for their spiritual needs. Although difficult to document in archaeological settings, McIntosh argues that the ideologies of power underlying social organization (especially those of hunters and smiths) are an integral part of this shared symbolic reservoir (McIntosh 1989, 1993; see also McIntosh n.d.).

Turning to oral traditions, McNaughton (1988), Tamari (1991), and Conrad (1992) have all suggested that by the thirteenth or fourteenth century, with the consolidation of power during the rise of the Mali empire as catalyst, endogamous occupational groups were part of the social landscape. In fact, oral traditions concerning the dispersal of peoples from Wagadu suggest that certain clans were already associated exclusively with leatherworking or smithing much earlier. The consistency with which these clans are identified as "pure," while others are said to have joined the profession at a later point in time, offers evidence of both the antiquity of the ideology and its capacity to respond to changing social and political circumstances. The fall of Ghana, the rise and expansion of the Mali empire, the hegemony of Songhay—these were times of crises, transitional periods when individuals and groups adjusted and adapted, suffered or prospered accordingly.

Charles Bird (1981; see also Bird, Kendall, and Tera 1995) has suggested that clues to the origin of *nyamakalaya* (i.e., the particular configuration of blacksmiths, potters, bards, and leatherworkers in the Mande world), and especially of *jeliya* (bardship), may be found in examining the character and distribution of these institutions. Bird notes that while smiths and praise singers are found throughout West Africa, "casted" bards appear only in relation to "casted" smiths, and only in the regions affected by the empires of Ghana and Mali. If Sumanguru Kanté represents an old and powerful alliance between hunters and blacksmiths, then his defeat by Sunjata Keita may herald the arrival of a new world order. The emergence of "casted" bards may mark a shift in allegiance to the new economic and religious power in the region—that of Islam. This theory is supported by persistent themes of the Islamic origins of the progenitors of bards, blacksmiths, and leatherworkers, even though we know from the archaeological record and from other oral traditions that the crafts of blacksmithing, pottery, and leatherworking predate Islam's arrival and diffusion in the region.

Although establishing a precise chronology for the dispersal of Mande leatherworkers may never be possible, the widespread distribution of both *garankew* and *jeliw*, the indigenous character of the technology of leatherworking, and the correspondence of a distinctive style throughout this same region, all support the notion of such a diaspora. *Garankew* began leaving their Soninke homeland perhaps as early as the tenth and eleventh centuries in search of opportunities south and west. They probably settled into communities as foreign specialists, competing with other leatherworkers for clients at local and regional markets. Leatherworking also seems to have been long established among Bamana and Maninka griot families, although oral traditions are largely silent about this specialization. Griots today choose to emphasize their oral artistry for its prominent role

FIGURE 143. Bamana potter Assa Coulibaly supervising the work of her granddaughter. Banamba, Mali, 1988.

FIGURE 144. Soninke leather-worker Nunka Soumanou is part of an extended family of leatherworkers whose ancestors came to the region in search of farmland and founded the nearby town of Garankébougou. They continue to attend local markets to offer their services as leatherworkers, but earn most of their livelihood from farming and trade. Sirakorola, Mali, 1983.

in the great events of Mande history. However, the craft is too widespread among *jeli* families to have been the result of its recent adoption by a few out of economic necessity. Furthermore, the subtle but significant differences between the short, hook-bladed knife used by *jeliw* and the long, straight-bladed knife preferred by *garankew* suggest the presence of at least two distinct technological traditions.

Similarly, the most salient feature to set Mande pottery production apart from others is the particular technology of the forming process. The Mande technique of forming the base of the pot over a convex mold is fundamentally different from the concave mold or direct-pull technologies used by other potter groups in the region. Even more distinctive is the complex identity of potters as *numumusow,* who, like their blacksmith husbands, are a critical presence at all stages of the life cycle, entrusted with the most dangerous of operations in turning child into adult. For potters, evidence of their participation in Mande history is tied less to geographical extent than to the intensity and constancy of their craft and identity in the heartland. Their sense of history is deep but very much locally based—quite a contrast to the far-reaching traditions of the leatherworkers.

Thus while potters and leatherworkers share in the same broad cultural experience, their histories are not identical. What the future holds for the descendants of these artists is hard to predict. The combined effects of drought and deforestation have limited the resources of all artists, especially potters and blacksmiths. The demand for the potters wares is increasingly limited, as imported metalware and plastics have become ubiquitous. Although the cooling effects of pottery water jars in this hot, dry climate will retain a market for these objects for the foreseeable future, there is less call for the other items potters produce. The women themselves are ambivalent about their current situation and prospects for their descendants (Figure 143). Making pottery is hard and dirty work. While they do not want their children to suffer as they have, they do want them to have the strength and wisdom to survive difficult times. Knowledge of pottery production and the capacity to carry it out are qualities that set pottery makers apart from others. They are proud of their heritage.

For leatherworkers, the situation is similar (Figure 144). With the exception of amulet covers and the occasional knife sheath, there is not much demand for the services leatherworkers once provided. Their heyday waned with the passing of the era of cavalry and warriors. In today's world, wealth and position are marked by cars and motorcycles, not by horses laden with the products of the leatherworkers' skills. Those leatherworkers who remain active in the trade are ones who have turned to providing European-style handbags, wallets, belts, and shoes for a Westernized clientele. They speak of the broader range of models available to them now, confident that they can make anything their patrons may demand. Indeed, these craftsmen have more in common with their ancestors than one might think, for it was just that kind of entrepreneurial spirit that allowed leatherworkers to play a significant role in Mande cultural history.

NOTES

I. MORE THAN OBJECTS

1. The main style regions identified by Sieber and Rubin (1968) for African sculptural traditions are the Western Sudan, Guinea Coast, Equatorial Forest, and Southern Savanna. The Guinea Coast style region stretches from the present-day country of Guinea all the way around the coast to the border between Nigeria and Cameroon; it includes Mende, Baule, and Yoruba arts among others. The Equatorial Forest style region extends from the coast of Gabon across northern Zaire to Lake Tanganyika and includes Fang and Kota, as well as Nbaka, Mangbetu, and Lega arts. The Southern Savanna style region includes the sculpture-producing groups of southern Zaire and Angola, including Chokwe, Kuba, Luba, and Songye among others. In the last decade, Eastern and Southern Africa have been added to this repertoire of style labels, as awareness of sculptural forms produced in these areas has increased and as non-sculptural media have been accepted into scholarly discussions.

2. The term *Mande* is a linguistic one that encompasses the related languages spoken by Bamana, Maninka, Mandinka, Soninke, Jula, and others in the north and west, as well as the more distantly related Konyaka, Kono, Loma, Mende, Dan, Mano, and oth-

ers in the south. Gur language groups include the Dogon, Senufo, Mossi, Bwa, and others of the Volta River regions of eastern Mali, Burkina Faso, Côte d'Ivoire, and Ghana.

3. In a 1984 critique, Jan Vansina chided art historians for their ahistorical approaches to African art. In a reasoned response, Marla Berns (1989b) explored the viability of using linguistics and art forms to reconstruct the history of population movements in the upper Benue region of Nigeria (see also Berns 1989a). The notion of open borders in the Western Sudan was the subject of a special issue of *African Arts*, for which I contributed an article (Frank 1987); see esp. in that issue McNaughton (1987), Roy (1987b), and Green (1987b).

4. Although they are best known for work that focuses on issues of social and symbolic content, a number of scholars of Mande art have recently turned their attention specifically to historical issues. See esp. Arnoldi (1989, 1995), Ezra (1984, 147-66; 1986a), Mark (1992), McNaughton (1991, 1992), and Weil (1995).

5. My use of the term *technological style* derives from the work of Heather Lechtman (1977). She argues that there is more to technology than materials and procedures. To better understand why people do things the way they do, one must recognize the sym-

bolic nature and cultural specificity of technological attitudes and behaviors. See also Merrill (1968).

6. See esp. Bonnie Wright's (1989) discussion of Wolof "caste" identities. I have consciously avoided using the term *caste* because it carries with it too much baggage from the Indian context with which the concept is most closely identified. Alternative labels such as "endogamous occupational group" are technically accurate but cumbersome. I prefer to introduce the reader to the Mande term *nyamakala,* which is already a loaded concept. See Conrad and Frank (1995), esp. the article by Bird, Kendall, and Tera (1995).

7. In this study Western Sudan designates a style region geographically and culturally distinct from the varied traditions east of the Niger bend (the central Sudan), encompassing the Hausa states and Bornu in present-day northern Nigeria, Niger, and western Chad. These traditions are also to be distinguished from the present-day country of Sudan in northeastern Africa, although they share a similar ecology.

8. Those linguistic rules that are common to Fulfulde and Soninke, but not northern Mande, were very likely borrowed by the Soninke from the Fula. The same is true of certain loan words. The linguistic relationship between Soninke and Fulfulde is reflected in the similarity of terms for leatherworking tools. See chap. 5 for a discussion of leatherworking tools and associated terminology.

9. Identifying Maraka, Jula, and Jakhanke simply as ethnic terms is problematic. For example, "true" Maraka *(Maraka-je)* of the regions of Segou and Kaarta claim to be Soninke, tracing their origins back to Wagadu and the empire of Ghana. Like their counterparts in the south and west, they are associated with commerce and orthodox Islam. But *Maraka* has also come to mean anyone who has adopted Islam, in contrast to nonbelievers generally referred to as *Bamana* or *Kado* (the Mande term for Dogon people). See Gallais (1962, 1967); Roberts (1978, 5-6); Arnoldi (1983, 88-89). Similarly, in southern Mali and northern Côte d'Ivoire, *Jula* (Dyula) has come to refer to anyone who has adopted Islam, in contrast to *Bamana* or *Senufo* as a label for someone who is non-Muslim. Furthermore, the generic term *jula* is the Mande word for trader, used usually in reference to those of Mande origin and most often Muslim, but it

also may be applied to other traders, regardless of ethnic origin or religious affiliation. See Green (1984); Launay (1982, 1-3); Person (1963, 1972); Curtin (1972); Lewis (1971, 1972); Perinbam (1974).

10. There are exceptions. During the heyday of the Mali empire, the relationship was one of economic, social, and political domination. The tables were turned in the nineteenth century with the rise of al-Ḥadj ʿUmar and the Fula state of Masina.

11. "Voltaic" refers to the region of the upper part of the Black, Red, and White Volta rivers (the former country of Upper Volta, now Burkina Faso).

12. Unfortunately, the credibility of the ethnographic information in this account is compromised by the inclusion of fanciful tales concerning the inhabitants of the Sudan, such as men who wear snakes as one would a turban or a belt, people without heads, and a race solely of women who become pregnant by bathing in a certain body of water and give birth only to girls (Levtzion and Hopkins 1981, 132-34).

13. According to De Moraes (1972), toward the end of the sixteenth century, the trade in hides along la Petite Côte (south of Cape Verde, Senegal) began to expand dramatically. A century later, in their efforts to establish a monopoly over the trade, the French eliminated the competition, causing the bottom to fall out of the market. Among the documents cited by De Moraes (37) concerning the trade in untanned hides is a 1588 agreement between the Portuguese king and a group of English merchants, one of whom was a tanner by profession.

14. There are few reports concerning the trade in hides and skins along the coast during the eighteenth and nineteenth centuries. If it continued at all, it was on a greatly diminished scale. The trade was revived by the French colonial administration at the beginning of the twentieth century (Correspondance sur les peaux 1900-1905). To this day hides and skins form a significant part of Mali's exports.

15. In the twelfth century al-Idrīsī described the people of Aghmat (in southern Morocco) as "opulent, wealthy merchants who go into the land of the Sūdān with numbers of camels bearing immense sums in red and coloured copper and garments and woollen cloth and turbans and waist-wrappers *(mi'zar)* and different kinds of beads of glass and

mother-of-pearl and precious stones and various kinds of spices and perfumes and tools of worked iron" (Levtzion and Hopkins 1981, 128).

16. However, the widespread distribution of a distinctive type of footed bowl in archaeological settings suggests that at least some pottery objects traveled. See chap. 2.

17. Ablution bowls (*sèlidagaw*) are still identified by potters among the products they make, even though have been largely replaced by plastic and aluminum teakettles.

18. In the Djenné corpus of sculpture, human figures predominate, single or in pairs, seated or kneeling, with hands resting on knees or crossed over the chest. Subsets include equestrians and warriors, pregnant females, and figures with distorted or bizarre features suggestive of disease or some supernatural malady, such as heads twisted to the side or snakes emerging from nostrils (de Grunne 1980, 1983, 1987; McIntosh and McIntosh 1979, 1982, 1986).

The Bankoni corpus to date is a much smaller one, thematically somewhat more limited and slightly later in date (14th-16th centuries). The name comes from the site a few miles northeast of Bamako excavated in the 1950s by Szumowski (1957-58) that yielded a nearly complete statue and several fragments. Bankoni-style figures tend to be more elongated, with small heads and less-detailed features.

Thermoluminescence testing on many of the pieces has suggested a range of dates between the 11th and 16th centuries. Unfortunately, almost all of these figures entered the international art market without clear provenance, let alone the valuable information that might have been gained had they been recovered during controlled archaeological investigations (McIntosh and McIntosh 1986). Recently the more general term *Inland Niger Delta* has been used to identify Djenné-style pieces without clear provenance (see *African Arts* 1995, a special issue devoted to "Protecting Mali's Cultural Heritage").

19. See, for example, the leather amulet-laden crown of a Kuranko paramount chief from Kabala, Koinadugu District, northern Sierra Leone (Prussin 1986, 84, fig. 4.9a).

20. For a discussion of the importance of the productive as opposed to reproductive capacities of female slaves, see Meillassoux (1983). For a table of comparative prices for male and female slaves, see Klein (1983, 74-75; 1992, 40-41); see also Roberts (1987, 116-18).

21. Biot implies that the disdain with which local potters are viewed is the result of negative attitudes the Mande Konyaka brought with them toward blacksmiths, griots, and potters.

22. In many ways my work responds to a call made by Claude Ardouin (1978) in an article on blacksmiths in the Sudanic region. He was dismayed by the lack of intellectual exchange among archaeologists, historians, art historians, and others and by the tendency of scholars to oversimplify the complexity of social and cultural relationships. He argued that close studies of particular contexts had to be made before broad cross-cultural generalizations about the position and status of the blacksmith in Sudanic societies could be attempted. The same cautions apply to the study of other artist groups, including potters and leatherworkers.

2. THE PLACE OF POTS

1. What is unusual about this early assemblage is the lack of sherds from cooking vessels, as would be indicated by signs of blackening from fire or by the presence of rim shapes commonly found on cooking vessels. These were quite prominent in later phases. Susan McIntosh (1995, 157-62) has suggested that this may indicate a shift in food preparation practices, away from baking, grilling, or roasting, toward steaming and boiling, which could accommodate an increasing population.

2. Susan McIntosh (1995, 157-64) takes exception to Gallay's characterization of the later assemblages as "diachronically homogeneous" (Gallay and Huysecom 1989; Gallay 1986). She argues that while overall concepts of design and vessel form remain remarkably stable, differences in decorative techniques and rim characteristics do reflect change over time.

3. Tellem is the name archaeologists have given to the peoples who inhabited the Bandiagara region prior to the arrival of the Dogon around the 15th to 16th centuries (Bedaux 1972, 1988). While some may have moved away, others probably were assimilated into Dogon culture. Koumbi Saleh (6th-15th century A.D.) was an important trading center thought by

some to have been the capital of the empire of Ghana; it is located near the border of present day Mali and Mauritania.

4. To my knowledge, there are no references to ceramics or ceramic production in any of the early Arab accounts, as these items were apparently not a major item of trade in either direction.

5. The term *Mandingo* was used extensively by early Anglophone writers as a general term for Mande peoples, including the Mandinka, Maninka, and Bamana, as well as those Mande immigrants to Sierra Leone and Liberia known today by the ethnic label Mandingo.

6. The fact that leather objects are much easier to transport than pottery certainly contributed to the discrepancy in the quantities of these two media in museum collections. Equally important, most of the early collections were made by military men and colonial officers with much greater interest in shot pouches, swords, and the like, than in domestic wares of the female domain.

7. Two such exhibitions are *Fired Brilliance: Ceramic Vessels from Zaire,* at the Gallery of Art, University of Missouri-Kansas City, in 1990, and *A Language of Hand and Heart: The African Pottery Collection of Keith Achepohl,* at the University of Iowa Museum of Art in 1994.

8. This approximation does not count the relatively recent flowerpots, ashtrays, and other oddities found in the markets of the capital or other large cities where there is a sizable civil servant and European community.

9. For example, reports on indigo dyeing made by students of the Ecole William Ponty (Sébikotane, Senegal) in the early 1940s identify pottery vessels for indigo dyeing in the Fouta Djallon region (Bah 1943-44; Barry 1943-44; M'baye 1941-43) and elsewhere (Dakar: Guèye 1942-43; Seck 1940-43; Kayes: Keita 1940-45; Benin: Nalla n.d.; Gao and Bourem: Maiga 1940-43). Today large metal barrels and plastic basins serve these purposes.

10. The collector and art dealer Charles D. Miller III has several Bamana vessels acquired in the 1970s with human and animal figures in high relief (Figure 26). They are similar in style to vessels identified as ritual pots photographed in Bamako by the Japanese anthropologist Jun Mori in the mid-1980s (conversa-

tion with the author during a conference on African pottery at the University of Iowa, April 8-9, 1994). See also Dawson (1993, cover, cat. nos. 23, 24).

11. In Hamdalaye, just north of Kangaba. Gauging from the condition of the vessel and what little information I could obtain about the late potter, I would estimate that it was about forty years old.

12. Olga Linares de Sapir (1969) identifies the *gargoulette* as a relatively new form among the Jola (Diola) of the Fogny region (north of the Casamance River) because it was not being made by older potters of this region, nor by the non-Muslim Jola (Diola) of the Kasa region to the south. She speculates that because of its wide distribution in Islamized areas, the *gargoulette* may have been introduced by the Muslim Mandingo. Dupuis and Echard (1971) report that Hausa potters claim the *garigulèti* to be of recent introduction, despite centuries-long contact with the Islamic world.

13. Boyer (1953, 105) identifies the Soninke term as *djinimiho;* Gallay (1970, 82) identifies it as *gérémé-nati.* In northern Cameroon it is known as *ngargulel* (David and Hennig 1972, 1-29), apparently the local pronunciation of *gargoulette.*

14. In many households in the region it is possible to see these large storage vessels lined up against the inner walls of kitchens, partially buried for stability. They are no longer made. Jula potters also make a variety of braziers based on metal prototypes. At least one potter has made tripod braziers *(singonw)* similar to those more common in the north.

15. This is a type of vessel I first encountered in the Kadiolo region. It has been documented not only among the Senufo (Spindel 1988, 1989), but as far west as Silaya, Guinea, among the Mande Jalonke (Dialonke) (Kivekäs et al. 1993, 106), among Banda and Mo potters of Ghana (Crossland and Posnansky 1978, 84-86), east into Burkina Faso among the Lobi (Schneider 1990, 166-85) and the Dagari (Dawson 1993, 18, 41), and among the Bassari of northern Togo (Hahn 1991a, 83; 1991b). Whether this type of sacred vessel may ultimately be historically related to the spherical pots covered with bumps from Inland Niger Delta archaeological contexts remains to be seen (see McIntosh 1989, 75, fig. 3).

16. I watched one potter in Bamako, never one to shy away from a difficult commission, attempt to

emulate a pancake griddle she had seen from Mopti, but without much success.

17. The mottled reddish brown surfaces of the Kalabougou pots, in fact, are more like those of Senufo potters in northern Côte d'Ivoire than those of their other Mande neighbors. The buff red surfaces of Somono pottery are more like those of the pots of their local Fula competitors.

18. This device has been documented among the Soninke by de Zeltner (1915), Boyer (1953), and Gallay (1970). Similar patterns are achieved in different ways by other potters. The textured surfaces of Dogon pots, for example, are made by pounding out the interior of the vessel against a knotted fiber mat (Bedaux 1986).

19. Similar plaited-fiber roulettes are found in the tool kits of Senufo and Bobo potters. These seem to fall somewhere between those that Soper (1985) has proposed calling "knotted" and "accordion pleat strip roulette." Designs apparently made from carved wooden roulettes appear on some pots from the Segou area available in the Bamako markets. The use of these tools by the potters of Kalabougou is confirmed by Raimbault (1980).

3. BEYOND THE FRINGE

1. Upper arm daggers with stamped designs, metal overlay, and appliqué with green leather typical of Tuareg and Hausa leatherwork can be found in museum collections. See also Gabus (1958, 250-51).

2. Wild animal skins frequently are found on various objects in museum collections, especially those associated with warfare and hunting. Such skins are still available in markets today. There is a method of partial tanning used to stabilize skins (usually sheep or goat) with the hair left on for prayer rugs. There is no way of knowing whether the skins to which these early Arab accounts refer were treated in this manner.

3. See also *Akhbār al-Zamān* (10th-11th century A.D.) and al-Zuhrī (after 1154) in Levtzion and Hopkins (1981, 35, 95, 97-99). In the 16th century, Leo Africanus ([1600] 1896, 3:827) reported that during the winter the common people of Gago (Gao) clothe themselves with the "skin of beasts."

4. Takrur is noted for being one of the earliest states of the Western Sudan to have adopted Islam and to have established relations with the Maghreb via the trans-Saharan trade. It was located in the westernmost region of the Sudan along the banks of the lower Senegal River; see Levtzion (1972, 1:135-37).

Al-Bakrī (early 11th century) commented on the distinction between the tailored or sewn garment and the wrapper. He reported that with the exception of foreigners (Muslims) the ruler of Ghana reserved the right to wear the sewn garment for himself and the royal line, while others draped themselves with "cotton, silk or brocade, according to their means" (Levtzion and Hopkins 1981, 80, 87).

5. Cadamosto went on to provide one of the earliest descriptions of locally produced strip-woven cloth. He wrote: "Their women spin it into cloth of a span in width. They are unable to make wider cloth because they do not understand how to card it for weaving. When they wish to make a larger piece, they sew four or five of these strips together" (Crone 1937, 31-32). It seems that Cadamosto was the one who did not understand the weaving process. While women spin the thread, the weaving of narrow strips is done by men on a horizontal loom. The strips are then sewn together to form a cloth wrapper.

6. The concept of protective amulets in West Africa is not strictly Islamic. Various natural substances, including the claws and teeth of powerful animals, birds, and animal skulls, as well as a variety of plants and mineral substances, sewn up in leather packets, also served as efficacious agents of power that very likely predated the introduction of Islam.

7. Most often mentioned as appropriate payment were slaves, cattle, and gold. In 1732 Jean Barbot noted that one amulet was worth as much as two or three slaves, and that the viceroy "constantly wore to the value of fifty slaves in these Grigris about his body; and so every other person of note proportionally. . . . To say the truth, some of the principal Blacks are so well furnish'd all over with Grigris in every part of their bodies, under their shirts and bonnets, that they cannot well be wounded with any Assagaia, or javelin; nay, they often stand in need of being helpd to mount their horses, which are also adornd with the same, to render them more sprightly, to prevent their being hurt" (cited in Sieber 1972, 40, 53; see also Bowdich [1819] 1966, 271).

8. Anderson came into contact frequently with Mande traders who "tried every method to induce me to trade; they carried me to their houses and would get out their small leathern bags; these bags contained from ten to fifteen large twisted gold rings, ('sannue')" (Anderson [1870/1912] 1971, 94-95). According to Mauny (1961, 375), leather sacks called *querbas* were used for transporting gold objects across the Sahara. Unfortunately, there is no way of knowing what early travel sacks or bags may have looked like.

9. The meaning of the term *sharki* is not entirely clear. Al-Idrīsī (Levtzion and Hopkins 1981, 108) previously mentions that there is a reed that grows along the banks of the "Nil" (the Niger River) known as *sharki*. Indeed, sandals of woven palm fiber are known among the Tuareg (Lhote 1950, 522, fig. 10). However, it is equally possible that this is a reference to leather sandals; in the 12th century, al-Zuhrī reported that skins from the region of Gao are known as *sharki* skins. He wrote: "This country is known in Ifriqiya and Egypt as the land of Shark and for this reason the skins which are imported from there are called *sharkī* skins" (Levtzion and Hopkins 1981, 97). In the 19th-century French translation of al-Idrīsī (1866, 8), Dozy and Jan de Goeje tentatively translated the last part of this passage somewhat differently: ". . . il porte aux pieds des souliers garnis de courroies (?)" (. . . he wears sandals ornamented with cowries [?] on his feet).

10. Because of the lower cost of sandals, the value of the trade was considerably less than that for cloth. In his discussion of the extent of the cloth trade, Barth (1857, 1:511) reported that the trade in indigo-dyed cloth extended well beyond Timbuktu, "the very inhabitants of Arguin [on the Atlantic coast just south of present-day Morocco] dressing in the cloth woven and dyed in Kanó." However, Barth does not provide evidence for the trade of Hausa sandals west of Timbuktu.

11. Cited above in chap. 1 (Levtzion and Hopkins 1981, 133).

12. See Levtzion and Hopkins (1981): al-Yaʿqūbī (9th century), p. 22; Ibn al-Faqīh (10th century), p. 28; Ibn Ḥawqal (10th century), p. 46; al-Bakrī (11th century), p. 67; al-Zuhrī (12th century), p. 95; al-Idrīsī (12th century), p. 127; Abū Ḥāmid al-Gharnāṭī (12th century), p. 134; *Kitāb al-Istibṣār* (12th century), p. 142; Yāqūt (13th century), pp. 169, 173, 174; al-Qazwīnī (13th century), p. 180; and Ibn Saʿīd (13th century), p. 191.

13. Horses are not indigenous to West Africa, but it remains uncertain when and by what routes the various breeds were introduced into the region (Law 1980; McCall 1979; Fisher 1973).

14. Law (1980, 89-91) has suggested that the introduction of the saddle and stirrup may be linked to the beginning of the trans-Saharan trade in horses during the 13th and 14th centuries.

15. Cadamosto had Spanish horses with him when he stopped at Cayor (Wolof) (Crone 1937, 35). The Portuguese purchase of Moroccan textiles for the African trade has been documented by John Vogt (1975).

16. On breeding and production of equipment, see Law (1980, 41-46, 89-118, passim); on production of equipment, see brief references in Echenberg (1971, 243, 247); Johnson (1976, 485); Legassick (1966); Person (1968-75).

17. Mande terms for sword include *npan, npanmuru,* and *muruba.*

18. Examples of this style saddletree were photographed on a research expedition undertaken by the Musée Nationale du Mali in the region known as Bakounou, the northwestern part of Mali toward the border with Mauritania. In Fatoma this style was said to be from the region of Nioro, belonging to either Soninke or Tuareg horsemen (interview with Ali Sango, Fatoma, 1984). This type of saddle is also called *gale.*

19. In the early 19th century in Morocco, James Grey Jackson (1809, 246-47) noted the importance of amulets for horses: "I have seen eleven round one horse's neck." He went on to say that when he purchased horses there and attempted to cut off these "incantations," the people looked upon him as a desperate infidel.

20. For example, there is a corpus of high status objects from Liberia consistently identified as Mandingo that may be said to represent an unusual Mande substyle. These elaborate horse trappings, hammock awnings, and pouches are made from black

and white leather, red cloth, and wild animal skins (monkey or leopard), using embroidery, appliqué, and patchwork techniques quite unlike the more common reddish brown, painted and embroidered Mande style.

21. There is no way of knowing whether the craftsmen Barth encountered were Arab foreigners, the descendants of mixed marriages between foreign trader-craftsmen and local women, or local craftsmen working in an Arabic style. Whatever their ethnic background, the fact that Barth identified them as Arab suggests a strong North African association, parallel to that of the Arma slipper makers of Djenné and Timbuktu.

22. The distribution of Hausa-style sandals clearly reflects their widespread trade relations (see Adamu 1978). According to Lhote (1950), the principle centers of manufacture were Kano, Zinder, Tessaoua, Tahoua, Maradi, and especially Agades, where the finest quality were produced. In the 19th century, Gustave Nachtigal ([1879-89] 1971, 2:184-85, 211) noted the presence of this style in Bornu. They have long been popular among the Saharan Tuareg groups and were traded as far north as the Algerian oasis of Wargla and even Touggourt (Lhote 1950, 514), southeast into Cameroons, and southwest along the kola trade routes through northern Benin, Togo, and into Ghana.

23. Especially Tauxier (1908, 1912, 1917); see also Lombard (1957).

24. The Olbrechts bags are now in the collection of the Musée Royal de l'Afrique Centrale, Tervuren (MRAC 79.1.277-278 and 79.1.711-712), along with three others with equally specific provenance—one collected by W. Verheyen among the Gurma of Nanergu, western Togo, identified as Mossi (MRAC 68.54.303), and a pair collected in 1933 by Houzeau de Lehaie in Bamako (MRAC 69.59.669-670). A similar bag was collected by Kunz Dittmer in Guiaro, southern Burkina Faso, between 1954 and 1956 and is now in the Hamburg Museum für Völkerkunde (57.8.311). Another was collected by Dittmer among the Mossi from the Koudougou region of Burkina Faso and is now in the American Museum of Natural History, New York (AMNH 90.1.7121). Gisela Völger purchased several in 1978, including a pair, identified as Mossi, purchased in the Kaya market,

Burkina Faso, and another identified as Dogon, purchased in Somadougou, south of Mopti, Mali (now in the Deutsches Ledermuseum/Deutsches Schuhmuseum, Offenbach am Main, Germany) (see Völger 1979, 102, no. 144). Bernhard Gardi purchased one in 1982 in Mopti, but it was from the region of Seno Mango (toward the border with Burkina Faso) and was identified as the work of either a Peul (Fula), Dogon, or Bwa craftsman; it is now in the collection of the Ethnography Department of the Berne Historical Museum, Berne, Switzerland (B.G.82.313.171) (see Gardi 1985, 303-18, illus. p. 317). In 1983 I collected one in Bamako that was identified as Dogon (Figure 78).

25. Translation mine. "Le travail en est fort original et absolument spécial. Je n'ai jamais RIEN VU d'analogue ni comme forme ni comme procédé d'ornementation, ni enfin comme couleur de cuir (blanc) chez les Maures, les Mandingka, les Soninka, les Bamana ou les Foulbé." This statement is clearly his own observation and therefore useful for my purposes since Tautain spent much of his time in the Mande region. Unfortunately, much of the data presented in the article is problematic. Tautain admitted that he had never actually seen a Bobo person, who, he said, were known for their cannibalism. His information came from several Jula traders, who may well have had a vested interest in protecting their sources by giving false testimony on the "savagery" of the Bobo.

4. THE TECHNOLOGY OF MANDE POTTERY

1. See McNaughton's discussion of Mande people's ambivalent attitudes toward *nyama* and especially the ability of blacksmiths to master it (1988, 15-21, passim).

2. One potter told me that there are both male and female *jinèw,* mirroring relationships in this world. They are often personalized with proper names. The *jinèw* of the clay pit she uses are known as Kondoron (male) and Sande (female). According to René Bravmann (1995), throughout the Islamic world spirits are conceptualized in human form, with human foibles and desires. Naming them is one of

the ways in which they are personalized and honored.

3. I do not have much evidence for how strictly these sacrifices are observed today. Some potters claimed that all of the various sacrifices, proscriptions, and taboos associated with the clay pit continue to be practiced or observed rigorously, while others suggested that in this day and age no one pays much attention to these rules of the past. However, most of the potters with whom I spoke about this topic did say that they had participated in these events in their lifetime, even if it had been in years past.

4. According to one of the potters, although they are not supposed to see the entry of the clay pit, Maninka women need fear no danger if they choose to help a potter friend transport the clay from the pit back to the compound. The potter might then return the favor by making a gift of a pottery vessel.

5. In response to a question about whether a menstruating woman could dig clay, I was told of a situation that arose several years ago when the potters of Somba (near Kolokani) had trouble with their pots breaking during firing for no apparent reason. It was determined that someone (probably from a neighboring village!) had broken the *tana* (taboo). An elder blacksmith performed the sacrifice, begging the pardon of the *jinèw* of the clay pit with an offering of seven white kola nuts, a white cock, and uncooked rice. The sacrifice completed, the women had no more problems with their pots breaking.

6. *Temper* is the term for the nonclay (nonplastic) elements in a clay body, usually added to the mixture by the potter to prevent cracking during drying and firing. These include such materials as ground shells, grasses, and sand. The term *grog* refers to temper made from previously fired materials such as old pots (Shepard [1956] 1985, 24-27).

7. According to Dieterlen (1951, 30-31, n. 3), there is great significance behind the related terms *kuru* (canoe), *kuruni* (spindle), and *kuruni* (stool) because the term *kuru* also designates the ark in which the mythical primordial blacksmith descended to the earth with the eight cereal grains provided by the creator god Faro, by means of which agriculture was introduced.

8. The wood is *lenge* or *dagan (Afzelia africana)*. Scientific names of trees cited here and below were obtained using Bamana/Maninka names recorded in the field and identified in Adam (1970), Bailleul (1981), Dalziel (1948), and Koné (1995). Brett-Smith (1994, 121-24) notes that *lenge (lènkè)* is known to be dangerous for the *nyama* it contains and says that it is identified as being the home of *jinèw* (spiritual forces).

9. I saw as few as four vessels being fired at one time. The largest firing for which I was able to record the numbers represented the work of four women and included seventy-two pieces.

10. *Wòlò (Terminalia sspp)* was most often identified as the best wood for firing; others included *geni, gènou,* or *guènye (Pterocarpus erinaceus), bumu* or *mboumboum (Bombax costatum), npekuba* or *npekou (Lannea microcarpa), nèrè (Parkia biglobosa), ntereni (Pteleopsis suberosa), sama, samagara,* or *so (Swartzia madagascariensis?), taba kumba (Parinari macrophylla* or *Detarium microcarpum?), cangèrèjè* or *tiangara (Combretum nigricans* or *Combretum geitonophyllum),* and *toro* or *toronyényé (Ficus capensis). Si* or *shi (Butyrospermum paradoxum* or *Butyrospermum parkii),* commonly known as karite, cannot be used because it sparks.

11. The term *wòlòsò* is derived from the resemblance of the shape of the iron hook to the sickle (also called *wòlòsò*) used in harvesting. The hook has other uses as well. According to the women of Kangaba, by stepping over the *wòlòsò* and having the prescribed prayers spoken, a Maninka woman can be cured of barrenness and miscarriage.

12. Various materials can be used to make the solution, including the seed pods of *bagana (Acacia nilotoca adansonii),* the seed pods or bark of *nèrè (Parkia biglobosa),* the bark of *npekuba (Lannea microcarpa)* or *geni (Pterocarpus erinaceus),* and the leaves of *kunjè (Guiera senegalensis).*

13. Person (1968-75, 1:57); Tamari (1991, 243, 246-49). Not all authors agree with blanket identifications of Mande origins for Senufo artist groups. Glaze (1981, 5, 31, 37, 227 n. 28) identifies the *tyeduno* (Tyeduno) artist group of blacksmiths and potters as being of Mande origin. She suggests that the *kpeene* (Kpeene) artist group of brass casters and potters and *kule* (Kule) group of wood and calabash carvers (following Richter) also may be of Mande origin. See

also Richter (1980, 15–17) for a discussion of *kule* (Kulebele) origins, and Spindel (1989, 68) for a word of caution on theories as to the origins of the *kpeene* (Kpeenbele).

14. Christopher Roy, who interviewed Bwa and Mossi potters, does not say whether they were of Mande origin (1987a, 50–60). However, he does identify some potters of Ouri (a village midway between Bobo Dioulasso and Ouagadougou) as the wives of blacksmiths, specifically of the Konaté clan. In another essay, Roy (1985, 3–7) discusses the migration of this well-known family of Mande smiths from their Mande homeland to Ouri via the Bobo Dioulasso region. It is likely that at least some of them brought their wives, skilled in pottery making, with them. The technology could then have been transmitted to other women who married into the family. From his descriptions and photographs of pottery forming and firing, the parallels to Bamana and Maninka pottery would support such a hypothesis.

15. The convex mold also appears among the Hausa (Dupuis and Echard 1971), Nupe (Nicholson 1934), Yoruba of Nigeria and Niger (Wahlman 1972), Nuna and Gurma (Gulmance) of Burkina Faso (Banaon 1990; Geis-Tronich 1989), and other ethnic groups.

16. Descriptions of the techniques employed by Mo potters are based on research by Roy Sieber in Branman, Ghana, in 1967, and by Marla Berns in Bonakire in 1978. See Crossland and Posnansky (1978, 82).

17. I have addressed some of the questions concerning what I believe to be the non-Mande origins of the Jula potters in Frank (1993). The multiple origins of the Somono have long been a subject of debate, but probably include Bamana, Marka or Soninke, Bobo, and Boso. See LaViolette (1987, 108–15); Roberts (1981); Sundstrom (1972). The fact that Somono potters use both convex mold and paddle and anvil techniques may reflect either these diverse ethnic origins or their working closely with Fula and Songhay potters in the pluralistic setting of Djenné.

18. Kathryn Green pointed out (letter to the author, April 1996) that the seven-day weekly calendar was an Islamic introduction and therefore could not have predated Islam. However, it is the concept of certain days as protected that was carried over from pre-Islamic tradition and incorporated into the new calendar.

5. THE TECHNOLOGY OF MANDE LEATHERWORK

1. In 1623 the British explorer Richard Jobson noted that leatherworkers in the Gambia region seemed to know how to tan and dye the smaller skins but not the larger hides, which they sold to Europeans. He wrote: ". . . whereby appeares, they have knowledge to dresse their leather. Howbeit I conceive, onely their goats and deare skinnes, which they can colour and dye: but to greater beasts hides, their apprehension cannot attaine, and some of these are held for curious persons, and deepe capacities: for they will bee feeling of some stuffe garments we weare, and do think, and will boldly say, that wee doe make them of the hides, we buy from them, and will not doe it in their sight, because they shall not learne" ([1623] 1904, 154).

2. Some leatherworkers say that their fathers employed slaves to assist them with tanning, while others are adamant that although slaves might be called upon to assist in particular chores, they never would be allowed to acquire the secrets of the trade. Among the Moors and Tuareg it is women, the wives of blacksmiths, who do both tanning and leatherworking. Moor women in the region of Kayes are especially renowned for their tanning skills. In the past they were seminomadic, traveling with their families and small herds of cattle, sheep, and goats, exchanging milk, salt, and possibly tanned skins for grains and other food stuffs. Many Moor families have now settled in towns, such as Kayes, Kita, and Kolokani, where they have become the principal tanners. Other leatherworkers now purchase their skins from them. Among the Hausa and the Yoruba, in contrast, tanning is the exclusive domain of men.

3. The most common breed of sheep in this region is the hair sheep. These are better for tanning than the various wool-bearing breeds because they have a tighter, firmer structure, more like that of goats (Reed 1972, 41–43).

4. The pelts of some animals (especially wild

ones) are prepared in such a way as to preserve the fur. In addition, prayer rugs are prepared from goat or sheep skins by washing and scraping the inner surface. Pounded acacia pods are then rubbed into the flesh side and wrapped up, hairy side out, and left for several hours. This is repeated several times until the skin is thoroughly washed and allowed to dry. This process partially stabilizes the skin but does not render it supple, as does the complete tanning process.

5. Certain trees are said to have been particularly effective because they produce strong potash. Among these are *ngalama (Anogeissus leiocarpus* or *Anogeissus schimperi)*, as well as *nyama (Bauhinia rediculata), nkunan (Sclerocarya birrea* or *Poupartia birrea)*, and *sira* or baobab *(Adansonia digitata)*. In Djenné, according to Monteil ([1932] 1971, 231), ashes are mixed with water and allowed to sit for a day or so and then placed in a basket or porous pottery jar. The water is filtered through the ashes several times. Leatherworkers also may use a lye soap produced locally by women, available in village markets and still used in indigo dyeing.

6. A number of vegetable substances may be used with or in place of chicken droppings, such as the sour leaves or fruit of *nsarani (Adenopus breviflorus)*, also called *basansarani* or *sarani* in Bamana.

7. Translation mine. "A ce sujet, il faut signaler une exception à la règle qui veut que les dialli-karangués cultivent une sorte de mil spécial qui ne se mange point, mais dont l'épi donne, par macération dans l'eau chaude, une teinture rouge brique qu'ils emploient pour leurs cuirs et qui est très estimée. Il leur suffit, du reste, d'un élever chaque année une vingtaine de pieds dans un coin de leur cour. C'est un travail à la hauteur de leur courage. Ce mil est cultivé exclusivement par eux, et, à chaque récolte, ils mettent de côté un ou deux épis pour les semailles de l'année à venir."

According to Ben Sai (1944b, 21), one of the terms for this type of millet is *diali-nio,* i.e., griot's millet.

8. A third source of yellow dye occasionally mentioned is the leaves of *ngalama (Anogeissus schimperi, Anogeissus leiocarpus)*. A maceration of the leaves, bark, or fruits was mixed with water and boiled. After the solution cooled, alum *(yerelen)* was added to

act as a mordant (de Zeltner 1915, 225; Saint-Père 1925, 50). However, some of my informants claimed that *ngalama* was used only for cloth, not leather. Ben Sai (1944a, 17-18; 1944b) includes it in his discussion of materials used in dyeing cloth but does not mention it in that for leather dyes.

9. According to Dalziel (1926, 234-37), the Hausa had several ways of obtaining green, including mixing indigo dye with one of the yellow vegetable dyes. A more complex method involved the use of copper or brass filings with a mineral salt on untanned skin. Green leather is especially popular among the Tuareg, who used similar materials in dyeing their own leather and may have imported some from the Hausa (Lhote 1950, 519). According to Nicolaisen (1963, 282), green was obtained by the Tuareg of Ahaggar and Tassili-n-Ajjer either from a mineral or powder introduced from the south or from a vegetable powder introduced from the north. Green leather also appears to have been imported into West Africa from Egypt. In Agades, Barth called on a man who had arrived several days earlier and found him busy "selling fine Egyptian sheep-leather called kurna (which is in great request here, particularly that of a green color) to a number of lively females, who are the chief artisans in leather-work" (1857, 1:330-31). Lyon (1821, 158) included green leather from Egypt as one of the imports into the Fezzan.

10. I am grateful to Bernard Gardi for sharing the results of his research in the Inland Niger Delta region prior to my own fieldwork. His work focused on this question of the relationship between artist identity and distinctive technologies. He brought to my attention the different tool forms used by leatherworkers of different ethnic identities. His findings were borne out by my own research farther south and west of the Inland Niger Delta. See Gardi 1985.

11. "Deja grâce à nos conseils et sur notre initiative, les cordonniers sont parvenus à l'aide de formes en bois à confectionner des bottes et pantouffles à la mode europeene" (Monographies du cercle de Djenné, 1895-1930, 73). This may be a misreading of Monteil's work; I was unable to locate a copy of the original text. One of the Djenné leatherworkers had among his tools a European-style boot tree (Figure

127). It was comprised of four parts, one piece in the shape of the toe and ball of the foot, two pieces forming the calf and heel of the boot, and a fourth piece that slides in from the top, acting as a wedge to stretch the leather tight. According to Salaman (1986, 97-98), this type of last was used in Europe primarily by the owner to keep his boots in shape. Although it had been used by the leatherworker in forming boots, it was not considered an essential tool.

12. Other materials used include the leaves of *tamat (Acacia seyal),* galls of *tabarekkat (Tamarix aphylla),* and the fruit of the *tedjoq (Pistacia atlantica).* The bark of the *tamat* acacia *(Acacia seyal)* is used especially for tanning water bags; see Nicolaisen (1963, 271-73).

13. Although Moor women tan the hides of cows and oxen in shallow pits, goat and sheep skins are tanned in pottery vessels above ground. Tuareg women also do their tanning above ground in a specially made receptacle of camel hide (Nicolaisen 1963, 270-71).

14. Nicolaisen (1963, 282) lists the dyes used by the Tuareg of Ahaggar and Tassili-n-Ajjer and mentions iron and water put in a container, shielded from the sun, and allowed to sit for several days, but he does not mention any other ingredients.

15. Roy Sieber identified such a material in use in Ghana in 1964 (conversation with the author prior to fieldwork, 1982).

16. The leaves of *Anogeissus schimperi,* known in Bamana as *ngalama,* are used to dye cloth in the Western Sudan, but Mande leatherworkers insisted that this dye would not work on leather.

17. In fact, I found this approach to be reasonably successful when interviewing leatherworkers in the markets and side streets of Bamako, where they had come in search of clients. It became somewhat of a game to greet a leatherworker, silently guessing his ethnic identity based on the tools scattered about before asking his name and setting up an interview.

18. A photograph taken by Jean Rouch in 1948 (Photothèque, Institut Fondamental d'Afrique Noire, Dakar [SN 49-388bis]) shows a Bella woman making amulets, in Zibane, Tillaberi, Niger. See Nicolaisen (1963, 275, fig. 219); Gabus (1958, fig. 274). The Bella are usually identified as a distinct ethnic population

historically subservient to the Tuareg of central Niger.

19. According to Lhote (1952, 923), the makers of *bata* in Agades use a wooden slate called *alcalib.*

20. He suggests, however, that the origin of this work may ultimately be Sonrhaï.

6. MANDE POTTERS: *NUMUMUSOW*

1. The problematic tendency for scholars to identify those who work metal but who also carry out a variety of other critical social and ritual functions, such as burying the dead, simply as smiths is viewed by Nigel Barley (1984) as part of a larger problem of ethnocentric bias in the anthropological literature toward men and smithing. He argues that to identify potters simply as "female smiths" denies us a fuller understanding of social metaphors "engendered" by the transformative processes involved in pottery forming and especially firing. See also Sterner and David (1991); Herbert (1993); and Barley (1994).

2. Translation by Kassim Koné. The literal translation is: "Sumaworo entered Mande / and a shirt of human skin entered Mande / Sumaworo entered Mande / and pants of human skin entered Mande."

3. Kanté drew a sharp distinction between *juguya* and *farinya.* While both are conditions to be feared and hence respected, the former is undeniably evil, while the latter is powerful but essentially good.

4. In a recent publication configured as a dictionary of famous Malian women, the historian Adame Ba Konaré (1993) chronicles the lives and reputations of the mythical women of oral tradition along with celebrated women of more recent Malian history, with a special tribute to the female martyrs of the 1991 coup d'état. I thank David Conrad for this reference.

5. Many of the following references to women in oral tradition are drawn from a paper by David Conrad titled "Mooning Armies and Mothering Heroes: Female Power in Mande Epic Tradition," presented at the International Conference on Mande Studies, Leiden, March 22-24, 1995. I am grateful to Conrad for providing me a copy of his paper prior to its publication (Conrad forthcoming). The title alludes to one Nyana Djoukoudoulaye, a woman possessed of sorcerous powers so strong that she could bring warfare to a complete stop by

pointing her exposed buttocks toward the battlefield.

6. Examples provided by Conrad include the slave girl Sijanma who contributes to the success of the Segou ruler Faama Da Jara by betrayal of her master Basi. The 19th-century ruler Samori's failure to defeat Sikasso is attributed to One-Breasted Demba, the lover of Samori's brother, Keme Brema, and sister of Sikasso's ruler, Mansa Keba. When Samori learns of the affair and questions his brother's loyalty, Keme is so distraught that, in a suicidal gesture, he goes into battle without his protective amulets and is killed. Upon learning of her lover's death, Demba angrily dons men's clothing and successfully leads the Sikasso forces against those of Samori. The tables are turned in another tale from Samori's exploits when Kagbe, wife of Gbankundo Saaji Kamara, provides information crucial to Samori's success over her husband.

7. References in the epic texts to "mothers" or "fathers" may signal generational difference but not necessarily biological relationships. This is true even in daily speech, for when someone cites elders or ancestors of previous unspecified generations, the phrase "our fathers" or "our mothers" may be used. Similarly, "sisters" and "brothers" may identify men and women of the same age grade but not necessarily siblings.

8. Conrad identifies these three as the Conde (Kondé) women, "sisters" of the powerful Mande ruler Donsamo'o Nyamo'o Diarra.

9. The best discussion of the Mande concepts of *fadenya* (literally, father-childness) and *badenya* (mother-childness) remains Bird and Kendall (1980). The *fadenya* spirit of competition and individual achievement contrasts with the communal values of cooperation and consensus captured in the notion of *badenya*.

10. One of the best known is the father memorialized in the autobiographical novel of Camara Laye, *L'enfant noir* (1953). For a discussion of Camara (Kamara) as the quintessential *fune* patronymic, see Conrad (1995).

11. In fact, with one exception, all of the potters I interviewed were from and had married into blacksmith families. The only exception is a woman from a leatherworker family in Guinea who had been mar-ried by her father to one of his blacksmith friends. In addition, there is another woman long since divorced from the husband of the arranged marriage of her childhood, now on her fourth or fifth nonblacksmith husband. All of the blacksmiths I interviewed had married only women from other blacksmith families, though not all were practicing potters any more than the men were practicing blacksmiths.

12. Excision in the Mande context involves surgical removal of the clitoris, traditionally performed on prepubescent girls. Efforts by medical professionals, social workers, and others to bring this practice to an end have increased in recent years. Despite these campaigns, sentiment remains strongly behind the importance of excision for a young woman's transition to adulthood and her future competitive relationship to her cowives. It is not my place here to present arguments for or against the practice. In conversations with potters, when I registered my concern for the health problems during childbirth suffered by young women who have been excised, the response was overwhelmingly in support of the practice. To be an unexcised woman implies being uncivilized, dirty, backward, open for ridicule and ostracism. As for the negative physical effects, I was told repeatedly that if the operation is done correctly, there will be no subsequent health problems for the young women. Nevertheless, fewer and fewer *numumusow* perform the service, though it is often done in medical clinics when the child is still a toddler.

13. Similarly, only certain blacksmith families have the right and the capacity to produce the exceptional individuals to head Komo, to become sculptors of the first rank, or to become renowned as diviners (Brett-Smith 1994).

14. The conversation in which these statements were embedded began with a long description by Koloko of meetings called by the local women's political organization and representatives from various government and nongovernment health organizations from the capital to convince women that the practice was detrimental to the general health of young women, especially during childbirth. She remained unconvinced of their arguments and convinced of her own ability to perform the procedure correctly.

15. Dieterlen acknowledges one potter, Nadyè Dambèlè of Konodimini (near Segou), in the list of people who contributed to the gathering of information for the book. While it is likely that at least some of her information on sacred pottery rites came from this woman, Dieterlen does not identify her in the description itself, nor does she specify the particular setting in the text.

16. Pâques's research was conducted primarily in N'Tentu (Bougouni region of southern Mali), the capital village of the Samake, reputed to be the most "pure" of Bamana peoples. The potters were generally of the Bagayoko clan of a neighboring village, married into the resident Jawara (Diawara) blacksmith families.

17. According to my informants, Mondays and Fridays were sacred days on which it was forbidden to dig clay (see chap. 4, above).

18. My information concerns the Nyagwan of the village of Gouala south of Bamako. My informants were one of the wives of the head of the Doumbia blacksmith family and one of his daughters, who had married into a blacksmith family in Kangaba. It is tempting to suggest that Nyagwan may be a variation on the Gwan institution as described by Ezra (1986b, 22-23) among the southern Bamana. However, there are some important differences in our information. While Nyagwan was capable of addressing fertility problems of its younger members and apparently non-initiated women who might seek advice and spiritual intervention from its leaders, that was not identified as its primary purpose. From our discussions, Nyagwan seems to have been directed more toward the spiritual health and solidarity of senior women, rather than toward fertility issues affecting younger women. However, my information was limited because younger women simply did not know much about it and older women who may well have participated in Nyagwan activities were generally unwilling to discuss it.

19. There are reports that lend credence to such seemingly miraculous acts. Included among the exceptional feats attributed to Komo masquerades is one during which the performer stamps the ground with his foot and a fountain of water shoots forth (McNaughton 1988, 142-43). McNaughton (1982, 495-98; 1988, 44-46) recounts in some detail a dra-

matic performance he witnessed of "fire" spitting. Fire manipulation figures prominently in accounts of Komo and other performances.

20. The wrapping of thread while speaking prayers is a common means of imbuing an object with spiritual force. This is the way in which Muslim clerics invest an amulet with powers over and above those contained in the sacred texts written on small pieces of paper, neatly folded. These amulets are generally brought to the leatherworker already wrapped in thread to be encased in a protective leather sheath.

21. Julianne Short witnessed a celebration (fura) not far from Kolokani during which seven young women were being prepared for marriage. It was called fini siri, "tying the cloth." According to Short, the role of the numumuso was critical, as it was she who tied the excision mud-cloth wrappers (symbolic of their status as marriageable adults) around each of the girls (telephone conversation with the author, 1994). See also Brett-Smith 1982.

22. Even in urban settings, numu identity is not forgotten. One of my interpreters was from a blacksmith family. She was a part of the well-educated urban middle class and did not wish to be singled out among her peers as a numumuso. She once told me of becoming somewhat embarrassed and annoyed while attending a social event where she and a woman from a griot family were presented with modest gifts of cash because they were both nyamakalaw.

23. This association has been highlighted in the titles of several recent exhibitions, including *Purpose and Perfection: Pottery as a Woman's Art in Central Africa,* National Museum of African Art, Smithsonian Institution, Washington, D.C. (1992-96); *Women's Art in Africa: Woodfired Pottery from Iowa Collections,* University of Iowa Museum of Art, Iowa City (October 23, 1991-June 28, 1992); and *In the Circle of African Women,* Newark Museum, Newark, N.J. (March 28-May 31, 1992).

24. De Zeltner identifies his potter informant as a member of both the Soninke blacksmith "caste" and that of woodworkers known as *lawBe (laobé)* among the Fula and as *sakke (saké)* among the Soninke. From my own fieldwork I can say that the occurrence of intermarriage within the various artisan groups was a rare phenomenon, despite the

assumption that social rules rigidly pronounced for ideological reasons tend to be more loosely adhered to in practice.

25. Diawara suggests that a sexual transgression may have caused the men to be forbidden to practice their craft, a broken taboo that apparently did not restrict the activities of women.

26. Soumbounou (Soumanou) is a family name that is most commonly associated with *garanke* and *jeli* families.

27. This is in contrast to information provided by Saint-Père (1925, 21) that it is the wives of leatherworkers who are "les coiffeuses officielles." According to de Zeltner (1908, 221), it is the wives of leatherworkers, not those of blacksmiths, who shave the heads of newborns for the baptism ceremonies, tattoo and dress the hair of women, and excise young girls. He notes later on that the vocations of hairdresser and tattooer are also held by other women.

28. However, there are other potters in the region whose identity falls outside the dominant blacksmith-potter paradigm. Spindel has documented pottery production among the Nafanra, where potters are the wives of farmers. These women use a forming technology that is fundamentally different from that of their *kpeene* and *tyeduno* neighbors but remarkably similar to that of the Jula potters of the Kadiolo region (see chap. 4).

29. However, in another publication, Holas (1957, 95) notes that excision is not universally practiced among the Senufo, and that when it is the operation is performed by someone within the family rather than by a specialist.

30. Among northern Mande peoples, it is generally the wives of *garanke* who perform gum tattooing and occasionally lip tattooing. According to Appia (1965), among the Fula (Peul) and Maninka (Malinké) populations of the Fouta Djallon region excision is performed by the wives of blacksmiths known by the Fulfulde name of *wayluBe (wailube;* s., *baylo, bailo).*

7. MANDE LEATHERWORKERS: *GARANKEW* AND *JELIW*

1. In his study of Mande oral traditions, David

Conrad (1985, 35) noted that "the high value placed on Muslim antecedents has given rise to such extensive manipulation of traditional genealogies that at some point in the chain of oral transmission, pre-Islamic forebears began to lose status in favour of relative late-comers from the Middle East." I would especially like to thank David Conrad for material he made available to me as this chapter was being written as well as for his close reading of different versions. Some of this material appeared in Frank 1995.

2. This claim is made despite the historical reality that Abraham lived hundreds of years before Muhammad. This is a good example of how historical personages and events can be telescoped in oral traditions.

3. According to N'Diayé (1970, 88), Surakata is the ancestor of the Kouyatés, not all griots. However, both Zemp (1966) and Conrad (1985) recorded traditions of Surakata as an ancestral figure for all *jeli.*

4. Translation mine. "Notre ancêtre est Sourakata. Il ne priait pas. En ce temps-là il y avait une grande guerre. Sourakata ne voulait pas prier et Mahomet lui demanda: 'Pourquoi ne pries-tu pas?' Sourakata répondit: 'Je ne prie pas!' Au plus forte de la guerre, Sourakata fut arrêté parce qu'il ne voulait pas prier. Lorsqu'on le tortura, il cria et demanda pardon. Alors Mahomet dit: 'Puisqu'il crie bien, ne le tuez pas! Il va rester chez nous et crier. Tous les enfants et les petits-enfants de Sourakata seront griots.'

"Mahomet donna à Sourakata une alêne et dit: 'Tu dois coudre la queue de mon cheval.' Puis il dit: 'Si les marabouts écrivent des papiers, enfermez ceux-ci dans de petits sachets en cuir et cousez la peau.' Et depuis ce jour-là nous travaillons la peau."

5. Wagadu is the name from oral traditions that scholars believe to be the ancient empire of Ghana, centered in northern Mali and eastern Mauritania, with its capital at the ancient city of Koumbi Saleh (see Map 2). Manden is the name from oral traditions that refers to the heartland of the Mali empire in southwestern Mali and Guinea.

6. The town of Diara was the capital of the Soninke kingdom also known as Diara, weakened in the 17th century by civil war between the Daabo and Sagone lineages and ultimately defeated by the Bamana in the 18th century (Boyer 1953; Webb 1995, 48-50).

7. In fact, the only active leatherworkers in Kangaba today are *jeliw*. There is one family of *garankew*, but they earn a living by trade and are considered as strangers.

8. According to Eric Pollet and Grace Winter (1971, 231 n. 91), there are 4 *garanke* clans—Ganesi, Diawara (Jawara), Mangasi, and Kalloga (Kaloga)—identified in Diafounou as having always been leatherworkers. Of these, only the Diawara are said to have been one of the 144 clans arriving from Wagadu at the end of the 12th century (Pollet and Winter 1971, 46, 198-204). The only other leatherworker lineage represented among the original 144 were the Simaga (Simaka).

9. Wane was citing an Arabic manuscript by Cheickh Moussa Kamara. The Tukulor name for these leatherworkers is *sakkeeBe alawBe* (s., *gaalabbo, galabo*).

10. This was also confirmed during conversations I had in the spring of 1984 with Gerald Cashion, who had done fieldwork in the Wasulu region in the 1970s.

11. The Diabaté patronymic in the Kadiolo region of southeastern Mali appears with two distinct associations, one noble and Senufo, one griot and Jula.

12. References to *garankew* include the following: in the Soninke regions of Diafounou (Jafunu, Diahounou) and Guidimakha (Saint-Père 1925; Pollet and Winter 1971); the Soninke Jawara (Diawara) of Bakounou (Boyer 1953); Senegambia (Weil 1984); among the Tukulor (Toucouleur) of Fouta Toro (Wane 1969); in Guinea among Fula (Peul) and Maninka (Mandingo, Manding) (Arcin 1907; Marty 1921; Durand 1932; Barry 1943-44; Prussin 1986, 1995; Rivière 1969); and in northern Sierra Leone (Winterbottom [1803] 1969; Prussin 1986). There are leatherworkers of other ethnic identities in this region, including the *sakkeeBe* (see n. 16, below) of Tukulor and Fula origin (see Wane 1969). According to Peter Weil (letter to the author, January 20, 1988), two of the leatherworker lineages in Wuli are identified with the early history of the state, although their association with Muslim cleric and trading lineages is unclear. The patronymic of one of these lineages is Silla (Sylla), a common Soninke family name recognized as either *garanke* or noble. The patronymic of the other lineage is Fati, a family name, to my knowledge, not found among the Soninke in Mali.

13. One of the links between the *garankew* and a Soninke heritage is that in Guinea and to some extent in Sierra Leone the wives of these leatherworkers are the principal indigo dyers, traditionally a specialization of Soninke women in the Sudanic region.

14. Joseph Opala told me this during conversations when I was doing fieldwork in Sierra Leone in 1988. In fact, when I asked my field assistant Chernoh Njai to ask a leatherworker in Kabala what his ethnicity was, he phrased the question "You're a Fula, aren't you?" The man's response was unequivocal, "No, I am Mandingo!" This was no surprise to me, as I already knew the man's patronymic to be Sylla, a common Mande *garanke* name. But it was a surprise to Njai, a man who is otherwise quite knowledgeable about craft traditions and local history (see Frank 1995).

15. Especially Sini Mansaray in Freetown, Muhammad Sylla in Kabala, and Muhammad Tounkara in Makenie, 1988.

16. *Sakke* (pl. *SakkeeBe*) is the Fulfulde term for Fula leatherworkers and saddle makers. On another occasion, a Dogon leatherworker in Sevaré recommended me to a saddle maker in Segou, whom he referred to as "Jeliba." When I asked if he was a *garanke,* he said yes, he was a *jeli-garanke,* and then that he was actually a *jeli* but that he practiced *garankeya*. He later identified himself by the Dogon "caste" term *gòòn* (Adama Gana, Sevaré, 1983).

17. Translation mine. ". . . enfin, quelques-uns sont karangués, ce qui comprend tout le travail du corroyeur, du tanneur, du sellier, du cordonnier, etc., et un mot la fabrication de tout objet en cuir. . . . Certains chants, certaines danses, la confection de certains instruments, de même que le métier de karangué, sont leur apanage exclusif."

18. Kourouma (Koroma) and Doumbouya (Doumbia) are common griot patronymics, though they also may be noble and blacksmith (see Sidibé 1959; Camara 1976, 103). Doumbia is identified by Amselle (1972, 10) as a common griot name in the Wasulu region; however, I found it to be more commonly a blacksmith patronymic in the region of Kangaba. Several of Zemp's Maninka (Malinké) griot informants among the Dan of west central Côte d'Ivoire were of the Doumaya clan (1966, 617-18).

Kamara is usually identified as a *fune* patronymic (N'Diayé 1970; Conrad 1995) or as a blacksmith name.

19. Translation mine. "En bambara cordonnier se dit *garanké* et *dieli* chez les Malinkes et les Ouassoulounkes (*Dieli* veut dire exactement griot, mais, commes chez les Malinkes et les Ouassoulounkes, il n'y a pas les griots qui exercent la métier de cordonnier, il n'y a pas d'autre nom pour designer ceux-ci)."

20. His use of the word *actuellement* suggests that he thinks it may be a recent trend. Earlier, in identifying the *garanke* as a Bamana caste of leatherworkers, Zahan admitted that they are not well understood from an ethnological point of view (1963, 127).

21. Translation mine. "Ce n'est pas le cas pour les *yeobo* chez les Dan . . . dont les resources proviennent pour la plus grand part de leur travail de cordonnier . . . ils ne chantent et ne tambourinent pas plus souvent que les musiciens dan qui sont agriculteurs . . . le *yeomi* chez les Dan exerce surtout son second métier de cordonnier."

22. Translation mine. "Mais les *yeli* gardent leurs distances des *garanké*, qui sont chez les peuples mandé les véritables travailleurs de la peau, et ils les consièrent avec mépris: 'Si les *garanké* demandent à quelqu'un un cadeau et qu'il leur est refusé, ils pissent sur lui ou salissent sa maison avec leur excréments. Mais nous, nous ne faisons pas cela, nous chantons!' "

23. Launay speculated on the issue of Dieli identity in a letter dated December 4, 1987, following our discussions during the African Studies Association meetings in Denver earlier that year, at which I presented a paper on the identity of Mande leatherworkers. This in part led him to develop his material from Côte d'Ivoire into a more formal discussion of the ambiguities of Dieli identity (Launay 1995).

24. This information from Kathryn Green came from our discussions following a panel at the 1987 African Studies Association meetings in Denver, for which we both presented papers (see Green 1987a).

25. What was surprising was that their wives were potters; see Frank 1993 and chap. 5, above.

26. Such was not the case for the Maraka (Soninke) towns of Banamba, Kiban, Touba, and Sirakorola, where leatherwork seems to be the exclusive domain of *garankew.* The one exception was an Arma leatherworker who primarily tanned skins for sale to other leatherworkers, occasionally taking commissions for slippers.

27. Bernhard Gardi's work in and around Mopti and Fatoma suggests that this kind of ethnic diversity is anything but exceptional. He has identified seven distinct leatherworking traditions in the Masina region. In addition to the *garankew,* whom he identifies as Mande (Bamana, Malinke, Soninke), his list includes *sakke* (male, Peul; i.e., Fula), Bella (male, Bella-Tuareg), *garasa* (female, Tuareg and Songhay), *arma* (male, Songhay), *jambu/gòòn* (male, Dogon), and *hanu* (male, Bwa). See Gardi 1985, 304.

There are also several families of Tuareg blacksmith-leatherworkers in the capital city of Bamako. While leatherwork is traditionally the domain of women among the Tuareg, the tourist market for cassette, video, and computer disk boxes is such that men have taken over production and distribution of the craft. When I first arrived in Bamako in 1983, these beautiful tooled leather-covered boxes were making quite a splash. According to the oral tradition of the time, the boxes were offered in a variety of none-too-specific shapes and sizes until a Peace Corps volunteer commissioned one for his cassette tapes.

28. There are some important differences. Both groups are recognized as having always been free, according to tradition protected from enslavement and warfare by their peculiar status. Perhaps the most prominent of the *nyeenyBe* are the *maabo* (pl., *maabuuBe*), male weavers and griots whose wives are often potters. In addition to the distinction of pairing potters with weavers rather than blacksmiths, Fula society is unusual in recognizing weaving as a specialized profession. Mande society considers weaving a task for slaves. Other *nyeenyBe* include the *baylo* (pl., *wayluBe*), who are blacksmiths and especially jewelers, and the *labbo* (pl., *lawBe*), who are woodworkers.

29. Translation mine. "Noumô, Garanké ou Diali vous êtes né, Noumô, Garanké ou Diali vous resterez jusqu'à votre dernier jour, même si vous n'exercez jamais la profession désignée sous un de ces noms et vous serez père, grand'père, bisaïeul, etc. . . . d'enfants qui, peut-être, ne seront jamais ni forgerons, ni cordonniers, ni musiciens, mais dont chacun restera Diali, Noumô, Garanké."

GLOSSARY OF MANDE POTTERY AND LEATHERWORKING TERMS

(Bamana-Maninka terms unless otherwise indicated)★

bagana, baanan   acacia *(Acacia nilotica andasonii, Acacia scorpioides adstringens); jabe* in Soninke

bamadaga   lidded ceramic vessel with raised nodules, used for storing sacred medicines; Kadiolo region; lit., crocodile pot

barama   ceramic skeuomorph of an iron or aluminum cooking pot; also *nègèdaga*

basidaga   ceramic couscous steamer; also *nyintin*

binyè, biyèn   leatherworker's awl; *bune* in Soninke

biyèlè   small ceramic bowl

bòrò, bòrè   generic term for bag

bunsan   generic term for fringe

coolo   ceramic rainspout; Kadiolo region

cooro   stirrup-handled ceramic cap used to protect the pinnacles of the old Sudanese-style mosques; Kadiolo region

coron   leather boot; *xuufi* in Soninke

daga   generic term for ceramic pot; *gine* in Soninke

dagajo, dagalo   pottery making; lit., raising a pot, making a pot stand

dunden   narrow-necked ceramic or calabash water vessel

faga   ceramic washbasin; also used in the Kadiolo region to close the tombs in non-Muslim burials

falamu   halter for a horse or donkey

farawòrò   special kind of millet cultivated by leatherworkers specifically for the red dye *(Sorghum caudatum* var. *colorans)*

finye   large ceramic water storage vessel; also *jifinye*

furadaga   ceramic vessel for preparing traditional herbal medicines; Kadiolo region; lit., leaf pot

furuno, furunè   ceramic brazier based on metal prototype (from the French *fourneau*)

gale   leather-covered wooden saddle with a forked back

garanke, karanke   Soninke leatherworker

garankeya   state or condition of being a *garanke*, encompassing leatherworker identity and practice

garigulèti   stirrup-spouted ceramic water jar (from the French *gargoulette*)

jeli, jali   Bamana/Maninka bard, musician, griot, and often leatherworker

---

★Bamana-Maninka terms are drawn primarily from fieldwork and verified in Bazin (1906), Bailleul (1981), and Koné (1995). I thank Kassim Koné for checking my conversion of the French orthography of Mande words into appropriate Bamana-Maninka orthography. Soninke terms are from Kendall, Soumare, and Soumare (1980).

jeliya, jaliya   state or condition of being a *jeli*, encompassing bard-griot identity and practice, especially praise singing but also leatherworking

jèmè, jèmèni   leather wallet; *xalasi-taxundi-fo* in Soninke

jidaga   ceramic water jar; *lalle* in Soninke

jifinye   large ceramic water storage vessel; also *finye*

jò   netted fiber wrapped around a tamper, used to impress a pattern into the bottom of a pot

karafejuru   reins, bridle; *xarabin-kacce* in Soninke

kemesu   scissors; also *masu* (from the Arabic *miqaṣṣ*; plural, *maqāṣṣ*)

kerike, kirike   leather-covered wooden saddle; *xirxi* in Soninke

kisèbòrò   leather shot pouch; also *nègèdenbòrò*

kurun, kurunmuso   wooden platter used by Maninka potters as a turntable

marifamugu binyèn   leather-covered powderhorn

masu   scissors; also *kemesu* (from the Arabic *miqaṣṣ*; plural, *maqāṣṣ*)

muke   leather slipper; *muqqu* in Soninke

mukeyiri   wooden form for making slippers; lit., slipper wood

muru   knife; *labo* or *xafa* in Soninke; or dagger; *joroxo-labo* in Soninke

muruba   sword; lit., big knife; also *npan*; *kaafa* in Soninke

murutan   leather-covered knife sheath

nadaga   ceramic saucepot

nègèdaga   ceramic skeuomorph of an iron or aluminum cooking pot; also *barama*

nègèdenbòrò   leather shot pouch; also *kisèbòrò*

nègètigi   title for *numu* men and women who perform circumcision and excision; lit., master of the iron (knife)

ngomifaga   ceramic pancake griddle; Kadiolo region

npalan   leather saddlebag

npan   sword; also *muruba*

npanmurutan, npantan   leather-covered sword sheath

ntiriba   plant root (*Cochlospermum tinctorium*) used to dye leather yellow

nugulan   wooden polisher used by leatherworkers to smooth, crease, and impress leather; *naxaade* in Soninke

numu   usually translated as blacksmith or blacksmith-sculptor, but term also encompasses other meanings, including potter when referring to women, as well as healer, diviner, master of Komo, and ones who perform circumcision and excision

numumuso   a more precise reference to potters than *numu*; lit., female *numu*, or blacksmith wife/woman

numuya   state or condition of being a *numu*, encompassing blacksmith-potter identity and practice

nyama   spiritual energy, life force resident in all things, animate and inanimate; also means garbage, refuse

nyamakala   collective term for artisan groups including *jeliw, garankew, numuw,* and *funew,* among others

nyamaku   turmeric (*Curcuma longa*); roots used to dye leather yellow

nyintin   ceramic couscous steamer; may be used in the preparation of locust bean paste (*sumbala*); also *basidaga*

sabara   leather sandal; *teppu* in Soninke

sèbèn   leather-covered gris-gris, amulet; *safaye* in Soninke

sèlidaga   ceramic ablution bowl; lit., prayer pot

sheminfaga, shedaga   ceramic chicken watering vessel; lit., chicken drinking pot

singon   ceramic brazier in the form of a low bowl with three prongs extending into the interior

tobidaga   ceramic cooking pot

tugura   Soninke term for quiver

wala, walaha   wooden slate used as a work surface by leatherworkers; also the ritual slate used by Muslim scholars for teaching literacy and for preparing ritual fluids for healing; *wallaxa* in Soninke

wòlòsò   sickle-shaped iron hook mounted on the end of a long, wooden pole, used by potters to pull pots hot from the fire

wusulanbèlè   ceramic incense burner

yerelen   alum used in tanning and dyeing leather

REFERENCES

Abitbol, Michel. 1979. *Tombouctou et les Arma*. Paris: G.-P. Maisonneuve et Larose.

Adam, J.-G. 1970. Noms vernaculaires de plantes du Sénégal. *Journal d'agriculture tropicale et de botanique appliquée* 17 (7-9): 1-112.

Adam, M. G. 1903. Legendes historiques du pays de Nioro (Sahel). *Revue coloniale* 14:232-48.

Adamu, Mahdi. 1978. *The Hausa Factor in West African History*. Zaria, Nigeria: Ahmadu Bello University Press.

Adandé, Alexis, and Goudjinou Métinhoué. 1981. *Potières et poterie de Sè (Mono)*. Benin: Ministère de l'enseignement supérieur et de la recherche scientifique.

African Arts. 1995. Protecting Mali's Cultural Heritage (special issue). 28 (4).

Africanus, Leo. [1600] 1896. *The History and Description of Africa*. Translated by John Pory in 1600, edited by Robert Brown. Works of the Hakluyt Society, 2d ser., nos. 92-94. 3 vols. London: Bedford Press for the Hakluyt Society.

Amselle, Jean-Loup. 1972. Histoire et structure social du Wasulu avant Samori. Paper presented at the Conference on Manding Studies, School of Oriental and African Studies, University of London.

Amselle, Jean-Loup, and Elikia M'Bokolo, eds. 1985. *Au coeur de l'ethnie: Ethnies, tribalisme, et état en Afrique*. Paris: Editions la Découverte.

Anderson, Benjamin. [1870/1912] 1971. *Narrative of a Journey to Musardu and Narrative of the Expedition Despatched to Musahdu in 1874*. 2d ed. London: Frank Cass & Company.

Appia, B. 1965. Les forgerons du Fouta-Djallon. *Journal de la Société des Africanistes* 35 (2): 317-52.

Arcin, André. 1907. *La Guinée francaise*. Paris: Augustin Challamel.

Ardouin, Claude Daniel. 1978. La caste des forgerons et son importance dans le Soudan occidental. *Etudes maliennes* 24:1-32.

Arnoldi, Mary Jo. 1983. Puppet Theater in the Segu Region in Mali. Ph.D. diss., Indiana University.

———. 1989. Reconstructing the History and Development of Puppetry in the Segou Region, Mali. In *Man Does Not Go Naked: Textilen und Handwerk aus Afrikanischen und Anderen Landern*, 221-34. Edited by B. Engelbrecht and B. Gardi. Basel: Universität Basel and Museum für Völkerkunde.

———. 1995. *Playing with Time: Art and Performance in Central Mali*. Bloomington and Indianapolis: Indiana University Press.

Bah, Mamadou. 1943-44. Deux industries locales: Tannage et teinturerie (Hamdallaye, Labé, Guinea). Cahiers du William Ponty, devoir de vacances, Ecole William Ponty, Sébikotane, Senegal. Bibliothèque (Documentation), Institut Français d'Afrique Noire, Dakar.

Bailleul, Pére Charles. 1981. *Petit dictionnaire: Bambara-Français, Français-Bambara.* Avebury, England: Avebury Publishing Company.

Ba Konaré, Adame. 1993. *Dictionnaire des femmes célébres du Mali.* Bamako: Editions Jamana.

Balfour, Henry. 1934. The Tandu Industry in Northern Nigeria and Its Affinities Elsewhere. In *Essays Presented to C. G. Seligman,* 5-18. Edited by E. E. Evans-Pritchard et al. London: Kegan Paul, Trench, Trubner.

Banaon, Kouamé Emmanuel. 1990. *Poterie et société chez les Numa de Tierkou.* Etudes sur l'histoire et l'archéologie du Burkina Faso, 2. Stuttgart: Franz Steiner.

Barley, Nigel. 1984. Placing the West African Potter. In *Earthenware in Asia and Africa,* 93-105. Colloquies on Art and Archaeology in Asia, 12. Edited by John Picton. London: University of London Percival David Foundation of Chinese Art.

———. 1994. *Smashing Pots: Works of Clay from Africa.* Washington, D.C.: Smithsonian Institution Press.

Barry, Ibrahima. 1943-44. Deux industries locales: Tannage et teinturerie du Fouta Djallon à Pita (Guinea). Cahiers du William Ponty, devoir de vacances, Ecole William Ponty, Sébikotane, Senegal. Bibliothèque (Documentation), Institut Français d'Afrique Noire, Dakar.

Barth, Heinrich. 1857. *Travels and Discoveries in North and Central Africa.* 3 vols. New York: Harper & Brothers.

Bathily, Mamadou. n.d. Tannage et teinturerie (Tuabou, Bakel, Senegal). Cahiers du William Ponty, devoir de vacances, Ecole William Ponty, Sébikotane, Senegal. Bibliothèque (Documentation), Institut Français d'Afrique Noire, Dakar.

Bazin, H. [1906] 1965. *Dictionnaire Bambara-Français.* Reprint, Ridgewood, N.J.: Gregg Press.

Bedaux, R. M. A. 1972. Tellem, reconnaissance archéologique d'une culture de l'ouest africain au moyen-âge: Recherches architectoniques. *Journal de la Société des Africanistes* 42 (2): 103-85.

———. 1980. The Geographic Distribution of Footed Bowls in the Upper and Middle Niger Region. In *West African Culture Dynamics: Archeological and Historical Perspectives,* 247-58. Edited by B. K. Swartz, Jr., and Raymond E. Dumett. The Hague: Mouton.

———. 1986. Recherches ethno-archéologiques sur la poterie des Dogon (Mali). In *Op Zoek Naar mens en materiëlle Cultuur,* 117-48. Groningen: Rijks Universiteit.

———. 1988. Tellem and Dogon Material Culture. *African Arts* 21 (4): 38-45, 91.

Bedaux, R. M. A., and A. G. Lange. 1983. Tellem, reconnaissance archéologique d'une culture de l'ouest africain au moyen-âge: la poterie. *Journal des Africanistes* 53 (1-2): 5-59.

Bedaux, R. M. A., and Diderik van der Waals. 1987. Aspects of Life-Span of Dogon Pottery. *Newsletter: Department of Pottery Technology* (Leiden) 5:137-53.

Bedaux, R. M. A., and Kitty Rompen. n.d. Leather for the Dead: Archaeological Evidence of Leatherworking in Central Mali from the Eleventh to the Fifteenth Centuries. Typescript.

Bedaux, R. M. A., and Michel Raimbault. 1993. Les grandes provinces de la céramique au Mali. In *Vallées du Niger,* 273-93. Edited by Jean Devisse et al. Paris: Editions de la Réunion des Musées Nationaux.

Bedaux, R. M. A., et al. 1978. Recherches archéologiques dans le delta intérieur du Niger (Mali). *Palaeohistoria* 20:91-220.

Ben Sai, S. 1944a. Plantes tinctoriales et teinture indigéne au Soudan. *Notes africaines* 23 (June): 17-19.

———. 1944b. Plantes à tannins: Tannage et teinture des cuirs au Soudan. *Notes africaines* 24 (October): 20-22.

Berns, Marla. 1989a. Ceramic Clues: Art History of the Gongola Valley. *African Arts* 22 (2): 48-59, 102.

———. 1989b. Cross-Cultural Perspectives: Art History in the Upper Benue. Paper presented at the 8th Triennial Symposium on African Art, Washington, D.C.

———. 1993. Art, History, and Gender: Women and Clay in West Africa. *African Archaeological Review* 11:133-53.

Biot, Bernadine. 1989. La poterie Wan et Mona dans la région de Mankono: Une contribution a l'étude de la céramique ivoirienne. *Annales d'histoire, Université d'Abidjan* 17:31-52.

Bird, Charles S. 1970. The Development of Mandekan (Manding): A Study of the Role of Extra-Linguistic Factors in Linguistic Change. In *Language and History in Africa,* 146-59. Edited by David Dalby. London: Frank Cass & Company.

———. 1981. Evolution of Bards and Blacksmiths: An Hypothesis. Lecture at Indiana University, Bloomington.

Bird, Charles S., and Martha B. Kendall. 1980. The Mande Hero: Text and Context. In *Explorations in African Systems of Thought,* 13-26. Edited by Ivan Karp and Charles S. Bird. Bloomington: Indiana University Press.

Bird, Charles S., Martha B. Kendall, and Kalilou Tera. 1995. Etymologies of "Nyamakala." In *Status and Identity in West Africa: "Nyamakalaw" of Mali,* 27-35. Edited by David C. Conrad and Barbara E. Frank. Bloomington and Indianapolis: Indiana University Press.

Bochet, Gilbert. 1959. Les Poro des Diéli. *Bulletin de l'I.F.A.N.,* ser. b, 21 (1-2): 61-101.

Boser-Sarivaxevanis, Renée. 1969. *Apercus sur la teinture à l'indigo en Afrique occidentale.* Basel: Museum für Völkerkunde. First published in *Verhandlungen der Naturforschenden Gesellschaft in Basel,* vol. 80, no. 1 (1969).

———. 1980. Research on the History of Traditional Woven and Dyed Textiles of West Africa. In *West African Textiles and Garments,* 5-27. Minneapolis: University of Minnesota.

Bowdich, Thomas E. [1819] 1966. *Mission from Cape Coast Castle to Ashantee.* Edited by W. E. F. Ward. 3d ed. New York: Barnes and Noble.

———. 1821. *An Essay on the Superstitions, Customs and Arts, Common to the Ancient Egyptians, Abyssinians and Ashantees.* Paris: J. Smith.

Boyer, G. 1953. *Un peuple de l'Ouest Soudanais: Les Diawara.* Mémoires de l'Institut Français d'Afrique Noire, no. 29. Dakar: Institut Français d'Afrique Noire.

Bravmann, René A. 1973. *Open Frontiers: The Mobility of Art in Black Africa.* Index of Art in the Pacific Northwest, no. 5. Seattle: University of Washington Press for the Henry Art Gallery.

———. 1974. *Islam and Tribal Art in West Africa.* Cambridge: Cambridge University Press.

———. 1995. Islamic Spirits and African Artistry in Trans-Saharan Perspective. In *Islamic Art and Culture in Sub-Saharan Africa,* 57-69. Edited by Karin Adahl and Berit Sahlström. Figura Nova Series, 27. Uppsala: Acta Universitatis Upsaliensis.

Bray, Jennifer M. 1976. The Tim-Tim Makers of Oyo. *Savanna* 5 (2): 127-37.

Brett-Smith, Sarah C. 1982. Symbolic Blood: Cloths for Excised Women. *RES* 3: 15-31.

———. 1994. *The Making of Bamana Sculpture.* Cambridge: Cambridge University Press.

Brooks, George E. 1985. Western Africa to c. 1860 A.D.: A Provisional Historical Schema Based on Climate Periods. Working papers, no. 1. Bloomington: African Studies Program, Indiana University.

Brunot, L. 1923. Vocabulaire de la tannerie indigéne à Rabat. *Hespéris* 3 (1): 83-124.

———. 1946. La cordonnerie indigéne à Rabat. *Hespéris* 33 (3-4): 227-321.

Büttikofer, Johann. 1890. *Reisebilder aus Liberia.* 2 vols. Leiden: E. J. Brill.

Caillie, René. [1830] 1968. *Travels through Central Africa to Timbuctoo.* 3 vols. Reprint, London: Frank Cass & Company.

Camara, Sory. 1976. *Gens de la parole: Essai sur la condition et le rôle des griots dans la société Malinké.* Paris: Mouton.

Cashion, Gerald A. 1982. Hunters of the Mande: A Behavioral Code and Worldview Derived from the Study of Their Folklore. Ph.D. diss., Indiana University.

Charry, Eric S. 1992. Musical Thought, History, and Practice among the Mande of West Africa. Ph.D. diss., Princeton University.

Conrad, David C. 1981. The Role of Oral Artists in the History of Mali. 2 vols. Ph.D. diss., School of Oriental and African Studies, University of London.

———. 1985. Islam in the Oral Traditions of Mali: Bilali and Surakata. *Journal of African History* 26 (1): 33-49.

———. 1992. Searching for History in the Sunjata Epic: The Case of Fakoli. *History in Africa* 19:147-200.

———. 1995. Blind Man Meets Prophet: Oral Tradition, Islam, and *Funé* Identity. In *Status and Identity in West Africa: "Nyamakalaw" of Mali,* 86-132. Edited by David C. Conrad and Barbara E. Frank. Bloomington and Indianapolis: Indiana University Press.

———. Forthcoming. Mooning Armies and Mothering Heroes: Female Power in Mande Epic Tradition. In *In Search of Sunjata: The Mande Epic as History, Literature, and Performance.* Edited by Ralph Austen. Bloomington and Indianapolis: Indiana University Press.

———. n.d. The Sabu of Dalilu: Sacred Sites and Spiritual Power in Mande History. Typescript.

Conrad, David C., and Barbara E. Frank, eds. 1995. *Status and Identity in West Africa: "Nyamakalaw" of*

Mali. Bloomington and Indianapolis: Indiana University Press.

Correspondance sur les peaux. 1900-1905. 2Q/6. Archives Nationales du Mali, Koulouba.

Crone, G. R., ed. and trans. 1937. *The Voyages of Cadamosto and Other Documents on Western Africa in the Second Half of the Fifteenth Century.* Works of the Hakluyt Society, 2d ser., no. 80. London: Bedford Press for the Hakluyt Society.

Crossland, L. B., and Merrick Posnansky. 1978. Pottery, People, and Trade at Begho, Ghana. In *The Spatial Organization of Culture,* 77-89. Edited by Ian Hodder. Pittsburgh: University of Pittsburgh Press.

Curtin, Philip D. 1972. The Western Juula in the Eighteenth Century. Paper presented at the Conference on Manding Studies, School of Oriental and African Studies, University of London.

Dalby, David. 1971. Introduction: Distribution and Nomenclature of the Manding Peoples and Their Language. In *Papers on the Manding,* 1-13. Edited by Carleton T. Hodge. African Series, vol. 3. Bloomington: African Studies Program, Indiana University.

Dalziel, J. M. 1926. African Leather Dyes. *Kew Bulletin* 6:225-38.

———. 1948. *The Useful Plants of West Tropical Africa.* London: Crown Agents for the Colonies.

Daniel, Fernand. 1910. Etude sur les Soninkés ou Sarakolés. *Anthropos* 5:27-49.

Dark, Philip J. C. 1973. *An Introduction to Benin Art and Technology.* Oxford: Clarendon Press.

David, Nicholas, and Hilke Hennig. 1972. *The Ethnography of Pottery: A Fulani Case Seen in Archeological Perspective.* McCaleb Module in Anthropology, no. 21. Reading, Mass.: Addison Wesley.

Davies, O. 1964. Gonja Painted Pottery. *Transactions of the Historical Society of Ghana* 7:4-11.

———. 1969. Painted Pottery in the Volta Basin. *West African Archaeological Newsletter* 11:22.

Dawson, Douglas. 1993. *African Ceramics: Ancient and Historic Earthenware Vessels.* Chicago: Douglas Dawson Gallery.

de Grunne, Bernard. 1980. *Terres cuites anciennes de l'Ouest Africain.* Publications d'histoire de l'art et d'archéologie de l'Université Catholique de Louvain, 22. Louvain-la-Neuve: Institut Supérieur d'Archéologie et d'Histoire de l'Art, Collège Erasme.

———. 1983. *Ancient Pottery from Mali: Some Prelimi-nary Remarks.* Munich: Galerie Biedermann and Fred and Jens Jahn.

———. 1987. *Divine Gestures and Earthly Gods: A Study of the Ancient Terra-Cotta Statuary from the Inland Niger Delta in Mali.* Ph.D. diss., Yale University.

———. 1991. Heroic Riders and Divine Horses: An Analysis of Ancient Soninke and Dogon Equestrian Figures from the Inland Niger Delta Region in Mali. *Minneapolis Institute of Arts Bulletin* 66 (1983-86): 78-96.

Delafosse, Maurice. 1912. *Haut-Sénégal-Niger (Soudan français).* 3 vols. Paris: Emile Larose.

De Moraes, Nize Izabel. 1972. Le commerce des peaux à la Petite Côte au XVIIe siècle (Sénégal). *Notes africaines* 134 (April): 37-45; 136 (October): 111-16.

Devisse, Jean, et al., eds. 1993. *Vallées du Niger.* Paris: Editions de la Réunion des Musées Nationaux.

de Zeltner, Frantz. 1908. Notes sur la sociologie soudanaise. *L'anthropologie* 19:217-33.

———. 1915. Notes sur quelques industries du Soudan français. *L'anthropologie* 26:219-34.

Diawara, Mamadou. 1990. *La graine de la parole: Dimension sociale et politique des traditions orales du royaume de Jaara (Mali) du XVème au milieu du XIXème siècle.* Stuttgart: Franz Steiner.

Dieterlen, Germaine. 1951. *Essai sur la religion bambara.* Paris: Presses Universitaires de France.

———. 1955. Mythe et organisation sociale au Soudan français. *Journal de la Société des Africanistes* 25 (1-2): 39-76.

———. 1957. The Mande Creation Myth. *Africa: Journal of the International African Insititute* 27 (2): 124-38.

———. 1959. Mythe et organisation sociale au Soudan français. *Journal de la Société des Africanistes* 29 (1): 119-38.

DNAFLA (Direction Nationale de l'Alphabetisation Fonctionnelle et de la Linguistique Appliquée). 1979. *Lexique Soninke-Français.* Bamako: Ministére de l'Education Nationale.

———. 1980. *Lexique Bambara-Français.* Bamako: Ministére de l'Education Nationale.

Dodwell, C. B. 1953. The Tim-Tim Makers of Oyo. *Nigeria* 2:126-31.

Drost, Dietrich. 1967. *Töpferei in Afrika: Technologie.* Berlin: Akademie-Verlag.

———. 1968. *Töpferei in Afrika: Okonomie und Soziologie.* Berlin: Akademie-Verlag.

Dudot, Bernard. 1969. Une production originale de l'artisanat d'Agadez: Les boîtes en peau non tannée dites "batta." *Notes africaines* 122 (April): 55–58.

Dupuis, Annie, and Nicole Echard. 1971. La poterie traditionnelle Hausa de l'Ader (Rep. du Niger). *Journal de la Société des Africanistes* 41 (1): 7–34.

Dupuis-Yacouba, Auguste-Victor. 1921. *Industries et principales professions des habitants de la région de Tombouctor.* Paris: Emile Larose

Durand, Oswald. 1932. Les industries locales au Fouta. *Bulletin du Comité d'Etudes Historiques et Scientifiques de l'Afrique Occidentale Francaise* 15:42–71.

Echenberg, Myron J. 1971. Late Nineteenth-Century Military Technology in Upper Volta. *Journal of African History* 12 (2): 241–54.

Elbl, Ivana. 1991. The Horse in Fifteenth-Century Senegambia. *International Journal of African Historical Studies* 24 (1): 85–110.

Ezra, Kate. 1984. Early Sources for the History of Bamana Art. Iowa Studies in African Art, vol. 1. Iowa City: School of Art and Art History, University of Iowa.

———. 1986a. Historical Dimensions of Bamana Figurative Sculpture. Paper presented at the 7th Triennial Symposium on African Art, University of California, Los Angeles.

———. 1986b. *A Human Ideal in African Art: Bamana Figurative Sculpture.* Washington, D.C.: Smithsonian Institution Press for the National Museum of African Art.

———. 1988. *Art of the Dogon.* New York: Metropolitan Museum of Art.

Fagerberg-Diallo, Sonja. 1984. *A Practical Guide and Reference Grammar to the Fulfulde of Maasina.* Jos, Nigeria: Joint Christian Ministry in West Africa.

Fagg, William. 1971. *The Living Arts of Nigeria.* London: Studio Vista.

Fernandes, Valentim. [fl. 1494–1516] 1938. *Description de la côte d'Afrique de Ceuta au Sénégal.* Translated and annotated by P. de Cenival and Th. Monod. Paris: Comité d'Etudes Historiques et Scientifiques de l'Afrique Occidentale Francaise, Librairie Larose.

Filipowiak, Wladyslaw. 1979. *Etudes archéologiques sur la capitale médiévale du Mali.* Szczecin: Muzeum Narodowe.

Fisher, Humphrey J. 1973. He Swalloweth the Ground with Fierceness and Rage: The Horse in the Central Sudan. *Journal of African History* 13 (3): 369–88; 14 (3): 355–79.

Forbes, R. J. 1966. *Studies in Ancient Technology.* Vol. 5. 2d ed. Leiden: E. J. Brill.

Frank, Barbara E. 1987. Open Borders: Style and Ethnic Identity. *African Arts* 20 (4): 48–55, 90.

———. 1988. Mande Leatherworking: A Study of Style, Technology, and Identity. Ph.D. diss., Indiana University.

———. 1993. Reconstructing the History of an African Ceramic Tradition: Technology, Slavery, and Agency in the Region of Kadiolo (Mali). *Cahiers d'études africaines* 33 (3): 381–401.

———. 1994. More Than Wives and Mothers: The Artistry of Mande Potters. *African Arts* 27 (4): 26–37, 93–94.

———. 1995. Soninke "Garankéw" and Bamana-Malinke "Jeliw": Mande Leatherworkers and the Diaspora. In *Status and Identity in West Africa: "Nyamakalaw" of Mali,* 133–50. Edited by David C. Conrad and Barbara E. Frank. Bloomington and Indianapolis: Indiana University Press.

———. Forthcoming. Recovering the Past: The Place of Pots and Potters in Mande Art History. In *Women's Art in Africa: The Sixth Stanley Conference on African Art.* Iowa City: School of Art and Art History, University of Iowa.

Gabus, Jean. 1958. *Au Sahara.* Vol. 1, *Arts et symboles.* Neuchâtel: Baconniére.

Gallais, Jean. 1962. Signification du groupe ethnique au Mali. *L'homme: Revue francaise d'anthropologie* 2 (2): 106–29.

———. 1967. *Le delta interieur du Niger: Etude de geographie regionale.* Dakar: Institut Français d'Afrique Noire.

Gallay, Alain. 1970. La poterie en pays Sarakolé (Mali, Afrique occidentale): Etude de technologie traditionnelle. *Journal de la Société des Africanistes* 40 (1): 7–84.

———. 1981. *Le Sarnyéré Dogon: Archéologie d'un isolat, Mali.* Recherche sur les grandes civilisations, no. 4. Paris: Editions ADPF.

———. 1986. Protohistoire et ethnologie ouest-africaine: (Non) pertinence du codage céramique. In *A propos des interprétations archéologiques de la poterie: Questions ouvertes,* 107–65. Edited by M. Th. Barrelet and J.-Cl. Gardin. Mémoire, no. 64. Paris: Editions Recherche sur les Civilisations.

———. 1991–92. Traditions céramiques et ethnies dans le delta intérieur du Niger (Mali): Approche ethnoarchéologique. *Bulletin du Centre Genevois d'Anthropologie* 3:23-46.

Gallay, Alain, and Eric Huysecom. 1989. *Ethno-archéologie africaine.* Document du Département d'Anthropologie et d'Ecologie, 14. Geneva: Université de Genève.

Gallieni, Joseph-Simon. 1885. *Voyage au Soudan français (Haut Niger et pays de Ségou), 1879-1881.* Paris: Hachette.

Gansser, A. 1950. The Early History of Tanning. *Ciba Review* 81 (August): 2938-62.

Gardi, Bernhard. 1985. *Ein Markt wie Mopti: Handwerkerkasten und traditionelle Techniken in Mali.* Basler Beiträge zur Ethnologie, vol. 25. Basel: Ethnologisches Seminar der Universität und Museum für Völkerkunde.

Geis-Tronich, Gudrun. 1989. *Les métiers traditionnels des Gulmance.* Weisbaden: Franz Steiner.

Glaze, Anita. 1981. *Art and Death in a Senufo Village.* Bloomington: Indiana University Press.

Goody, Jack. 1967. The Over-Kingdom of Gonja. In *West African Kingdoms in the Nineteenth Century,* 179-205. Edited by Daryll Forde and P. M. Kaberry. Oxford: Oxford University Press.

————. 1971. The Impact of Islamic Writing on the Oral Cultures of West Africa. *Cahiers d'études africaines* 11 (3): 355-466.

Gosselain, Olivier. 1992. Technology and Style: Potters and Pottery among Bafia of Cameroon. *Man,* n.s., 27 (3): 559-86.

Green, Kathryn Lee. 1984. The Foundation of Kong: A Study in Dyula and Sonongui Ethnic Identity. Ph.D. diss., Indiana University.

————. 1987a. Mansaya and the Role of the Jeliw in Southern Sudanic States. Paper presented at the 30th annual meeting of the African Studies Association, Denver, Colo., November 22.

————. 1987b. Shared Masking Traditions in Northeastern Ivory Coast. *African Arts* 20 (4): 62-69, 92.

Greenberg, Joseph H. 1966. *The Languages of Africa.* Bloomington: Indiana University Press.

Guèye, Samba N'Doucoumane. 1942-43. Deux industries locales: Teinturerie et tannage (Dakar, Senegal). Cahiers du William Ponty, devoir de vacances, Ecole William Ponty, Sébikotane, Senegal. Bibliothèque (Documentation), Institut Français d'Afrique Noire, Dakar.

Guyot, R., R. LeTourneau, and L. Paye. 1936. Les cordonniers de Fes. *Hespéris* 23 (1): 9-54.

Hahn, Hans Peter. 1991a. *Die Materielle Kultur der Bassar (Nord Togo).* Stuttgart: Franz Steiner.

————. 1991b. Die Töpferei der Bassar, Konkomba, Kabyè, und Lamba in Nord-Togo. *Paideuma* 37:25-54.

Hardin, Kris L. 1996. Technological Style and the Making of Culture: Three Kono Contexts of Production. In *African Material Culture,* 31-50. Edited by Mary Jo Arnoldi, Christraud M. Geary, and Kris L. Hardin. Bloomington and Indianapolis: Indiana University Press.

Hardin, Kris L., and Mary Jo Arnoldi. 1996. Introduction: Efficacy and Objects. In *African Material Culture,* 1-28. Edited by Mary Jo Arnoldi, Christraud M. Geary, and Kris L. Hardin. Bloomington and Indianapolis: Indiana University Press.

Hardy, André. 1938a. Les babouchiers de salé. *Bulletin economique du Maroc* 5:257-64.

————. 1938b. Les tanneurs de salé. *Bulletin economique du Maroc* 5:190-99.

Heathcote, David. 1974. A Leatherworker of Zaria City. *Nigerian Field* 39 (1): 12-26; 39 (3): 99-117.

Herbert, Eugenia. 1993. *Iron, Gender, and Power: Rituals of Transformation in African Societies.* Bloomington and Indianapolis: Indiana University Press.

Hodge, Alison. 1982. *Nigeria's Traditional Crafts.* London: Ethnographica.

Hoffman, Barbara. 1990. The Power of Speech: Language and Social Status among Mande Griots and Nobles. Ph.D. diss., Indiana University.

————. 1995. Power, Structure, and Mande "Jeliw." In *Status and Identity in West Africa: "Nyamakalaw" of Mali,* 36-45. Edited by David C. Conrad and Barbara E. Frank. Bloomington and Indianapolis: Indiana University Press.

Holas, Bohumil. 1957. *Les Sénoufo (y compris les Minianka).* Paris: Presses Universitaires de France.

————. 1966. *Les Sénoufo (y compris les Minianka).* 2d ed. Paris: Presses Universitaires de France.

————. 1968. The Sacred in Social Life: The Senufo Example. *Diogenes* 61 (spring): 114-31.

Hopkins, A. G. 1973. *An Economic History of West Africa.* London: Longman Group.

Hopkins, Nicholas S. 1971. Mandinka Social Organization. In *Papers on the Manding,* 99-128. Edited by Carleton T. Hodge. African Series, vol. 3. Bloomington: African Studies Program, Indiana University.

Huysecom, Eric, and Anne Mayor. 1993. Les traditions céramiques du delta intérieur du Niger:

Présent et passé. In *Vallées du Niger, 297-313.* Edited by Jean Devisse et al. Paris: Editions de la Réunion des Musées Nationaux.

Idiens, Dale. 1981. *The Hausa of Northern Nigeria.* Edinburgh: Royal Scottish Museum.

al-Idrīsī. 1866. *Description de l'Afrique et de l'Espagne.* Translated and edited by R. Dozy and M. J. de Goeje. Leiden: Brill.

Imperato, Pascal James. 1983. *Buffoons, Queens, and Wooden Horsemen: The Dyo and Gouan Societies of the Bamana of Mali.* New York: Kilima House.

Innes, Gordon. 1976. *Kaabu and Fuladu: Historical Narratives of the Gambian Mandinka.* London: School of Oriental and African Studies, University of London.

Jackson, James Grey. 1809. *An Account of the Empire of Morocco and the District of Suse.* London: W. Bulmer and Company.

Jemma, D. 1971. *Les tanneurs de Marrakech.* Mémoires du Centre de Recherches Anthropologiques Prehistoriques et Ethnographiques, 19. Algiers: Centre National de la Recherche Scientifique.

Jobson, Richard. [1623] 1904. *The Golden Trade, or A Discovery of the River Gambra, and the Golden Trade of the Aethiopians.* Edited by Charles G. Kingsley. Reprint, Teignmouth, England: E. E. Speight and R. H. Walpole.

Johnson, John William. 1986. Part One: The Study. In *The Epic of Son-Jara: A West African Tradition,* 3-83. Bloomington: Indiana University Press.

Johnson, Marion. 1976. The Economic Foundations of an Islamic Theocracy: The Case of Masina. *Journal of African History* 17 (4): 481-95.

Joly, A. 1906. L'industrie à Tétouan. *Archives marocaines* 8:203-63.

Kasfir, Sidney. 1984. One Tribe, One Style? Paradigms in the Historiography of African Art. *History in Africa* 2:163-93.

Keita, Amara Boubacar. 1940-45. Deux industries locales: Tannage et teinturerie (Kayes, Mali). Cahiers du William Ponty, devoir de vacances, Ecole William Ponty, Sébikotane, Senegal. Bibliothèque (Documentation), Institut Français d'Afrique Noire, Dakar.

Kendall, Martha B., Mamadou Soumare, and Saloum Soumare, comps. 1980. *Soninke: Special Skills Handbook.* Peace Corps Language Handbook Series. Brattleboro, Vt.: Experiment in International Living for Action/Peace Corps.

Kivekäs, Eila, et al. 1993. *Savi: Keramiikan ja arkkiteh-tuurin perinne Länsi-Afrikassa (Poterie et architecture en Afrique de l'Ouest).* Tampere, Finland: F. G. Lönnberg for Pyynikinlinna.

Kjersmeier, Carl. 1935-38. *Centres de style de la sculpture nègre africaine.* Paris: Albert Morancé.

Klein, Martin. 1983. Women in Slavery in the Western Sudan. In *Women and Slavery in Africa,* 67-92. Edited by Claire C. Robertson and Martin A. Klein. Madison: University of Wisconsin Press.

———. 1992. The Slave Trade in the Western Sudan during the Nineteenth Century. *Slavery and Abolition* 13 (1): 39-60.

Koné, Kassim. 1995. *Bamanankan Dangègafe.* West Newbury, Mass.: Mother Toungue Editions.

Kreamer, Christine Mullen. 1989. The Social and Economic Implications of Moba Male and Female Pottery Traditions (Northern Togo). Paper presented at the 8th Triennial Symposium on African Art, Washington, D.C.

Labouret, Henri. 1934. *Les Manding et leur langue.* Paris: Librarie Larose.

Lamb, Malcolm. 1981. The Hausa Tanners of Northern Nigeria (and the production of Sokoto Tanned Goatskins). *New Bookbinder* 1:58-62.

Launay, Robert. 1982. *Traders without Trade.* Cambridge: Cambridge University Press.

———. 1995. The Dyeli of Korhogo: Identity and Identification. In *Status and Identity in West Africa: "Nyamakalaw" of Mali,* 153-69. Edited by David C. Conrad and Barbara E. Frank. Bloomington and Indianapolis: Indiana University Press.

LaViolette, Adria. 1987. An Archaeological Ethnography of Blacksmiths, Potters, and Masons in Jenne, Mali (West Africa). Ph.D. diss., Washington University.

———. 1995. Women Craft Specialists in Jenne: The Manipulation of Mande Social Categories. In *Status and Identity in West Africa: "Nyamakalaw" of Mali,* 170-81. Edited by David C. Conrad and Barbara E. Frank. Bloomington and Indianapolis: Indiana University Press.

Law, Robin. 1980. *The Horse in West African History. The Role of the Horse in the Societies of Pre-colonial West Africa.* London: Oxford University Press.

Laye, Camara. 1953. *L'enfant noir.* Paris: Plon.

Lechtman, Heather. 1977. Style in Technology: Some Early Thoughts. In *Material Culture. Styles, Organization, and Dynamics of Technology,* 3-20. Edited by

Heather Lechtman and Robert S. Merrill. St. Paul, Minn.: West Publishing Company.

Legassick, Martin. 1966. Firearms, Horses, and Samorian Army Organization, 1870–1898. *Journal of African History* 7 (1): 95–115.

Levtzion, Nehemia. 1968. *Muslims and Chiefs in West Africa.* Oxford: Clarendon Press.

———. 1972. The Early States of the Western Sudan to 1500. In *History of West Africa,* vol. 1, 114–51. Edited by J. F. A. Ajayi and Michael Crowder. 2 vols. London: Longman Group, 1971; New York: Columbia University Press.

Levtzion, Nehemia, and J. F. P. Hopkins, eds. 1981. *Corpus of Early Arabic Sources for West African History.* Translated by J. F. P. Hopkins. Cambridge: Cambridge University Press.

Lewis, Barbara C. 1971. The Dioula in the Ivory Coast. In *Papers on the Manding,* 273–307. Edited by Carleton T. Hodge. African Series, vol. 3. Bloomington: African Studies Program, Indiana University.

———. 1972. The Dioula Diaspora in the Ivoirian South. Paper presented at the Conference on Manding Studies, School of Oriental and African Studies, University of London.

Lhote, Henri. 1950. Les sandales. In *Contribution à l'étude de l'air,* 512–33. Mémoires de l'Institut Français d'Afrique Noire, no. 10. Paris: Librarie Larose.

———. 1952. Les boites moulées en peau du Soudan, dites "Bata." *Bulletin de l'I.F.A.N.,* ser. b, 14 (3): 919–55.

———. 1955. *Les Touaregs du Hoggar (Ahaggar).* Paris: Payot.

Linares de Sapir, Olga. 1969. Diola Pottery of the Fogny and the Kasa. *Expedition* 11 (3): 2–11.

Lombard, J. 1957. Aperçu sur la technologie et l'artisanat Bariba. *Etudes dahomennes* 18:7–59.

Louis, André. 1968. Sellerie d'apparat et selliers de Tunis. *Cahiers des arts et traditions populaires* 1 (1): 41–100.

Lucas, A. 1948. *Ancient Egyptian Materials and Industries.* 3d ed. London: Edward Arnold.

Lyon, Captain G. F. 1821. *A Narrative of Travels in Northern Africa in the Years 1818, 19, and 20.* London: John Murray.

MacDonald, Kevin C. 1995. When Worlds Collide: A Consideration of the Holcene Peopling of Sub-Saharan West Africa. Paper presented at the 3d International Conference on Mande Studies, Rijksmuseum voor Volkenkunde, Leiden.

———. Forthcoming. Korounkorokalé Revisted: The "Pays Mande" and the Peopling of West Africa. *African Archaeological Review.*

Maiga, Attaher. 1940–43. Tannage et teinturerie (Bourem, Gao, Mali). Cahiers du William Ponty, devoir de vacances, Ecole William Ponty, Sébikotane, Senegal. Bibliothèque (Documentation), Institut Français d'Afrique Noire, Dakar.

Mark, Peter. 1992. *The Wild Bull and the Sacred Forest.* Cambridge: Cambridge University Press.

Marty, Paul. 1921. *L'Islam in Guinèe: Fouta Diallon.* Paris: Ernest Leroux.

Mathewson, R. D. 1968. The Painted Pottery Sequence in the Volta Basin. *West African Archaeological Newsletter* 8:24–31.

Mauny, Raymond. 1961. *Tableau géographique de l'Ouest Africain au moyen âge.* Mémoires de l'Institut Français d'Afrique Noire, no. 61. Dakar: Institut Français d'Afrique Noire.

M'Baye, Ibrahima. 1941–43. La teinturerie et la cordonnerie (Kindia, Guinea). Cahiers du William Ponty, devoir de vacances, Ecole William Ponty, Sébikotane, Senegal. Bibliothèque (Documentation), Institut Français d'Afrique Noire, Dakar.

McCall, Daniel F. 1979. The Horse in West African History. *L'uomo* 3 (1): 41–69.

McIntosh, Roderick J. 1989. Middle Niger Terracottas before the Symplegades Gateway. *African Arts* 22 (2): 74–83, 103–4.

———. 1993. Unearthing the Early Mande World of Authority. Paper presented at the annual meeting of the African Studies Association, Boston.

———. Forthcoming. The Mande Weather Machine and Its Social Memory Engine. In *Global Change in History and Prehistory.* Edited by Joseph Tainter, Roderick J. McIntosh, and Susan Keech McIntosh.

McIntosh, Roderick J., and Susan Keech McIntosh. 1979. Terracotta Statuettes from Mali. *African Arts* 12 (2): 51–53.

———. 1986. Dilettantism and Plunder: Illicit Traffic in Ancient Malian Art. *Unesco Museum* 149:49–57.

McIntosh, Susan Keech. nd. Blacksmiths and the Evolution of Political Complexity in Mande Society: An Hypothesis. Typescript.

———, ed. 1995. *Excavations at Jenné-jeno, Hambarketolo, and Kaniana (Inland Niger Delta, Mali), the 1981 Season.* University of California Publications in

Anthropology, 20. Berkeley, Los Angeles, and London: University of California Press.

McIntosh, Susan Keech, and Roderick J. McIntosh. 1980. *Prehistoric Investigations at Jenne, Mali*. Cambridge Monographs in African Archaeology, 2. Oxford: B.A.R.

———. 1982. Finding West Africa's Oldest City. *National Geographic,* September, 396-418.

———. 1983. Current Directions in West African Prehistory. *Annual Review of Anthropology* 12:215-58.

McLeod, M. D. 1984. Akan Terracotta. In *Earthenware in Asia and Africa,* 365-81. Colloquies on Art and Archaeology in Asia, 12. Edited by John Picton. London: University of London Percival David Foundation of Chinese Art.

McNaughton, Patrick R. 1977. The Bamana Blacksmiths: A Study of Sculptors and Their Art. Ph.D. diss., Yale University.

———. 1979. Secret Sculptures of Komo: Art and Power in Bamana (Bambara) Initiation Associations. Working Papers in the Traditional Arts, 4. Philadelphia: Institute for the Study of Human Issues.

———. 1982. Language, Art, Secrecy, and Power: The Semantics of "Dalilu." *Anthropological Linguistics* 24 (4): 487-505.

———. 1987. African Borderland Sculpture. *African Arts* 20 (4): 76-77, 91-92.

———. 1988. *The Mande Blacksmiths: Knowledge, Power, and Art in West Africa.* Bloomington and Indianapolis: Indiana University Press.

———. 1991. Is There History in Horizontal Masks? A Preliminary Response to the Dilemma of Form. *African Arts* 24 (2): 40-53, 88-90.

———. 1992. From Mande Komo to Jukun Akuma: Approaching the Difficult Question of History. *African Arts* 25 (2): 76-85, 99-100.

———. 1995. The Semantics of "Jugu": Blacksmiths, Lore, and "Who's Bad" in Mande. In *Status and Identity in West Africa: "Nyamakalaw" of Mali,* 46-57. Edited by David C. Conrad and Barbara E. Frank. Bloomington and Indianapolis: Indiana University Press.

Meakin, Budgett. 1902. *The Moors: A Comprehensive Description.* London: S. Sonnenschein & Company; New York: Macmillan.

Meillassoux, Claude. 1975. *L'esclavage en Afrique pré-coloniale.* Paris: François Maspero.

———. 1983. Female Slavery. In *Women and Slavery in Africa,* 49-66. Edited by Claire C. Robertson and Martin A. Klein. Madison: University of Wisconsin Press.

Merrill, Robert S. 1968. The Study of Technology. Vol. 15 of *International Encyclopedia of the Social Sciences.* Edited by David L. Sills. New York: Crowell and Macmillan.

Monographies du cercle de Djenné. 1895-1930. ID 38. Archives Nationales du Mali, Koulouba.

Monteil, Charles. [1932] 1971. *Une cité soudanaise: Djenné.* 2d ed. Paris: Editions Anthropos et Institut International Africain, 1971.

———. 1953. La légende du Ouagadou et l'origine des Soninké. In *Mélanges ethnologiques,* 359-408. Mémoires de l'Institut Français d'Afrique Noire, no. 23. Dakar: Institut Français d'Afrique Noire.

Morfit, Campbell. 1853. *The Arts of Tanning, Currying, and Leather-Dressing.* Edited from the French of J. De Fontenelle and F. Malepeyre, with numerous emendations and additions. Philadelphia: Henry Carey Baird.

Nachtigal, Gustave. [1879-89] 1971. *Sahara and Sudan.* Translated by Allan G. B. Fisher, Humphrey J. Fisher, and Rex S. o'Fahey. 4 vols. London: C. Hurst.

Nalla, Taïrou. n.d. Tannage et teinturerie (Porto Novo, Nagot, Dahomey). Cahiers du William Ponty, devoir de vacances, Ecole William Ponty, Sébikotane, Senegal. Bibliothèque (Documentation), Institut Français d'Afrique Noire, Dakar.

N'Diayé, Bokar. 1970. *Les castes au Mali.* Bamako: Editions Populaires.

Nicholson, W. E. 1934. Bida (Nupe) Pottery. *Man* 34: 71-73.

Nicolaisen, Johannes. 1963. *Ecology and Culture of the Pastoral Tuareg, with Particular Reference to the Tuareg of Ahaggar and Ayr.* Nationalmuseets Skrifter, Etnografisk Raekke, 9. Copenhagen: Glydendal.

Normand, Robert. 1902-3. L'art et l'habitation en Guinée française. *L'Ami des Monuments et des Arts* 16-17:67-74.

Pâques, Viviana. 1954. *Les Bambara.* Paris: Universitaires de France.

———. 1956. Les "Samake." *Bulletin de l'I.F.A.N.,* ser. b, 18 (3-4): 369-90.

Park, Mungo. 1799. *Travels in the Interior Districts of Africa.* London: W. Bulmer and Company.

———. 1815. *The Journal of a Mission to the Interior of Africa in the Year 1805.* 2d ed. London: John Murray.

Pereira, Duarte Pacheco. [d. 1533] 1937. *Esmeraldo de Situ Orbis.* Translated and edited by George H. T. Kimble. London: Hakluyt Society.

Perinbam, B. Marie. 1974. Notes on Dyula Origins and Nomenclature. *Bulletin de l'I.F.A.N.,* ser. b, 36 (4): 676-90.

———. 1980. The Julas in Western Sudanese History: Long Distance Traders and Developers of Resources. In *West African Culture Dynamics: Archaeological and Historical Perspectives,* 455-76. Edited by B. K. Swartz, Jr., and Raymond E. Dummett. The Hague: Mouton.

Person, Yves. 1963. Les ancêtres de Samori. *Cahiers d'études africaines* 4 (1): 125-56.

———. 1964. Enquête d'une chronologie ivoirienne. In *The Historian in Tropical Africa,* 322-37. Edited by J. Vansina, R. Mauny, and L. V. Thomas. London: Oxford University Press for the International African Institute.

———. 1968-75. *Samori: Une révolution dyula.* 3 vols. Dakar: Institut Français d'Afrique Noire.

———. 1972. The Dyula and the Manding World. Paper presented at the Conference on Manding Studies, School of Oriental and African Studies, University of London.

Pierre, C. 1906. *L'élevage dans l'Afrique occidentale francaise.* Paris: Challamel.

Plenderleith, H. J., and A. E. A. Werner. 1971. *The Conservation of Antiquities and Works of Art.* 2d ed. London: Oxford University Press.

Pollet, Eric, and Grace Winter. 1971. *La société Soninké (Dyahunu, Mali).* Brussels: Institut de Sociologie, Université Libre de Bruxelles.

Prussin, Labelle. 1986. *Hatumere: Islamic Design in West Africa.* Berkeley, Los Angeles, and London: University of California Press.

———. 1995. Architectural Facets of Islam in the Futa-Djallon. In *Islamic Art and Culture in Sub-Saharan Africa,* 21-56. Edited by Karin Adahl and Berit Sahlström. Figura Nova Series, 27. Uppsala: Acta Universitatis Upsaliensis.

Quarcoo, A. K., and Marion Johnson. 1968. Shai Pots: The Pottery Industry of the Shai People of Southern Ghana. *Baessler-Archiv,* n.s., 16:47-88.

Quimby, Lucy G. 1972. The Psychology of Magic among the Dyula. Paper presented at the Conference on Manding Studies, School of Oriental and African Studies, University of London.

Quinn, Charlotte A. 1972. *Mandingo Kingdoms of the Senegambia.* Evanston, Ill.: Northwestern University Press.

Raimbault, Michel. 1980. La poterie traditionnelle au service de l'archéologie: Les ateliers de Kalabougou (cercle de Ségou, Mali). *Bulletin de l'I.F.A.N.,* ser. b, 42 (3): 441-74.

Raffenel, Anne. 1856. *Nouveau voyage dans le pays des negres.* 2 vols. Paris: Imprimerie et Librarie Centrales des Chemins de Fer.

Ratzel, Friedrich. 1896-98. *The History of Mankind.* 3 vols. Translated by A. J. Butler. London: Macmillan and Company.

Ravenhill, Philip. 1996. The Passive Object and the Tribal Paradigm: Colonial Museography in French West Africa. In *African Material Culture,* 265-82. Edited by Mary Jo Arnoldi, Christraud M. Geary, and Kris L. Hardin. Bloomington and Indianapolis: Indiana University Press.

Reed, R. 1972. *Ancient Skins, Parchments, and Leathers.* London: Seminar Press.

Richter, Delores. 1980. *Art, Economics, and Change. The Kulebele of Northern Ivory Coast.* La Jolla, Calif.: Psych/Graphic Publishers.

Rivière, Claude. 1967. Dixinn-Port: Enquête sur un quartier de Conakry (République de Guinée). *Bulletin de l'I.F.A.N.,* ser. b, 29 (1-2): 446-47.

———. 1969. Guinée: La difficile émergence d'un artisanat casté. *Cahiers d'études africaines* 9 (4): 600-625.

Roberts, Richard. 1978. The Maraka and the Economy of the Middle Niger Valley, 1790-1908. Ph.D. diss., University of Toronto.

———. 1981. Ideology, Slavery, and Social Formation: The Evolution of Maraka Slavery in the Middle Niger Valley. In *The Ideology of Slavery in Africa,* 171-99. Edited by Paul E. Lovejoy. Beverly Hills, Calif.: Sage Publications.

———. 1984. Women's Work and Women's Property: Household Social Relations in the Maraka Textile Industry of the Nineteenth Century. *Comparative Studies in Society and History* 26 (2): 229-50.

———. 1987. *Warriors, Merchants, and Slaves: The State and the Economy in the Middle Niger Valley, 1700–1914.* Stanford: Stanford University Press.

Robertson, Claire C., and Martin A. Klein, eds. 1983. *Women and Slavery in Africa.* Madison: University of Wisconsin Press.

Rondeau, Chantal. 1980. La société Senufo du Sud Mali (1870-1950) de la tradition à la dependence. Ph.D. diss., University of Paris.

Rouch, Jean. 1954. *Les Songhay.* Paris: Presses Universitaires de France.

Rovine, Victoria. 1995. An African Textile Abroad: The Bogolan Explosion in Mali and the United States. Paper presented at the 10th Triennial Symposium on African Art, New York, April 19-23.

———. 1997. "Bogolanfini" in Bamako: The Biography of a Malian Textile. *African Arts* 30 (1): 40-51, 94-96.

Roy, Christopher D. 1975. West African Pottery Forming and Firing Techniques. Master's thesis, Indiana University.

———. 1985. *Art and Life in Africa.* Iowa City: University of Iowa Museum of Art.

———. 1987a. *Art of the Upper Volta Rivers.* Meudon, France: A. and E. Chaffin.

———. 1987b. The Spread of Mask Styles in the Black Volta Basin. *African Arts* 20 (4): 40-47, 89-90.

Saint-Père, J.-H. 1925. *Les Sarakollé du Guidimakha.* Paris: Emile Larose.

Salaman, R. A. 1986. *Dictionary of Leather-working Tools, c. 1700-1950.* New York: Macmillan.

Sanneh, Lamin O. 1976. The Origins of Clericalism in West African Islam. *Journal of African History* 17 (1): 49-72.

———. 1979. *The Jakhanke: The History of an Islamic Clerical People of the Senegambia.* London: International African Institute.

Schneider, Klaus. 1990. *Handwerk und Materialisierte Kultur der Lobi in Burkina Faso.* Stuttgart: Franz Steiner.

SCOA. 1984. *Rapport du moyen Niger avec le Ghana ancien.* Actes du premiere seminaire international de l'Association SCOA, Niamey, 1981. Paris: Société Commerciale de l'Afrique Occidentale.

Seck, Mamadou. 1940-43. Teinturerie et tannage (Bargny, Dakar, Senegal). Cahiers du William Ponty, devoir de vacances, Ecole William Ponty, Sébikotane, Senegal. Bibliothèque (Documentation), Institut Français d'Afrique Noire, Dakar.

Shea, Philip James. 1975. The Development of an Export Oriented Dyed Cloth Industry in Kano Emirate in the Nineteenth Century. Ph.D. diss., University of Wisconsin-Madison.

Shepard, Anna O. [1956] 1985. *Ceramics for the Archaeologist.* Publication 609. Reprint, Washington, D.C.: Carnegie Institution of Washington.

Shinnie, P. L., and F. J. Kense. 1989. *Archaeology of Gonja, Ghana: Excavations at Daboya.* Calgary: University of Calgary Press.

Sidibé, Mamby. 1959. Les gens de caste ou "nyamakala" au Soudan français. *Notes africaines* 81 (January): 13-17.

Sieber, Roy. 1972. *African Textiles and Decorative Arts.* New York: Museum of Modern Art.

———. 1973. Ede: Crafts and Surveys. *African Arts* 6 (4): 44-49, 94.

Sieber, Roy, and Arnold Rubin. 1968. *Sculpture of Black Africa: The Paul Tishman Collection.* Los Angeles: Los Angeles County Museum of Art.

Sissoko, Samballa. 1942-43. La teinture et le tannage en A.O.F. (Bafoulabé, Mali). Cahiers du William Ponty, devoir de vacances, Ecole William Ponty, Sébikotane, Senegal. Bibliothèque (Documentation), Institut Français d'Afrique Noire, Dakar.

So, Lamine. 1943-44. Tannage et teinturerie (Rufisque and Saint Louis, Senegal). Cahiers du William Ponty, devoir de vacances, Ecole William Ponty, Sébikotane, Senegal. Bibliothèque (Documentation), Institut Français d'Afrique Noire, Dakar.

Soper, Robert. 1985. Roulette Decoration on African Pottery: Technical Considerations, Dating, and Distributions. *African Archaeological Review* 3:29-51.

Soppelsa, Robert. Forthcoming. A Comparison of Baule and Senufo Pottery Techniques and Forms. In *Women's Art in Africa: The Sixth Stanley Conference on African Art.* Iowa City: School of Art and Art History, University of Iowa.

Spindel, Carol. 1988. "Our Mothers Had More Courage": Style and Technology among Senufo Potters. Master's thesis, University of Illinois.

———. 1989. Kpeenbele Senufo Potters. *African Arts* 22 (2): 66-73, 103.

Sterner, Judy, and Nicholas David. 1991. Gender and Caste in the Mandara Highlands: Northeastern Nigeria and Northern Cameroon. *Ethnology* 30 (4): 355-69.

Sundstrom, Lars. 1972. *Ecology and Symbiosis: Niger Water Folk.* Studia Ethnographica Upsaliensia, 35. Uppsala: Institutionen för Allmän och Jäm förande Etnografi, Uppsala Universitet.

Szumowski, G. 1957-58. Pseudotumulus des environs de Bamako. *Notes Africaines* 75 (July): 66-73; 77 (January): 1-11.

Tamari, Tal. 1991. The Development of Caste Systems in West Africa. *Journal of African History* 32 (2): 221-50.

Tautain, Louis. 1885. Notes sur les castes chez les Mandingues et en particulier chez les Banmanas. *Revue d'ethnographie* 3:343-52.

———. 1887. Quelques renseignments sur les Bobo. *Revue d'ethnographie* 6:228-33.

Tauxier, Louis. 1908. *Le noir de Guinée.* Paris: Bureaux de la Science Sociale.

———. 1912. *Le noir au Soudan.* Paris: Emile Larose.

———. 1917. *Le noir du Yatenga.* Paris: Emile Larose.

Tellier, Georges. 1898. *Autour de Kita: Etude soudanaise.* Paris: Henri Charles-Lavauzelle.

Thomas, L. 1957. Réflexions sur quelques activités techniques en basse Casamance (Sénégal). *Bulletin de l'I.F.A.N.,* ser. b, 19 (3-4): 507-57.

Vansina, Jan. 1984. *Art History in Africa.* London and New York: Longman.

Vogel, Susan, ed. 1981. *For Spirits and Kings: African Art from the Paul and Ruth Tishman Collection.* New York: Metropolitan Museum of Art.

Vogt, John. 1975. Notes on the Portuguese Cloth Trade in West Africa, 1480-1540. *International Journal of African Historical Studies* 8 (4): 623-51.

Völger, Gisela. 1979. *Markt in Der Sahel.* Offenbach am Main: Deutsches Ledermuseum.

Wahlman, Maude. 1972. Yoruba Pottery-Making Techniques. *Baessler-Archiv,* n.s., 20: 312-46.

Wane, Yaya. 1969. *Les Toucouleur du Fouta Tooro (Sénégal).* Initiations et études africaines, 25. Dakar: Institut Français d'Afrique Noire.

Waterer, John W. 1956. Leather. In *A History of Technology,* 147-87. Edited by Charles Singer et al. Vol. 2. Oxford: Clarendon Press.

Webb, James L. A. 1995. *Desert Frontier: Ecological and Economic Change along the Western Sahel, 1600–1850.* Madison: University of Wisconsin Press.

Weil, Peter M. 1984. Slavery, Groundnuts, and European Capitalism in the Wuli Kingdom of Senegambia, 1820-1930. *Research in Economic Anthropology* 6:77-119.

———. 1995. The "Kankurang" Mask Category: A Problem of Mande Cultural History. Paper presented at the 3d International Conference on Mande Studies, Rijksmuseum voor Volkenkunde, Leiden.

Winterbottom, Thomas. [1803] 1969. *An Account of the Native Africans in the Neighborhood of Sierra Leone.* 2 vols. 2d ed. New York: Frank Cass & Company.

Wright, Bonnie L. 1989. The Power of Articulation. In *Creativity of Power: Cosmology and Action in African Societies,* 39-57. Edited by W. Arens and Ivan Karp. Washington, D.C.: Smithsonian Institution Press.

Wright, Rita P. 1991. Women's Labor and Pottery Production in Prehistory. In *Engendering Archaeology: Women and Prehistory,* 194-223. Edited by Joan M. Gero and Margaret W. Conkey. Oxford: Basil Blackwell.

Zahan, Dominique. 1963. *La dialectique du verbe chez les Bambara.* Paris: Mouton.

———. 1974. *The Bambara.* Leiden: E. J. Brill.

Zemp, Hugo. 1964. Musiciens autochtones et griots malinké chez les Dan de Côte d'Ivoire. *Cahiers d'études africaines* 4 (3): 370-82.

———. 1966. La légende des griots malinké. *Cahiers d'études africaines* 6 (4): 611-42.

INDEX